Fix-It and Forget-It™ Recipes for Entertaining

FIX-IT and FORGET-IT™ RECIPES for ENTERTAINING

Slow Cooker Favorites for All the Year Round

Phyllis Pellman Good
& Dawn J. Ranck

Good  Books®

Intercourse, PA 17534
800/762-7171
www.goodbks.com

Cover design and illustrations by Cheryl Benner
Design by Dawn J. Ranck

FIX-IT AND FORGET-IT RECIPES FOR ENTERTAINING
Copyright © 2002 by Good Books, Intercourse, PA 17534

International Standard Book Number: 1-56148-377-X (paperback edition)
International Standard Book Number: 1-56148-378-8 (comb-bound paperback edition)
International Standard Book Number: 1-56148-379-6 (hardcover gift edition)
Library of Congress Catalog Card Number: 2002073876

Library of Congress Cataloging-in-Publication Data
Good, Phyllis Pellman
　　Fix-it and forget-it recipes for entertaining : slow cooker favorites for all the year
round / Phyllis Pellman Good & Dawn J. Ranck.
　　p. cm.
　　Includes index.
　　ISBN 1-56148-379-6 -- ISBN 1-56148-377-X (pbk.) -- ISBN 1-56148-378-8 (plastic
comb.)
　　1. Electric cookery, Slow. 2. Entertaining. I. Ranck, Dawn J. II. Title.
TX827.G66 2002
641.5′884-dc21　　　　　　　　　　　　　　　　　　　　　2002073876

Table of Contents

About
Fix-It and Forget-It
Recipes for Entertaining

Can you lead a busy life and still have guests for dinner?

Can you have people over without spending hours in the kitchen?

Would you love to try some new recipes in your slow cooker—maybe just for your own household?

Fix-It and Forget-It Recipes for Entertaining answers "yes" to all those questions.

This cookbook—in the *Fix-It and Forget-It* tradition—has more than 580 irresistible recipes (and no duplicates with the original *Fix-it and Forget-It Cookbook*).

Use these wonderful recipes to share dinner with your neighbors, with your summer weekend visitors, with friends after a chilly soccer game, with family for a birthday party.

All the dishes in this bountiful collection share two qualities—little fuss and lots of flavor.

Most of the recipes in this collection will fit in a 4-qt. or a 5-qt. slow cooker. We indicate those that require a larger cooker; with those we suggest that you use a 6-qt. cooker, or two smaller ones.

Many stove-top or oven recipes can be adapted for a slow cooker. If you want to experiment, use these conversion factors:

- Low (in a slow cooker) = 200°, approximately (in an oven)
- High (in a slow cooker) = 300°, approximately (in an oven)
- In a slow-cooker, 2 hours on Low = 1 hour, approximately, on High

And don't forget, every time you lift the lid and peek, you need to add 15 minutes to the cooking time.

So, relieve the pressures of hosting. Get rid of the last-minute stress of putting food on the table.

Visit with your guests until it's time to eat—then lift the lids of your steaming slow cookers—and offer them Fruited Pork Chops, Garlic Lime Chicken, Navy Bean Soup, Oriental Shrimp Dish, Hot Cranberry Punch—and more.

Fix-It and Forget-It Recipes for Entertaining is bursting with absolutely delicious recipes, as well as Tips for Hosting, Menus for Meals with Friends, and Ideas for Go-Alongs that complement slow cooker dishes.

You'll love cooking, hosting, and eating from this treasure of good food.

— Phyllis Pellman Good and Dawn J. Ranck

Beef
Main Dishes

Beef and Gravy

Arlene Groff
Lewistown, PA

Makes 8 servings

1 onion, chopped
1 Tbsp. butter
3-4-lb. beef roast, cubed
1 tsp. salt
1/4 tsp. pepper
2 cups water
3 beef bouillon cubes
1/2 cup flour

1. Saute onion in skillet in butter until brown. Place onion in slow cooker, but reserve drippings.

2. Brown roast in skillet in drippings. Add meat to slow cooker, again reserving drippings.

3. Combine salt, pepper, water, bouillon, and flour. Add to meat drippings. Cook until thickened. Pour over meat.

4. Cover. Cook on low 6-8 hours.

5. Serve over noodles.

Hickory Smoked Brisket

Janet Roggie
Lowville, NY

Makes 12-14 servings

3-4-lb. beef brisket
1/4 cup liquid smoke
1/2 tsp. celery salt
1/2 tsp. garlic salt
1/2 tsp. onion powder

1. Place beef on piece of foil.

2. Sprinkle with remaining ingredients. Wrap foil securely around beef. Place in slow cooker.

3. Cover. Cook on low 8-12 hours.

4. Serve warm with juice ladled over each slice.

Can-It-Really-Be-So-Easy? Roast Beef

Laverne Stoner
Scottdale, PA

Makes 8 servings

4-lb. beef roast
10¾-oz. can cream of mushroom soup
1 pkg. dry onion soup mix
1 cup water

1. Place beef roast on double layer of aluminum foil.
2. Combine soup and dry soup mix. Spread on all sides of roast. Wrap foil around roast. Place in slow cooker. Pour water around roast.
3. Cover. Cook on low 6-8 hours.

Rich and Tasty Beef Roast

Reita F. Yoder
Carlsbad, NM

Makes 6-8 servings

10¾-oz. can cream of mushroom soup
3-5-lb. beef roast
oil
1 pkg. dry onion soup mix

1. Spread mushroom soup in bottom of slow cooker.
2. Sear roast on all sides in oil in hot skillet. Add to slow cooker.
3. Sprinkle meat with dry onion soup mix.
4. Cook on high 5-6 hours.

Easy Stroganoff

Vicki Dinkel
Sharon Springs, KS

Makes 6-8 servings

10¾-oz. can cream of mushroom soup
14½-oz. can beef broth
1 lb. beef stewing meat or round steak, cut in 1″ pieces
1 cup sour cream
2 cups cooked noodles

1. Combine soup and broth in slow cooker. Add meat.
2. Cover. Cook on high 3-4 hours. Reduce heat to low and cook 3-4 hours.
3. Stir in sour cream.
4. Stir in noodles.
5. Cook on high 20 minutes.

Since I'm in school part-time and work two part-time jobs, this nearly complete meal is great to come home to. It smells wonderful when you open the door. A vegetable or salad and some crispy French bread are good additions.

Garlic Beef Stroganoff

Sharon Miller
Holmesville, OH

Makes 6-8 servings

2 tsp. beef bouillon granules
2 4½-oz. jars sliced mushrooms, drained
  with juice reserved
1 cup mushroom juice, with boiling water
  added to make a full cup
10¾-oz. can cream of mushroom soup
1 large onion, chopped
3 garlic cloves, minced
1 Tbsp. Worcestershire sauce
1½-2-lb. boneless round steak, cut into
  thin strips
2 Tbsp. oil
8-oz. pkg. cream cheese, cubed and
  softened

1. Dissolve bouillon in mushroom juice and water in slow cooker.
2. Add soup, mushrooms, onion, garlic, and Worcestershire sauce.
3. Saute beef in oil in skillet. Transfer to slow cooker and stir into sauce.
4. Cover. Cook on low 7-8 hours. Turn off heat.
5. Stir in cream cheese until smooth.
6. Serve over noodles.

Home-Style Beef Cubes

Dorothy Horst
Tiskilwa, IL

Makes 8-10 servings

½ cup flour
1 tsp. salt
⅛ tsp. pepper
4 lbs. beef cubes
½ cup chopped shallots or green onions
2 4-oz. cans sliced mushrooms, drained,
  or ½ lb. fresh mushrooms, sliced
14½-oz. can beef both
1 tsp. Worcestershire sauce
2 tsp. ketchup
¼ cup water
3 Tbsp. flour

1. Combine ½ cup flour, salt, and pepper. Toss beef in flour mixture to coat. Place in slow cooker.
2. Cover with onions and mushrooms.
3. Combine broth and Worcestershire sauce. Pour into slow cooker. Mix well.
4. Cover. Cook on low 7-12 hours.
5. One hour before serving, make a smooth paste of water and 3 Tbsp. flour. Stir into slow cooker. Cover and cook until broth thickens.
6. Serve over hot buttered noodles.

Menu Idea

Home-Style Beef Cubes
Hot Buttered Noodles
Tossed Salad with Oil and Vinegar
  Dressing
    To make Dressing combine:
      ½ cup red wine vinegar
      ½ cup olive oil
      1 tsp. salt
      1 cup sugar

Machaca Beef

Jeanne Allen
Rye, CO

Makes 10-12 servings

1 1/2-lb. beef roast
1 large onion, sliced
4-oz. can chopped green chilies
2 beef bouillon cubes
1 1/2 tsp. dry mustard
1/2 tsp. garlic powder
1 tsp. seasoning salt
1/2 tsp. pepper
1 cup salsa

1. Combine all ingredients except salsa in slow cooker. Add just enough water to cover.
2. Cover cooker and cook on low 10-12 hours, or until beef is tender. Drain and reserve liquid.
3. Shred beef using two forks to pull it apart.
4. Combine beef, salsa, and enough of the reserved liquid to make of desired consistency.
5. Use this filling for burritos, chalupas, quesadillas, or tacos.

After living in New Mexico for the past 30 years, I get homesick for New Mexican cuisine now that I live in Colorado. I keep memories of New Mexico alive by cooking foods that remind me of home.

Menu Idea

Machaca Beef
Refried Beans or Mexican Rice
Guacamole with Greens or Chips

Salsa Chuck Roast

Hazel L. Propst
Oxford, PA

Makes 6 servings

3-4-lb. chuck or round roast
1 Tbsp. oil
1 pkg. dry onion soup mix
2 cups water
1 cup salsa

1. Brown meat in skillet in oil on both sides. Place in slow cooker.
2. Add remaining ingredients to drippings in pan. Simmer 2-3 minutes. Add to slow cooker.
3. Cover. Cook on low 7-8 hours.
4. Serve with broth over noodles or rice.

Salsa Beef

Sarah Niessen
Akron, PA

Makes 5-6 servings

2-2 1/2 lbs. beef, cut up in bite-sized cubes
1 Tbsp. oil
16-oz. jar salsa
8-oz. can tomato sauce
2 garlic cloves, minced
2 Tbsp. brown sugar
1 Tbsp. soy sauce
1 cup canned tomatoes

1. Brown beef in skillet in oil. Place in slow cooker.
2. Add remaining ingredients.
3. Cover. Cook on low 6-8 hours.
4. Serve over rice.

Variation: For added flavor, use Italian tomato sauce.

Melt-in-Your-Mouth Mexican Meat Dish

Marlene Bogard
Newton, KS

Makes 6 servings

4-lb. chuck roast
1 tsp. salt
1 tsp. pepper
2 Tbsp. oil
1 onion, chopped
1 tsp. chili powder
1 tsp. garlic powder
1¼ cups diced green chili peppers
¾ cup hot pepper sauce
water

1. Season roast with salt and pepper. Sear on all sides in oil in skillet. Place in slow cooker.
2. Mix together remaining ingredients, except water, and spoon over meat. Pour in water down along the side of the cooker (so as not to wash off the topping) until roast is one-third covered.
3. Cover. Cook on high 6 hours. Reduce to low 2-4 hours, until meat falls apart.
4. Thicken sauce with flour if you like.
5. This highly seasoned meat is perfect for shredded beef Mexican tacos, burritos, etc.

Green Chili Roast

Anna Kenagy
Carlsbad, NM

Makes 8-10 servings

3-4-lb. beef roast
1 tsp. seasoned meat tenderizer
oil, optional
1 tsp. salt
3-4 green chili peppers, or 4-oz. can green chilies, undrained
1 Tbsp. Worchestershire sauce
½ tsp. black pepper

1. Sprinkle roast with meat tenderizer. Brown under broiler or in skillet in oil. Place in slow cooker.
2. Pour in water until roast is half covered.
3. Add remaining ingredients over top.
4. Cover. Cook on low 8 hours.
5. Serve with mashed potatoes and green beans.

Hosting Idea

Get two slow cookers going—one with this beef dish and one with the same recipe, but using chicken as the meat. Host a Mexican fiesta and let guests build their own combinations. Prepare bowls of olives, cheese (either shredded or cubed), chopped tomatoes, shredded lettuce, a variety of beans, and guacamole as go-alongs.

Apple and Onion Beef Pot Roast

Betty K. Drescher
Quakertown, PA

Makes 8-10 servings

3-lb. boneless beef roast, cut in half
oil
1 cup water
1 tsp. seasoning salt
1/2 tsp. soy sauce
1/2 tsp. Worcestershire sauce
1/4 tsp. garlic powder
1 large tart apple, quartered
1 large onion, sliced
2 Tbsp. cornstarch
2 Tbsp. water

1. Brown roast on all sides in oil in skillet. Transfer to slow cooker.
2. Add water to skillet to loosen browned bits. Pour over roast.
3. Sprinkle with seasoning salt, soy sauce, Worcestershire sauce, and garlic powder.
4. Top with apple and onion.
5. Cover. Cook on low 5-6 hours.
6. Remove roast and onion. Discard apple. Let stand 15 minutes.
7. To make gravy, pour juices from roast into saucepan and simmer until reduced to 2 cups. Combine cornstarch and water until smooth in small bowl. Stir into beef broth. Bring to boil. Cook and stir for 2 minutes until thickened.
8. Slice pot roast and serve with gravy.

Menu Idea

Apple and Onion Beef Pot Roast with Gravy
Mashed Potato Filling (page 214)
Peas or Green Beans

Fruited Beef Tagine

Naomi E. Fast
Hesston, KS

Makes 6-8 servings

1 Tbsp. oil
2 lbs. beef, cut into 2" cubes
4 cups sliced onions
2 tsp. ground coriander
1 1/2 tsp. ground cinnamon
3/4 tsp. ground ginger
14 1/2-oz. can beef broth, plus enough water to equal 2 cups
16 ozs. pitted prunes
salt to taste
fresh ground pepper to taste
juice of one lemon

1. Brown beef cubes in oil in skillet. Place beef in slow cooker. Reserve drippings.
2. Saute onions in drippings until lightly browned, adding more oil if needed. Add to slow cooker.
3. Add remaining ingredients, except lemon juice.
4. Simmer on low 5-6 hours, adding lemon juice during the last 10 minutes.
5. This recipe, accompanied with a tossed green salad and rolls, makes a complete meal.

Variations:
1. Mix in a few very thin slices of lemon rind to add flavor and eye appeal.

2. You can substitute lamb cubes for the beef.

There's-No-Easier Roast Beef

Sue Pennington
Bridgewater, VA

Makes 6-8 servings

12-oz. bottle barbecue sauce
3-4-lb. beef roast

1. Pour half of barbecue sauce into bottom of slow cooker.
2. Add roast. Top with remaining barbecue sauce.
3. Cover. Cook on low 6-8 hours.
4. Slice roast and serve with sauce.

Variation: Use an 18-oz. bottle of barbecue sauce if you prefer a juicier outcome.

Barbecue Roast Beef

Vicki Dinkel
Sharon Springs, KS

Makes 6-8 servings

1 1/2-2-lb. beef roast, cooked

Sauce:
1 cup ketchup
1/2 cup minced onions
2 tsp. Worcestershire sauce
1 cup water
1 Tbsp. brown sugar

1. Cut roast into cubes and place in slow cooker.
2. Combine sauce ingredients and pour over meat.

3. Cover. Cook on high 2 hours, then on low for 4. Return to high 30 minutes before serving.

8-Hour Tangy Beef

Mary Martins
Fairbank, IA

Makes 6-8 servings

3 1/2-4-lb. beef roast
12-oz. can ginger ale
1 1/2 cups ketchup

1. Put beef in slow cooker.
2. Pour ginger ale and ketchup over roast.
3. Cover. Cook on low 8-9 hours.
4. Shred with 2 forks and serve on buns. Or break up into chunks and serve over rice, potatoes, or pasta.

Variations:
1. This recipe produces a lot of juice. You can add chopped onions, potatoes, and green beans in Step 2, if you want. Or stir in sliced mushrooms and/or peas 30 minutes before the end of the cooking time.

2. For a tangier finished dish, add chili powder or cumin, along with black pepper, in Step 2.

Beef Roast in Beer

Evelyn Page
Riverton, WY

Makes 5-6 servings

2-3-lb. beef roast
1 can beer
1 onion, sliced

1. Place roast in slow cooker. Poke all over surface with fork.
2. Pour beer over roast. Cover. Refrigerate for 8 hours.
3. Add sliced onion to slow cooker.
4. Cover. Cook on low 6-8 hours.

Variations:

1. Brown roast in oil in skillet on top and bottom before placing in cooker.

2. Mix together 1 cup cider vinegar and 2 Tbsp. Worcestershire sauce. Marinate roast in mixture in refrigerator for 2-4 hours. Either discard marinade when placing roast in cooker, or add it to the cooker.

To thicken broth, mix together 1/4 cup flour and 1 cup water until smooth. Twenty minutes before end of cooking time, remove roast from cooker. Stir flour paste into beef broth until smooth. Return roast to cooker and continue cooking. When finished, cut roast into chunks and serve with gravy.

Italian Beef Au Jus

Carol Sherwood
Batavia, NY

Makes 8 servings

3-5-lb. boneless beef roast
10-oz. pkg. au jus mix
1 pkg. Italian salad dressing mix
14 1/2-oz. can beef both
half a soup can water

1. Place beef in slow cooker.
2. Combine remaining ingredients. Pour over roast.
3. Cover. Cook on low 8 hours.
4. Slice meat and spoon onto hard rolls with straining spoon to make sandwiches. Or shred with 2 forks and serve over noodles or rice in broth thickened with flour.

Note: To thicken broth, mix 3 Tbsp. cornstarch into 1/4 cup cold water. Stir until smooth. Remove 1/2 cup beef broth from cooker and blend into cornstarch-water. Stir back into broth in cooker, stirring until smooth. Cook 10-15 minutes on high until broth becomes of gravy consistency.

Saucy Italian Roast

Sharon Miller
Holmesville, OH

Makes 8-10 servings

3-3½-lb. boneless rump roast
½ tsp. salt
½ tsp. garlic powder
¼ tsp. pepper
4½-oz. jar mushroom pieces, drained
1 medium onion, diced
14-oz. jar spaghetti sauce
¼-½ cup beef broth
hot cooked pasta

1. Cut roast in half.
2. Combine salt, garlic powder, and pepper. Rub over both halves of the roast. Place in slow cooker.
3. Top with mushrooms and onions.
4. Combine spaghetti sauce and broth. Pour over roast.
5. Cover. Cook on low 8-9 hours.
6. Slice roast. Serve in sauce over pasta.

Simply Super Supper

Anne Townsend
Albuquerque, NM

Makes 4 servings

2 ribs celery, sliced
3 carrots, cut in strips
2 potatoes, cubed
2 onions, coarsely chopped
2-lb. beef roast
1 pkg. dry onion soup mix
1 Tbsp. liquid smoke
1½ cups water

1. Place vegetables in slow cooker.
2. Place roast on top of vegetables.
3. Sprinkle with dry soup mix.
4. Combine liquid smoke and water. Pour over roast.
5. Cover. Cook on low 7-8 hours, or until vegetables are tender.
6. Slice meat and serve with cole slaw and French bread. Lemon pie makes a nice finish.

This is a welcoming dinner to come home to because the house smells so yummy as you walk in. And the wonderful aroma lingers.

Tomato-y Beef Stew

Janie Steele
Moore, OK

Makes 6-8 servings

5 lbs. stewing meat, cubed
2 onions, chopped
14½-oz. can chopped tomatoes
10¾-oz. can tomato soup
5-6 carrots, sliced
5-6 potatoes, peeled and cubed
1 cup sliced celery
1 bell pepper, sliced
2 tsp. salt
½ tsp. pepper
2 cloves minced garlic

1. Combine all ingredients in slow cooker.
2. Cover. Cook on low 8 hours.
3. Serve with warm bread or cornbread.

Note: This recipe is very adaptable. You can reduce the amount of meat and increase the vegetables as you wish.

After-Work Stew

Vera M. Kuhns
Harrisonburg, VA

Makes 5 servings

3 medium-sized potatoes,
  pared and cubed
4 medium-sized carrots, quartered
2 celery ribs, sliced
2 medium-sized onions, sliced
1 1/2 lbs. beef, cut into 1 1/2" cubes, browned
2 tsp. salt
1/2 tsp. dried basil
1/2 tsp. pepper
10 3/4-oz. can tomato soup
half a soup can water

1. Layer potatoes, carrots, celery, and onions in slow cooker.
2. Mix beef with salt, basil, and pepper in bowl and place on top of vegetables.
3. Combine soup and water. Pour into slow cooker.
4. Cover. Bake on low 8-9 hours, or until vegetables and meat are tender.

Best Ever Beef Stew

Barbara Walker
Sturgis, SD

Makes 6 servings

2 cups water
1 pkg. beef stew mix
2 lbs. stewing meat, cubed
3 15-oz. cans whole new potatoes,
  or 3 lbs. fresh new potatoes
1 cup sliced celery
10-12 small white onions, peeled
1-1 1/2 cups sliced carrots
8 ozs. fresh mushrooms

1. Combine water and beef stew mix in slow cooker.
2. Layer meat in slow cooker.
3. Add remaining ingredients.
4. Cover. Cook on high 6-7 hours.

Favorite Sunday Pot Roast

Amber Swarey
Donalds, SC

Makes 6 servings

4-lb. chuck roast
meat tenderizer
1 pkg. dry onion soup mix
fresh mushrooms, sliced
carrots, sliced
potatoes, chunked
1 cup boiling water

1. Place roast in slow cooker. Sprinkle with meat tenderizer and onion soup mix.
2. Layer mushrooms over roast.
3. Add carrots and potatoes around roast.

4. Pour water over vegetables.
5. Cover. Cook on high 4-5 hours.
6. Add a fresh salad and your meal is ready.

This is a recipe I grew up with at home. When Sunday came around, we looked forward to roast, potatoes, and carrots.

New Mexico Stew
Helen Kenagy
Carlsbad, NM

Makes 8 servings

2 lbs. stewing meat or steak, cubed
salt to taste
pepper to taste
1 Tbsp. oil
5-6 potatoes, cubed
6-8 carrots, diced
other vegetables — diced
1-2 4.25-oz. cans chopped green chilies
1½ lbs. raw pork sausage, crumbled

1. Salt and pepper stewing meat. Brown in oil in skillet.
2. Place half the stewing meat in bottom of slow cooker.
3. Layer half the vegetables and chilies over the beef. Crumble half the sausage over top. Sprinkle each layer with salt and pepper.
4. Continue layering until all ingredients are used.
5. Cover. Cook on high until ingredients begin to boil. Then turn cooker to low for 8-10 hours. Do not lift lid and do not stir during cooking.
6. Serve with a green salad and fresh bread.

Beef Stew with Shiitake Mushrooms
Kathy Hertzler
Lancaster, PA

Makes 4-6 servings

12 new potatoes, cut into quarters
½ cup chopped onions
8-oz. pkg. baby carrots
3.4-oz. pkg. fresh shiitake mushrooms, sliced, or 2 cups regular white mushrooms, sliced
16-oz. can whole tomatoes
14½-oz. can beef broth
½ cup flour
1 Tbsp. Worcestershire sauce
1 tsp. salt.
1 tsp. sugar
1 tsp. dried marjoram leaves
¼ tsp. pepper
1 lb. beef stewing meat, cubed

1. Combine all ingredients except beef in slow cooker. Add beef.
2. Cover. Cook on low 8-9 hours. Stir well before serving.

Menu Idea

Beef Stew with Shiitake Mushrooms
Tossed Salad of Mesclun Greens,
    sauteed almonds, mandarin oranges
    and a Caesar dressing
Homemade Multigrain Bread
Fresh Fruit

Sunday Roast Beef

Beverly Flatt-Getz
Warriors Mark, PA

Makes 8 servings

4 potatoes, peeled and quartered
1/2 cup peeled small onions
1 cup carrot chunks
4-lb. beef chuck roast
1 Tbsp. olive oil
1 pkg. G. Washington Seasoning
1/2 tsp. onion salt
1/2 tsp. minced garlic
1/2 tsp. garlic salt
1 cup water
few drops Worcestershire sauce
1/2 cup cold water
1 Tbsp. cornstarch

1. Place potatoes, onions, and carrots in bottom of slow cooker.
2. Sear beef in olive oil in skillet. Add to vegetables in slow cooker.
3. Sprinkle with seasonings.
4. Pour water around roast.
5. Cover. Cook on low 8-10 hours.
6. Remove meat and vegetables from juice. Season juice with Worcestershire sauce.
7. Dissolve cornstarch in cold water. Add to slow cooker. Cook on high until thick and bubbly.

When I was growing up we often had this for Sunday lunch after church. Mom put it in the oven very early. I adapted the recipe for making it in a slow cooker.

Menu Idea

Sunday Roast Beef
Creamed Onions, or Creamed Peas and
   Onions
Dinner Rolls with Butter
Hot Apple Pie with Vanilla Ice Cream
   and Cinnamon Sauce

Slow Cooker Stew

Arlene Groff
Lewistown, PA

Makes 10 servings

1 qt. canned stewing beef, or 2 lbs.
   stewing beef, cut into 1" pieces
1 qt. tomato soup
1 cup diced carrots
1/2 cup diced celery
1/2 cup chopped onions
2-3 cups diced potatoes
1 cup diced cabbage
1 qt. canned green beans,
   or 2 1-lb. pkgs. frozen green beans
1 tsp. salt
1/2 tsp. pepper
1/2 tsp. Italian seasoning
2 cups water or tomato juice

1. Combine all ingredients in slow cooker.
2. Cover. Cook on low 7-8 hours.

Easy Beef Stew

Janie Steele
Moore, OK

Makes 14-18 servings

2-3 lbs. beef, cubed
16-oz. pkg. frozen green beans
  or mixed vegetables
16-oz. pkg. frozen corn
16-oz. pkg. frozen peas
2 lbs. carrots, chopped
1 large onion, chopped
4 medium potatoes, peeled and chopped
10¾-oz. can tomato soup
10¾-oz. can celery soup
10¾-oz. can mushroom soup
bell pepper chopped, optional

1. Combine all ingredients in 2 4-qt. slow cookers (this is a very large recipe).
2. Cover. Cook on low 10-11 hours.

Bavarian Beef

Naomi E. Fast
Hesston, KS

Makes 6 servings

3-3½-lb. boneless beef chuck roast
oil
3 cups sliced carrots
3 cups sliced onions
2 large kosher dill pickles, chopped
1 cup sliced celery
½ cup dry red wine or beef broth
⅓ cup German-style mustard
2 tsp. coarsely ground black pepper
2 bay leaves
¼ tsp. ground cloves
1 cup water
⅓ cup flour

1. Brown roast on both sides in oil in skillet. Transfer to slow cooker.
2. Add remaining ingredients.
3. Cover. Cook on low 6-7 hours.
4. Remove meat and vegetables to large platter. Cover to keep warm.
5. Mix flour with 1 cup of broth until smooth. Return to cooker. Turn on high and stir, cooking until broth is smooth and thickened.
6. Serve over noodles or spaetzle.

Menu Idea

Bavarian Beef
Buttered Noodles or Spaetzle
Gingerbread with Custard Sauce

Italian Beef Stew

Kathy Hertzler
Lancaster, PA

Makes 4-6 servings

2 Tbsp. flour
2 tsp. chopped fresh thyme
1 tsp. salt
1/4-1/2 tsp. freshly ground pepper
2 1/4 lbs. beef stewing meat, cubed
3 Tbsp. olive oil
1 onion, chopped
1 cup tomato sauce
1 cup beef stock
1 cup red wine
3 garlic cloves, minced
2 Tbsp. tomato paste
2 cups frozen peas, thawed but not cooked
1 tsp. sugar

1. Spoon flour into small dish. Season with thyme, salt, and pepper. Add beef cubes and coat evenly.
2. Heat oil in slow cooker on high. Add floured beef and brown on all sides.
3. Stir in remaining ingredients except peas and sugar.
4. Cover. Cook on low 6 hours.
5. Add peas and sugar. Cook an additional 30 minutes, or until beef is tender and peas are warm.

Dawn's Mushroom Beef Stew

Dawn Day
Westminster, CA

Makes 8-10 servings

1 lb. sirloin, cubed
2 Tbsp. flour
oil
1 large onion, chopped
2 garlic cloves, minced
1/2 lb. button mushrooms, sliced
2 ribs celery, sliced
2 carrots, sliced
3-4 large potatoes, cubed
2 tsp. seasoning salt
14 1/2-oz. can beef stock, or 2 bouillon cubes dissolved in 1 2/3 cups water
1/2-1 cup good red wine

1. Dredge sirloin in flour and brown in skillet. Reserve drippings. Place meat in slow cooker.
2. Saute onion, garlic, and mushrooms in drippings just until soft. Add to meat.
3. Add all remaining ingredients.
4. Cover. Cook on low 6 hours. Test to see if vegetables are tender. If not, continue cooking on low for another 1-1 1/2 hours.
5. Serve with crusty bread.

Beef Mushroom Casserole

Susan Stephani Smith
Monument, CO

Makes 12 servings

4 lbs. lean beef sirloin, cut into 1″ cubes
2 10¾-oz. cans cream of mushroom soup
2 pkgs. dry onion soup mix
¼-1 tsp. pepper, according to your taste
    preference
½ tsp. salt
1-2 cups red Burgundy wine, optional
1½ lbs. fresh mushrooms, quartered
¼ cup sour cream, optional

1. Combine all ingredients except wine, mushrooms, and sour cream in slow cooker.
2. Cover. Cook on low 4-5 hours, stirring occasionally.
3. Add mushrooms and wine. Cook 30 minutes longer.
4. Ten minutes before end of cooking time, stir in sour cream, if you wish.
5. Serve over egg noodles.

Beef Burgundy

Joyce Kaut
Rochester, NY

Makes 6 servings

2 slices bacon, cut in squares
2 lbs. sirloin tip or round steak, cubed
¼ cup flour
1 tsp. salt
½ tsp. seasoning salt
¼ tsp. dried marjoram
¼ tsp. dried thyme
¼ tsp. pepper
1 garlic clove, minced
1 beef bouillon cube, crushed
1 cup burgundy wine
¼ lb. fresh mushrooms, sliced
2 Tbsp. cornstarch
2 Tbsp. cold water

1. Cook bacon in skillet until browned. Remove bacon, reserving drippings.
2. Coat beef with flour and brown on all sides in bacon drippings.
3. Combine steak, bacon drippings, bacon, seasonings, garlic, bouillon, and wine in slow cooker.
4. Cover. Cook on low 6-8 hours.
5. Add mushrooms.
6. Dissolve cornstarch in water. Add to slow cooker.
7. Cover. Cook on high 15 minutes.
8. Serve over noodles.

Beef Stew with Wine

Andrea O'Neil
Fairfield, CT

Makes 8-10 servings

1 lb. stewing meat, cubed
oil
2 onions, quartered
4 carrots, sliced
4-5 potatoes, cubed
28-oz. can crushed tomatoes
1/2 cup wine
1 pkg. dry onion soup mix
1 cup water
2 tsp. salt
3/4 tsp. pepper
3 Tbsp. cornstarch
1/4 cup water

1. Brown beef cubes in skillet in oil.
2. Place in slow cooker. Add other ingredients and stir to combine.
3. Cover. Cook on low 9-10 hours.
4. Ten minutes before serving, stir cornstarch into water until smooth. Stir into hot stew.

Variation: For added zest, add 1/2 tsp. Old Bay Seasoning and 1 rib celery, diced, in Step 2.

Tempting Beef Stew

Patricia Howard
Albuquerque, NM

Makes 10-12 servings

2-3 lbs. beef stewing meat
3 carrots, sliced thin
1-lb. pkg. frozen green peas with onions
1-lb. pkg. frozen green beans
16-oz. can whole or stewed tomatoes
1/2 cup beef broth
1/2 cup white wine
1/2 cup brown sugar
4 Tbsp. tapioca
1/2 cup bread crumbs
2 tsp. salt
1 bay leaf
pepper to taste

1. Combine all ingredients in slow cooker.
2. Cover. Cook on low 10-12 hours.
3. Serve over noodles, rice, couscous, or biscuits.

Variation: In place of the tapioca, thicken stew with 1/4 cup flour dissolved in 1/3-1/2 cup water. Mix in and turn cooker to high. Cover and cook for 15-20 minutes.

Prepare this Tempting Beef Stew before your guests arrive. Give yourself time to relax instead of panicking in a last-minute rush.

Beef Pot Roast

Nancy Wagner Graves
Manhattan, KS

Makes 6-8 servings

4-5-lb. beef chuck roast
1 garlic clove, cut in half
salt to taste
pepper to taste
1 carrot, chopped
1 rib celery, chopped
1 small onion, sliced
3/4 cup sour cream
3 Tbsp. flour
1/2 cup dry white wine

1. Rub roast with garlic. Season with salt and pepper. Place in slow cooker.
2. Add carrots, celery, and onion.
3. Combine sour cream, flour, and wine. Pour into slow cooker.
4. Cover. Cook on low 6-7 hours.

Pot-Roast Complete

Naomi E. Fast
Hesston, KS

Makes 6-8 servings

3-3 1/2-lb. arm roast, boneless
2 large onions, sliced
1/2 cup brown sugar
1/3 cup soy sauce
1/3 cup cider vinegar
2 bay leaves
2-3 garlic cloves, minced
1 tsp. grated fresh ginger
1 cup julienned carrots, matchstick size
2 cups sliced button mushrooms
2-3 cups fresh spinach leaves,
    or 2 10-oz. pkgs. frozen spinach, drained
2 Tbsp. cornstarch

1. Place meat, topped with onions, in slow cooker.
2. Combine brown sugar, soy sauce, and vinegar. Pour over beef.
3. Add bay leaves, garlic, and ginger
4. Cover. Cook on high 6-7 hours.
5. Spread carrots, mushrooms, and spinach over beef.
6. Cover. Cook on high 20 minutes.
7. Mix cornstarch with 1/2 cup broth from slow cooker. Return to slow cooker.
8. Cover. Cook 10 minutes more.
9. Serve over rice.

I can't count how many times I have used this recipe over the last 15-20 years as a guest meal.

Hungarian Barley Stew

Naomi E. Fast
Hesston, KS

Makes 8 servings

2 Tbsp. oil
1½ lbs. beef cubes
2 large onions, diced
1 medium-sized green pepper, chopped
28-oz. can whole tomatoes
½ cup ketchup
⅔ cup dry small pearl barley
1 tsp. salt
½ tsp. pepper
1 Tbsp. paprika
10-oz. pkg. frozen baby lima beans
3 cups water
1 cup sour cream

1. Brown beef cubes in oil in skillet. Add onions and green peppers. Saute. Pour into slow cooker.
2. Add remaining ingredients except sour cream.
3. Cover. Cook on high 5 hours.
4. Stir in sour cream before serving.
5. Serve with your favorite cabbage slaw.

Hungarian Beef Stew

Esther Becker
Gordonville, PA

Makes 6 servings

2 lbs. beef cubes
1 onion, chopped
2 medium potatoes, peeled and cubed
2 carrots, sliced
10-oz. pkg. frozen lima beans
2 tsp. parsley
½ cup beef broth
2 tsp. paprika
1 tsp. salt
16-oz. can diced tomatoes

1. Combine beef, onion, potatoes, carrots, lima beans, and parsley in slow cooker.
2. Combine remaining ingredients and pour into slow cooker.
3. Cover. Cook on low 10-12 hours.
4. Serve with Seven Layer Salad and Homemade Rolls.

Crockery Cooking
Betty Sue Good
Broadway, VA

Makes 8 servings

2 lbs. beef cubes
oil
1 large onion, chopped
2 potatoes, cubed
2 carrots, sliced
1 pt. frozen lima beans, thawed
1 qt. stewed tomatoes
1-1½ tsp. salt, according to your taste
   preference
¼-½ tsp. pepper, according to your taste
   preference

1. Brown beef on all sides in oil in skillet.
Place in slow cooker.
2. Layer onions, potatoes, carrots, and lima
beans over beef.
3. Mix tomatoes and seasonings together in
bowl. Pour over meat and vegetables.
4. Cover. Cook on low 8-10 hours.
5. Serve over rice with warm rolls, pickles,
pecan pie, and vanilla ice cream.

Wash-Day Stew
Naomi E. Fast
Hesston, KS

Makes 8-10 servings

1½-2 lbs. lean lamb or beef, cubed
2 15-oz. cans garbanzo beans, drained
2 15-oz. cans white beans, drained
2 medium onions, peeled and quartered
1 qt. water
1 tsp. salt
1 tomato, peeled and quartered
1 tsp. turmeric
3 Tbsp. fresh lemon juice
8-10 pita bread pockets

1. Combine ingredients in slow cooker.
2. Cover. Cook on high 6-7 hours.
3. Lift stew from cooker with a strainer
spoon and stuff in pita bread pockets.

*I learned to prepare this nutritious meal from a
student from Iran, who was attending graduate
school at the University of Nebraska. Fatimeh
explained to me that her family prepared this dish
every wash day. Very early in the morning, they
made a fire in a large rock-lined pit outside. Then
they placed a large covered kettle, filled with the
above ingredients, over the coals to cook slowly all
day. At the end of a day of doing laundry, the food
was ready with a minimum of preparation. Of
course, they started with dry beans and dry
garbanzos, presoaked the night before. They
served this Wash-Day Stew spooned into pita
bread and ate it with their hands.*

Menu Idea

Wash-Day Stew
**Cucumber/Onion Salad with sour
   cream, salt, and mint**

Pepper Beef Goulash
Anna Stoltzfus
Honey Brook, PA

Makes 4-6 servings

1/2 cup water
6-oz. can tomato paste
2 Tbsp. vinegar
1 pkg. dry sloppy Joe seasoning
2-2¼ lbs. beef stewing meat, cubed
1 rib celery, sliced
1 medium green pepper,
    cut into 1/2" pieces

1. Combine water, tomato paste, vinegar, and seasoning mix in slow cooker.
2. Stir in beef, celery, and green peppers.
3. Cover. Cook on high 4-5 hours.
4. Serve over noodles.

Tender Texas-Style Steaks
Janice Muller
Derwood, MD

Makes 4-6 servings

steaks or chops
1 cup brown sugar
1 cup ketchup
salt to taste
pepper to taste
few dashes of Worcestershire sauce

1. Lay steaks in bottom of slow cooker.
2. Combine sugar and ketchup. Pour over steaks
3. Sprinkle with salt and pepper and a few dashes of Worcestershire sauce.

4. Cover. Cook on high 3 hours and low 3 hours.
5. Serve with wide egg noodles, green beans, and applesauce. Use some of the juice from the cooker over the noodles. Thicken the juice if you like with a little flour.

Swiss Steak
Judi Manos
West Islip, NY

Makes 6 servings

1½ lbs. boneless beef round steak
1 tsp. peppered seasoning salt
6-8 potatoes, cubed
1½ cups baby carrots
1 medium onion, sliced
14½-oz. can diced tomatoes with basil,
    garlic, oregano
12-oz. jar home-style beef gravy
chopped fresh parsley

1. Cut beef into 6 pieces. Sprinkle with seasoning salt. Brown in skillet for about 8 minutes.
2. Layer potatoes, carrots, onions, and beef in slow cooker.
3. Combine tomatoes and gravy. Pour over beef and vegetables.
4. Cover. Cook on low 7-9 hours.
5. Sprinkle with parsley.

Variation: For more flavor add 1/2 tsp. dried basil, 1/2 tsp. dried oregano, and 2 minced garlic cloves to the tomatoes and gravy in Step 3.

Swiss Steak

Marie Shank
Harrisonburg, VA

Makes 6-8 servings

2-lb. round steak, cut into serving pieces
1 tsp. salt
½ tsp. pepper
1 large onion, sliced, or 1 pkg. dry onion
    soup mix
16-oz. can tomatoes

1. Combine ingredients in slow cooker.
2. Cover. Cook on low 6-10 hours or high 3-4 hours.

Note: You may want to omit the salt if you use the onion soup mix.

Slow Cooker Pepper Steak

Esther Hartzler
Carlsbad, NM

Makes 6-8 servings

1½-2 lbs. round beef steak
2 Tbsp. oil
¼ cup soy sauce
1 cup chopped onions
1 garlic clove, minced
1 tsp. sugar
½ tsp. salt
¼ tsp. pepper
¼ tsp. ground ginger
4 tomatoes, cut in eighths,
    or 16-oz. can tomatoes
2 large green peppers, cut in strips
½ cup cold water
1 Tbsp. cornstarch

1. Cut beef into 3" x 1" strips. Brown in oil in skillet. Drain. Transfer to slow cooker.
2. In separate bowl, combine soy sauce, onions, garlic, sugar, salt, pepper, and ginger. Pour over beef.
3. Cover. Cook on low 5-6 hours.
4. Add tomatoes and green peppers. Cook 1 hour longer.
5. Combine cold water and cornstarch to make paste. Stir into slow cooker. Cook on high until thickened.
6. Serve over noodles or rice.

Savory Pepper Steak

Grace W. Yoder
Harrisonburg, VA

Makes 6 servings

1½-lb. beef round steak, cut ½" thick
¼ cup flour
½ tsp. salt
⅛ tsp. pepper
1 medium onion, chopped or sliced
1 garlic clove, minced
2 large green peppers, sliced in ½" strips
29-oz. can whole tomatoes
1 Tbsp. beef flavor base, or 1 beef
   bouillon cube
1 Tbsp. soy sauce
2 tsp. Worcestershire sauce
3 Tbsp. flour
3 Tbsp. water

1. Cut beef into strips.
2. Combine ¼ cup flour, salt, and pepper. Toss with beef until well coated. Place in slow cooker.
3. Add onions, garlic, and half the green pepper slices. Mix well.
4. Combine tomatoes, beef base, soy sauce, and Worcestershire sauce. Pour into slow cooker.
5. Cover. Cook on low 8-10 hours.
6. One hour before serving, turn to high and stir in remaining green pepper.
7. Combine 3 Tbsp. flour and water to make smooth paste. Stir into slow cooker. Cover. Cook until thickened.
8. Serve over rice.

Slow Cooker Beef with Mushrooms

Grace W. Yoder
Harrisonburg, VA

Makes 6 servings

2 medium onions, thinly sliced
½ lb. mushrooms, sliced, or 2 4-oz. cans
   sliced mushrooms, drained
2½-lb. beef flank or round steak
salt to taste
pepper to taste
1 Tbsp. Worcestershire sauce
1 Tbsp. oil
paprika to taste

1. Place sliced onions and mushrooms in slow cooker.
2. Score top of meat about ½" deep in diamond pattern.
3. Season with salt and pepper. Rub in Worcestershire sauce and oil. Sprinkle top with paprika.
4. Place meat on top of onions.
5. Cover. Cook on low 7-8 hours.
6. To serve, cut beef across grain in thin slices. Top with mushrooms and onions.

Barbecued Chuck Steak

Rhonda Burgoon
Collingswood, NJ

Makes 4 servings

1½-lb. boneless chuck steak, 1½" thick
1 clove garlic, minced
¼ cup wine vinegar
1 Tbsp. brown sugar
1 tsp. paprika
2 Tbsp. Worcestershire sauce
½ cup ketchup
1 tsp. salt
1 tsp. prepared mustard
¼ tsp. black pepper

1. Cut beef on diagonal across the grain into 1"-thick slices. Place in slow cooker.
2. Combine remaining ingredients. Pour over meat. Stir to mix.
3. Cover. Cook on low 3-5 hours.

Fruited Flank Steak

Ruth A. Feister
Narvon, PA

Makes 6 servings

1 flank steak
salt to taste
pepper to taste
14½-oz. can mixed fruit,
    or your choice of canned fruit
1 Tbsp. salad oil
1 Tbsp. lemon juice
¼ cup teriyaki sauce
1 tsp. vinegar
1 garlic clove, minced

1. Sprinkle steak with salt and pepper. Place in slow cooker.
2. Drain fruit, saving ¼ cup syrup. Combine ¼ cup syrup with remaining ingredients. Pour over steak.
3. Cover. Cook on low 6-8 hours. Add drained fruit during the last 15 minutes of cooking.
4. Lift from cooker onto platter. Using sharp knife slice across the grain making thin slices. Spoon fruit over meat.
5. Serve with baked rice.

Pigs in Blankets

Linda Sluiter
Schererville, IN

Makes 4-6 servings

2-3-lb. round steak, cut about 1" thick
1 lb. bacon
1 cup ketchup
¾ cup brown sugar
1 cup water
half a yellow onion, chopped

1. Cut steak into strips 1" thick x 3" long.
2. Lay a bacon strip down, then a strip of beef on top of the bacon slice. Roll up and secure with toothpick. Place in slow cooker.
3. Combine remaining ingredients. Pour over meat roll-ups.
4. Cover. Cook on high 8 hours.

Apple and Brown Sugar Corned Beef

Mary Seielstad
Sparks, NV

Makes 8-10 servings

2½-3-lb. corned beef brisket
8 small red potatoes
3 medium carrots, peeled and sliced
1 large onion, cut in 6-8 pieces
1 small head cabbage, cut in chunks
1 qt. apple juice
1 cup brown sugar
1 Tbsp. prepared mustard

1. Place meat, potatoes, carrots, onion, and cabbage in 6-qt. slow cooker, or divide between 2 4- or 5-qt. cookers.
2. Combine apple juice, brown sugar, and mustard. Pour into slow cooker(s).
3. Cover. Cook on high 6-6½ hours or low 10-12 hours, or until vegetables and meat are tender.
4. Remove meat and vegetables from slow cooker. Thinly slice meat across the grain. Serve topped with vegetables.
5. Delicious eaten with cornbread.

Note: If potatoes are not small, quarter them.

Corned Beef

Elaine Vigoda
Rochester, NY

Makes 8 servings

3 large carrots, cut into chunks
1 cup chopped celery
1 tsp. salt
½ tsp. pepper
1 cup water
3-4-lb. corned beef
1 large onion, cut into pieces
half a small head of cabbage, cut in wedges
4 potatoes, peeled and chunked

1. Place carrots, celery, seasonings, and water in slow cooker.
2. Add beef. Cover with onions.
3. Cover. Cook on low 8-10 hours, or on high 5-6 hours.
4. Lift corned beef out of cooker and add cabbage and potatoes, pushing them to bottom of slow cooker. Return beef to cooker.
5. Cover. Cook on high 2 hours.
6. Remove corned beef. Cool and slice on the diagonal. Serve surrounded by vegetables.

Corned Beef and Cabbage with Potatoes and Carrots

Rosaria Strachan
Fairfield, CT

Makes 6-7 servings

3-4 carrots, sliced
3-4 potatoes, cubed
1 onion, sliced
2½-3½-lb. corned beef brisket
10-12 peppercorns
4-6 cabbage wedges

1. Place carrots, potatoes, and onions in bottom of slow cooker.
2. Place beef over vegetables.
3. Cover with water.
4. Add peppercorns.
5. Cover. Cook on low 8-10 hours or on high 5-6 hours.
6. Add cabbage. Cook on high 2-3 hours more.
7. Cut up meat and serve on large platter with mustard or horseradish as condiments. Pass vegetables with meat or in their own serving dish.

Corned Beef Dinner

Shirley Sears
Tiskilwa, IL

Makes 6 servings

2 onions, sliced
2 garlic cloves, minced
3 potatoes, pared and quartered
3 carrots, sliced
2 bay leaves
1 small head cabbage, cut into 4 wedges
3-4-lb. corned beef brisket
1 cup water
½ cup brown sugar
1 Tbsp. prepared mustard
dash of ground cloves

1. Layer onions, garlic, potatoes, carrots, bay leaves, and cabbage in slow cooker.
2. Place brisket on top.
3. Add water.
4. Cover. Cook on low 10-11 hours.
5. During last hour of cooking, combine brown sugar, mustard, and cloves. Spread over beef.
6. Discard bay leaves. Slice meat and arrange on platter of vegetables.

Slow-Cooked Short Ribs

Jean A. Shaner
York, PA
Barbara L. McGinnis
Jupiter, FL

Makes 12 servings

2/3 cup flour
2 tsp. salt
1/2 tsp. pepper
4-4 1/2 lbs. boneless beef short ribs,
   or 6-7 lbs. bone-in beef short ribs
oil, or 1/3 cup butter
1 large onion, chopped
1 1/2 cups beef broth
3/4 cup wine or cider vinegar
1/2-3/4 cup packed brown sugar,
   according to your taste preference
1/2 cup chili sauce
1/3 cup ketchup
1/3 cup Worcestershire sauce
5 garlic cloves, minced
1 1/2 tsp. chili powder

1. Combine flour, salt, and pepper in plastic bag. Add ribs and shake to coat.
2. Brown meat in small amount of oil, or in butter, in batches in skillet. Transfer to slow cooker.
3. Combine remaining ingredients in saucepan. Cook, stirring up browned drippings, until mixture comes to boil. Pour over ribs.
4. Cover. Cook on low 9-10 hours.
5. Debone and serve.
6. It is ideal to cook these ribs one day in advance of serving. Refrigerate for several hours or overnight. Remove layer of congealed fat before serving over rice or noodles.

Beef Ribs with Sauerkraut

Rosaria Strachan
Fairfield, CT

Makes 8-10 servings

3-4 lbs. beef short ribs
32-oz. bag, or 27-oz. can, sauerkraut,
   drained
2 Tbsp. caraway seeds
1/4 cup water

1. Put ribs in 6-qt. slow cooker.
2. Place sauerkraut and caraway seeds on top of ribs.
3. Pour in water.
4. Cover. Cook on high 3-4 hours or on low 7-8 hours.
5. Serve with mashed potatoes.

Variation: If you really enjoy sauerkraut, double the amount of sauerkraut, and divide the recipe between 2 4- or 5-qt. cookers.

Ribs and Limas

Miriam Friesen
Staunton, VA

Makes 6 servings

3 lbs. beef short ribs
2 Tbsp. oil
1 onion, chopped
4 carrots, sliced
1/4 cup packed brown sugar
2 Tbsp. flour
2 tsp. dry mustard
1 1/2 tsp. salt
1/4 tsp. pepper
1 1/4 cups water
1/4 cup cider vinegar
1 large bay leaf, broken in half
10-oz. pkg. frozen lima beans or peas,
   cooked

1. Cut ribs into serving-size pieces. Brown ribs in skillet in oil.
2. Place onions and carrots in slow cooker. Add ribs.
3. Combine brown sugar, flour, mustard, salt, and pepper. Stir in water and vinegar until smooth. Pour over ribs. Push bay leaves into liquid.
4. Cover. Cook on high 5-6 hours or on low 10-12 hours.
5. Stir in lima beans.
6. Cover. Cook on high 20-30 minutes.
7. Remove bay leaf before serving.
8. Serve with a citrus salad and crusty rolls.

Potluck Beef Barbecue Sandwiches

Carol Sommers
Millersburg, OH

Makes 16 servings

4-lb. beef chuck roast
1 cup brewed coffee or water
1 Tbsp. cider or red-wine vinegar
1 tsp. salt
1/2 tsp. pepper
14-oz. bottle ketchup
15-oz. can tomato sauce
1 cup sweet pickle relish
2 Tbsp. Worcestershire sauce
1/4 cup brown sugar

1. Place roast, coffee, vinegar, salt, and pepper in slow cooker.
2. Cover. Cook on high 6-8 hours, or until meat is very tender.
3. Pour off cooking liquid. Shred meat with two forks.
4. Add remaining ingredients. Stir well.
5. Cover. Cook on high 30-45 minutes. Reduce heat to low for serving.

Barbara Jean's Junior Beef

Barbara Jean Fabel
Wausau, WI

Makes 8 servings

3 1/2-5 lb. beef roast
1/2 tsp. salt
1/2 tsp. cayenne pepper
1/2 tsp. black pepper
1 tsp. seasoned salt
1 medium onion, chopped
1 qt. dill pickle juice
4 dill pickles, chopped
8 hamburger rolls
1/2 lb. fresh mushrooms,
   sliced and sauteed
2 cups grated cheddar or Swiss cheese

1. Combine all ingredients except rolls, mushrooms, and cheese in slow cooker.
2. Cover. Cook on high 4-5 hours.
3. Shred meat using two forks. Reduce heat to low and cook 1 hour, or until meat is very tender.
4. Serve on hamburger buns with sauteed, sliced, fresh mushrooms and grated cheddar or Swiss cheese.

Beef Barbecue Sandwiches

Melba Eshleman
Manheim, PA

Makes 12-16 servings

3-4 lb. beef roast (bottom round or rump
   is best)
1/2 cup water
1/2 cup ketchup
1 tsp. chili powder
1 1/2 Tbsp. Worcestershire sauce
2 Tbsp. vinegar
1 tsp. salt
1 Tbsp. sugar
1 tsp. dry mustard
1 medium onion, finely chopped
1/2 cup water
10-12 kaiser rolls

1. The night before serving, place roast in slow cooker with 1/2 cup water.
2. Cover. Cook on low 10-12 hours.
3. Also the night before serving, combine remaining ingredients and refrigerate 8-10 hours.
4. In the morning, shred roast with fork and return to cooker. Pour remaining ingredients over top. Mix together.
5. Heat on low until mealtime.
6. Serve on kaiser rolls.

Ranch Hand Beef

Sharon Timpe
Mequon, WI

Makes 10-12 servings

3-3½-lb. boneless beef chuck roast
1 cup thinly sliced onions
10¾-oz. can cream of celery soup
4-oz. can sliced mushrooms
12-oz. can beer
½ cup ketchup
1 large bay leaf
½ tsp. salt
¼ tsp. lemon pepper
2 Tbsp. chopped fresh parsley,
   or 1½ tsp. dried parsley

1. Place roast in slow cooker.
2. Combine remaining ingredients. Pour over roast.
3. Cover. Cook on low 7-9 hours or on medium setting 4-6 hours, until meat is tender.
4. Remove bay leaf.
5. Shred roast with two forks. Mix meat through sauce.
6. Serve on buns for sandwiches or over cooked noodles as a main dish.

Variation: If you prefer a thicker sauce, stir 2 Tbsp. cornstarch into ¼ cup water. When smooth, sitr into hot sauce, 15 minutes before serving.

Note: To give this dish a Mexican theme, serve the beef over tortilla chips or fritos and have bowls of shredded lettuce, diced avocado, sliced green onions, sliced ripe olives, sour cream, diced tomatoes, and shredded cheese for garnishing the meat.

Menu Idea

For a Mexican theme:
   Ranch Hand Beef
   Sliced Tomatoes marinated in oil,
      vinegar, and herb dressing
   Cornbread
   Fresh Fruit with Yogurt Dip
   Buffalo Chip Cookies
   Mexican Fruitcake

Easy Roast Beef Barbecue

Rose Hankins
Stevensville, MD

Makes 12-16 servings

3-4-lb. beef roast
12-oz. bottle barbecue sauce
½ cup water
½ cup ketchup
½ cup chopped onions
½ cup chopped green pepper
12-16 sandwich rolls

1. Combine ingredients in slow cooker.
2. Cover. Cook on low 12 hours.
3. Shred meat using 2 forks. Mix thoroughly through sauce.
4. Serve on rolls with cole slaw.

Hot Beef Sandwiches
Evelyn L. Ward
Greeley, CO

Makes 10 servings

3 lbs. beef chuck roast
1 large onion, chopped
¼ cup vinegar
1 clove garlic, minced
1-1½ tsp. salt
¼-½ tsp. pepper

1. Place meat in slow cooker. Top with onions.
2. Combine vinegar, garlic, salt, and pepper. Pour over meat.
3. Cover. Cook on low 8-10 hours.
4. Drain broth but save for dipping.
5. Shred meat.
6. Serve on hamburger buns with broth on side.

I volunteer with Habitat for Humanity. I don't do construction, but I provide lunch sometimes for work crews. This sandwich is a favorite. I make the most colorful tossed salad that I can and serve fresh fruit that is in season and pie.

Herby Beef Sandwiches
Jean A. Shaner
York, PA

Makes 10-12 servings

3-4-lb. boneless beef chuck roast
3 Tbsp. fresh basil, or 1 Tbsp. dried basil
3 Tbsp. fresh oregano,
    or 1 Tbsp. dried oregano
1½ cups water
1 pkg. dry onion soup mix
10-12 Italian rolls

1. Place roast in slow cooker.
2. Combine basil, oregano, and water. Pour over roast.
3. Sprinkle with onion soup mix.
4. Cover. Cook on low 7-8 hours. Shred meat with fork.
5. Serve on Italian rolls.

Middle Eastern Sandwiches (for a crowd)
Esther Mast
East Petersburg, PA

Makes 10-16 sandwiches

4 lbs. boneless beef or venison, cut in
    ½" cubes
4 Tbsp. cooking oil
2 cups chopped onions
2 garlic cloves, minced
1 cup dry red wine
6-oz. can tomato paste
1 tsp. dried oregano
1 tsp. dried basil
½ tsp. dried rosemary
2 tsp. salt

dash of pepper
¼ cup cold water
¼ cup cornstarch
pita pocket breads
2 cups shredded lettuce
1 large tomato, seeded and diced
1 large cucumber, seeded and diced
8-oz. carton plain yogurt

1. Brown meat, 1 lb. at a time, in skillet in 1 Tbsp. oil. Reserve drippings and transfer meat to slow cooker.

2. Saute onion and garlic in drippings until tender. Add to meat.

3. Add wine, tomato paste, oregano, basil, rosemary, salt, and pepper.

4. Cover. Cook on low 6-8 hours.

5. Turn cooker to high. Combine cornstarch and water in small bowl until smooth. Stir into meat mixture. Cook until bubbly and thickened, stirring occasionally.

6. Split pita breads to make pockets. Fill each with meat mixture, lettuce, tomato, cucumber, and yogurt.

7. Serve with jello salad or applesauce.

Meat Loaf

Colleen Heatwole
Burton, MI

Makes 8 servings

2 lbs. ground beef
2 eggs
⅔ cup quick oats
1 pkg. dry onion soup mix
½-1 tsp. liquid smoke
1 tsp. ground mustard
½ cup ketchup, divided

1. Combine ground beef, eggs, dry oats, dry soup mix, liquid smoke, ground mustard, and all but 2 Tbsp. ketchup. Shape into loaf and place in slow cooker.

2. Top with remaining ketchup.

3. Cover. Cook on low 8-10 hours or on high 4-6 hours.

Hosting Idea

I like to invite guests for Sunday evening supper and suggest they come by 3:30-4:00. That gives me time to prepare the place, so that when they arrive we have time to relax and visit before the meal. After the meal we have time for games and the evening doesn't get late.

—Esther Mast

Comfort Meat Loaf

Trudy Kutter
Corfu, NY

Makes 6 servings

2 eggs, beaten
1/2 cup milk
2/3 cup bread crumbs
2 Tbsp. grated or finely chopped onion
1 tsp. salt
1/2 tsp. sage
1 1/2 lbs. ground beef
2-3 Tbsp. tomato sauce or ketchup

1. Combine everything but tomato sauce.
Shape into 6″ round loaf and place in cooker.
2. Cover. Cook on low 6 hours.
3. Spoon tomato sauce over meat loaf.
4. Cover. Cook on high 30 minutes.

Savory Meat Loaf

Betty B. Dennison
Grove City, PA

Makes 6-8 servings

2 lbs. ground beef or turkey
1 cup dry rolled oats
tomato juice (just enough to moisten meat
   if needed)
2 eggs
1 onion, diced
1 Tbsp. prepared mustard
1 tsp. garlic salt
2 Tbsp. ketchup
1 Tbsp. Worcestershire sauce
1 tsp. salt

Sauce:
26-oz. can, or 2 10 3/4-oz. cans, mushroom
   soup
6-10 fresh mushrooms, diced
1 Tbsp. onion flakes
half soup can water
1/4 tsp. salt
1/8 tsp. pepper

1. Combine all meat loaf ingredients. Shape
into either a round or an oval loaf, to fit the
shape of your slow cooker, and place in
greased cooker.
2. Cover. Cook on high 1 hour.
3. Combine sauce ingredients. Pour over
meat loaf.
4. Cover. Cook on low 6 hours.

*Note: Be careful when you remove the lid, not to
let the moisture that has gathered on the lid drop
back into the sauce, thereby thinning it.*

Magic Meat Loaf

Carolyn Baer
Conrath, WI

Makes 6 servings

1 egg, beaten
¼ cup milk
1½ tsp. salt
2 slices bread, crumbled
1½ lbs. ground beef
half a small onion, chopped
2 Tbsp. chopped green peppers
2 Tbsp. chopped celery
ketchup
green pepper rings
4-6 potatoes, cubed
3 Tbsp. butter, melted

1. Combine egg, milk, salt, and bread crumbs in large bowl. Allow bread crumbs to soften.
2. Add meat, onions, green peppers, and celery. Shape into loaf and place off to the side in slow cooker.
3. Top with ketchup and green pepper rings.
4. Toss potatoes with melted butter. Spoon into cooker alongside meat loaf.
5. Cover. Cook on high 1 hour, then on low 8-10 hours.

Gourmet Meat Loaf

Anne Townsend
Albuquerque, NM

Makes 8 servings

2 medium potatoes, cut in strips

Meat loaf:
2 lbs. ground beef
½ lb. bulk sausage
1 onion, finely chopped
2-3 cloves garlic, minced, according to your taste preference
½ cup ketchup
¾ cup crushed saltines
2 eggs
2 tsp. Worcestershire sauce
2 tsp. seasoning salt
¼ tsp. pepper

Sauce:
½ cup ketchup
¼ cup brown sugar
1½ tsp. dry mustard
½ tsp. ground nutmeg

1. Place potatoes in bottom of slow cooker.
2. Combine meat loaf ingredients. Form into loaf and place on top of potatoes.
3. Combine sauce ingredients. Spoon over meat loaf.
4. Cover. Cook on low 8-12 hours.

Note: The potatoes take longer to cook than the meat so make sure you allow enough time.

My husband has this at the top of his list of favorite meat loaf recipes.

Menu Idea

Gourmet Meat Loaf
Spinach Salad
Grilled Tomatoes

Cheese Meat Loaf

Mary Sommerfeld
Lancaster, PA

Makes 8 servings

2 lbs. ground chuck or ground beef
2 cups shredded sharp cheddar or
   American cheese
1 tsp. salt
1 tsp. dry mustard
1/4 tsp. pepper
1/2 cup chili sauce
2 cups crushed cornflakes
2 eggs
1/2 cup milk

1. Combine all ingredients. Shape into loaf. Place in greased slow cooker.
2. Cover. Cook on low 6-8 hours.
3. Slice and serve with your favorite tomato sauce or ketchup.

Variation: Before baking, surround meat loaf with quartered potatoes, tossed lightly in oil.

Festive Meatballs

Jean Butzer
Batavia, NY

Makes 5-7 servings

1 1/2 lbs. ground beef
4 1/2-oz. can deviled ham
2/3 cup evaporated milk
2 eggs, beaten slightly
1 Tbsp. grated onion
2 cups soft bread crumbs
1 tsp. salt
1/4 tsp. allspice
1/4 tsp. pepper
1/4 cup flour
1/4 cup water
1 Tbsp. ketchup
2 tsp. dill weed
1 cup sour cream

1. Combine beef, ham, milk, eggs, onion, bread crumbs, salt, allspice, and pepper. Shape into 2" meatballs. Arrange in slow cooker.
2. Cover. Cook on low 2 1/2-3 1/2 hours. Turn control to high.
3. Dissolve flour in water until smooth. Stir in ketchup and dill weed. Add to meatballs, stirring gently.
4. Cook on high 15-20 minutes, or until slightly thickened.
5. Turn off heat. Stir in sour cream.
6. Serve over rice or pasta.

Easy Meatballs
Carlene Horne
Bedford, NH

Makes 10-12 servings

2 10¾-oz. cans cream of mushroom soup
2 8-oz. pkgs. cream cheese, softened
4-oz. can sliced mushrooms, undrained
1 cup milk
2-3 lbs. frozen meatballs

1. Combine soup, cream cheese, mushrooms, and milk in slow cooker.
2. Add meatballs. Stir.
3. Cover. Cook on low 4-5 hours.
4. Serve over noodles.

Swedish Meat Balls
Zona Mae Bontrager
Kokomo, IN

Makes 6-8 servings

1 lb. ground beef
½ lb. ground pork
½ cup minced onions
¾ cup fine dry bread crumbs
1 Tbsp. minced parsley
1 tsp. salt
⅛ tsp. pepper
½ tsp. garlic powder
1 Tbsp. Worcestershire sauce
1 egg
½ cup milk
¼ cup oil

Gravy:
¼ cup flour
¼ tsp. salt
¼ tsp. garlic powder
⅛ tsp. pepper
1 tsp. paprika
2 cups boiling water
¾ cup sour cream

1. Combine meats, onions, bread crumbs, parsley, salt, pepper, garlic powder, Worcestershire sauce, egg, and milk.
2. Shape into balls the size of a walnut. Brown in oil in skillet. Reserve drippings, and place meatballs in slow cooker.
3. Cover. Cook on high 10-15 minutes.
4. Stir flour, salt, garlic powder, pepper, and paprika into hot drippings in skillet. Stir in water and sour cream. Pour over meatballs.
5. Cover. Reduce heat to low. Cook 4-5 hours.
6. Serve over rice or noodles.

Italian Meatball Subs
Bonnie Miller
Louisville, OH

Makes 6-7 servings

2 eggs, beaten
1/4 cup milk
1/2 cup dry bread crumbs
2 Tbsp. grated Parmesan cheese
1 tsp. salt
1/4 tsp. pepper
1/8 tsp. garlic powder
1 lb. ground beef
1/2 lb. bulk pork sausage

Sauce
15-oz. can tomato sauce
6-oz. can tomato paste
1 small onion, chopped
1/2 cup chopped green bell pepper
1/2 cup red wine, or beef broth
1/3 cup water
2 garlic cloves, minced
1 tsp. dried oregano
1 tsp. salt
1/2 tsp. pepper
1/2 tsp. sugar

1. Make meatballs by combining eggs and milk. Add bread crumbs, cheese and seasonings. Add meats. Mix well. Shape into 1" balls. Broil or saute until brown. Put in slow cooker.
2. Combine sauce ingredients. Pour over meatballs.
3. Cover. Cook on low 4-6 hours.
4. Serve on rolls with creamy red potatoes, salad, and dessert.

Arlene's BBQ Meatballs
Arlene Groff
Lewistown, PA

Makes 12 servings

2 lbs. ground beef
2 eggs
1 small onion, chopped
1/4 cup milk
1 1/2 cup crushed crackers (equal to one packaged column of saltines)
1 tsp. prepared mustard
1 tsp. salt
1/2 tsp. pepper
oil
1 1/2 cups tomato juice
1/3 cup vinegar
1 Tbsp. soy sauce
1 Tbsp. Worcestershire sauce
3/4 cup brown sugar
2 Tbsp. cornstarch
1 tsp. prepared mustard

1. Combine beef, eggs, onion, milk, crackers, 1 tsp. mustard, salt, and pepper. Form into small balls. Brown in oil in skillet. Place in slow cooker.
2. Combine remaining ingredients. Pour over meatballs.
3. Cover. Cook on high 2 hours. Stir well. Cook an additional 2 hours.

Menu Idea

Arlene's BBQ Meatballs
Macaroni and Cheese (page 145)
Vegetable of your choice

Cocktail Meatballs

Kathy Purcell
Dublin, OH

Makes 10-12 servings

3 lbs. ground beef
1 pkg. dry onion soup mix
14-oz. can sweetened condensed milk

Sauce:
18-oz. bottle ketchup
1/2 cup brown sugar
1/4 cup Worcestershire sauce

1. Combine beef, soup mix, and condensed milk. Form into about 3 dozen meatballs, each about 1 1/2" around.
2. Place meatballs on baking sheet. Brown in 350° oven for 30 minutes. Remove from oven and drain. Place meatballs in slow cooker.
3. Combine sauce ingredients. Pour over meatballs.
4. Cover. Cook on low 3-4 hours.

I have made these meatballs for many different parties and events and they are always a big hit. Everyone asks for the recipe.

Easy Meatballs for a Group

Penny Blosser
Beavercreek, OH

Makes 10-12 main-dish servings

80-100 frozen small meatballs
16-oz. jar barbecue sauce
16-oz. jar apricot jam

1. Fill slow cooker with meatballs.
2. Combine sauce and jam. Pour over meatballs.
3. Cover. Cook on low 4 hours, stirring occasionally.
4. This works well as an appetizer, or as a main dish over rice.

Sweet 'n Tangy Meatballs

Donna Lantgen
Rapid City, SD

Makes 8 servings

1 1/2 lbs. ground beef
1/4 cup plain dry bread crumbs
3 Tbsp. prepared mustard
1 tsp. Italian seasoning
3/4 cup water
1/4 cup ketchup
2 Tbsp. honey
1 Tbsp. red-hot cayenne pepper sauce
3/4-oz. pkg. brown gravy mix

1. Combine ground beef, bread crumbs, mustard, and Italian seasoning. Shape into 1" balls. Bake or microwave until cooked. Drain. Place meatballs in slow cooker.
2. Cover. Cook on low 3 hours.
3. Combine remaining ingredients in saucepan. Cook for 5 minutes. Pour over meatballs.
4. Cover. Cook on low 2 hours.

Variation: For a fuller flavor, use orange juice instead of water in sauce.

Meat Balls and Spaghetti Sauce

Carol Sommers
Millersburg, OH

Makes 6-8 servings

Meatballs:
1½ lbs. ground beef
2 eggs
1 cup bread crumbs
oil

Sauce:
28-oz. can tomato puree
6-oz. can tomato paste
10¾-oz. can tomato soup
¼-½ cup grated Romano or Parmesan
  cheese
1 tsp. oil
1 garlic clove, minced

sliced mushrooms (either canned or fresh),
  optional

1. Combine ground beef, eggs, and bread crumbs. Form into 16 meatballs. Brown in oil in skillet.
2. Combine sauce ingredients in slow cooker. Add meatballs. Stir together gently.
3. Cover. Cook on low 6-8 hours. Add mushrooms 1-2 hours before sauce is finished.
4. Serve over cooked spaghetti.

Mexican Meatballs

Anna Kenagy
Carlsbad, NM

Makes 4-5 servings

1 lb. ground beef
4 slices bread, torn into small pieces
1 onion, chopped
⅓ cup milk
1 egg yolk, beaten (reserve white)
1 tsp. salt
dash of pepper
1 egg white, beaten
1 cup cornflakes, crushed
oil
10¾-oz. can tomato soup
1 small green bell pepper, chopped
½ cup water

1. Combine ground beef, bread, onion, milk, egg yolk, salt, and pepper. Form into balls.
2. Roll balls in egg white and then in crumbs. Brown in hot oil in skillet and then place in slow cooker.
3. Combine soup, pepper, and water. Pour over meatballs.
4. Cover. Cook on low 8 hours or high 3-4 hours.

Snappy Meatballs
Clara Newswanger
Gordonville, PA

*Makes 6-8 main-dish servings,
or 25 appetizer servings*

Meatballs:
2 lbs. ground beef
1/2 cup chopped onions
1 cup bread crumbs
2 eggs
1 tsp. salt

Sauce:
3 1/2 cups tomato juice
1 cup brown sugar
1/4 cup vinegar
1 tsp. grated onion
12 gingersnap cookies, crushed

1. Combine meatball ingredients. Shape into balls. Brown in skillet. Drain well. Spoon into slow cooker.
2. Combine sauce ingredients in slow cooker. Pour over meatballs. Mix gently.
3. Cover. Cook on low 4 hours.

Our son married a woman from the West Coast. He brought his new bride "home" on their honeymoon. We held an informal reception for friends who could not attend their wedding. Served with a light lunch, this recipe brought raves! Now we think of our children 3000 miles away whenever we make these meatballs.

Sweet and Sour Meatballs
Alice Miller
Stuarts Draft, VA

Makes 4 servings

1 lb. ground beef
1/2 cup dry bread crumbs
1/4 cup milk
1 tsp. salt
1 egg, beaten
2 Tbsp. finely chopped onions
1/2 tsp. Worcestershire sauce

Sauce:
1/2 cup packed brown sugar
2 Tbsp. cornstarch
13 1/4-oz. can pineapple chunks, undrained
1/3 cup vinegar
1 Tbsp. soy sauce
1 green pepper, chopped

1. Combine meatball ingredients. Shape into 1 1/2" balls. Brown in skillet. Drain. Place in slow cooker.
2. Add brown sugar and cornstarch to skillet. Stir in remaining ingredients. Heat to boiling, stirring constantly. Pour over meatballs.
3. Cover. Cook on low 3-4 hours.

Note: If you like pineapples, use a 20-oz. can of chunks, instead of the 13 1/4-oz. can.

Chinese Meatballs

Evelyn L. Ward
Greeley, CO

Makes 6 servings

1 lb. ground beef
1 egg
5 Tbsp. cornstarch, divided
1/2 tsp. salt
2 Tbsp. minced onions
2 cups pineapple juice
2 Tbsp. soy sauce
1/2 cup wine vinegar
3/4 cup water
1/2 cup sugar
1 green pepper, cut in strips
1 can water chestnuts, drained
canned chow mein noodles
6 slices pineapple, cut into halves

1. Combine beef, egg, 1 Tbsp. cornstarch, salt, and onions. Mix well. Shape into 1" meatballs. Brown on all sides under broiler.
2. Mix remaining cornstarch with pineapple juice. When smooth, mix in soy sauce, vinegar, water, and sugar. Bring to boil. Simmer, stirring until thickened.
3. Combine meatballs and sauce in slow cooker.
4. Cover. Cook on low 2 hours.
5. Add green peppers and water chestnuts.
6. Cover. Cook 1 hour.
7. Serve over chow mein noodles and garnish with pineapple slices.

Applesauce Meatballs

Mary E. Wheatley
Mashpee, MA

Makes 6 servings

3/4 lb. ground beef
1/4 lb. ground pork
1 egg
3/4 cup soft bread crumbs
1/2 cup unsweetened applesauce
3/4 tsp. salt
1/4 tsp. pepper
oil
1/4 cup ketchup
1/4 cup water

1. Combine beef, pork, egg, bread crumbs, applesauce, salt, and pepper. Form into 1 1/2" balls.
2. Brown in oil in batches in skillet. Transfer meat to slow cooker, reserving drippings.
3. Combine ketchup and water and pour into skillet. Stir up browned drippings and mix well. Spoon over meatballs.
4. Cover. Cook on low 4-6 hours.
5. Serve with steamed rice and green salad.

Holiday Meat Balls

Jean Robinson
Cinnaminson, NJ

Makes 20 servings

2 15-oz. bottles hot ketchup
2 cups blackberry wine
2 12-oz. jars apple jelly
2 lbs. frozen, precooked meatballs, or your
    own favorite meatballs, cooked

1. Heat ketchup, wine, and jelly in slow cooker on high.
2. Add frozen meatballs.
3. Cover. Cook on high 4-6 hours. (If the meatballs are not frozen, cook on high 3-4 hours.)

Variations:
1. For those who like it hotter and spicier, put a bottle of XXXtra hot sauce on the table for them to add to their individual servings.

2. If you prefer a less wine-y flavor, use 1 cup water and only 1 cup wine.

Swedish Meatballs

Arlene Leaman Kliewer
Lakewood, Co

Makes 8-10 servings, or 60 very small meatballs

2 lbs. ground beef
2 eggs, slightly beaten
1 cup bread crumbs
2 tsp. salt
1/4 tsp. pepper

Sauce:
12-oz. bottle chili sauce
10-oz. jar grape jelly
1/2 cup ketchup
1 tsp. Worcestershire sauce

1. Combine ground beef, eggs, bread crumbs, salt, and pepper. Form into 60 small balls. Place on baking sheet.
2. Bake at 400° for 15-17 minutes. Place in slow cooker.
3. Combine sauce ingredients in saucepan. Heat. Pour over meatballs.
4. Heat on low until ready to serve.

We often make this recipe for our family's Christmas evening snack.

Variations:
1. Liven up the meatballs by adding 2/3 cup chopped onions, 2 Tbsp. snipped fresh parsley, and 1 tsp. Worcestershire sauce in Step 1.
   —Joan Rosenberger, Stephens City, VA

2. Add juice of half a lemon to the Sauce in Step 3.

   —Linda Sluiter, Schererville, IN

3. Use 1/2 cup crushed cornflakes in place of the 1 cup bread crumbs in the meatball mixture. Add 1 Tbsp. bottled lemon juice to the Sauce in Step 3.

   —Alice Miller, Stuarts Draft, VA

Meatball-Barley Casserole

Marjorie Y. Guengerich
Harrisonburg, VA

Makes 6 servings

²/₃ cup pearl barley
1 lb. ground beef
¹/₂ cup soft bread crumbs
1 small onion, chopped
¹/₄ cup milk
¹/₄ tsp. pepper
1 tsp. salt
oil
¹/₂ cup thinly sliced celery
¹/₂ cup finely chopped sweet peppers
10³/₄-oz. can cream of celery soup
¹/₃ cup water
paprika

1. Cook barley as directed on package. Set aside.
2. Combine beef, bread crumbs, onion, milk, pepper, and salt. Shape into 20 balls. Brown on all sides in oil in skillet. Drain and place in slow cooker.
3. Add barley, celery, and peppers.
4. Combine soup and water. Pour into slow cooker. Mix all together gently.
5. Sprinkle with paprika.
6. Cover. Cook on low 6-8 hours or on high 4 hours.

Barbecue Sauce and Hamburgers

Dolores Kratz
Souderton, PA

Makes 6 servings

14³/₄-oz. can beef gravy
¹/₂ cup ketchup
¹/₂ cup chili sauce
1 Tbsp. Worcestershire sauce
1 Tbsp. prepared mustard
6 grilled hamburger patties
6 slices cheese, optional

1. Combine all ingredients except hamburger patties and cheese slices in slow cooker.
2. Add hamburger patties.
3. Cover. Cook on low 5-6 hours.
4. Serve in buns, each topped with a slice of cheese if you like.

Notes:
1. Freeze leftover sauce for future use.

2. This is both a practical and a tasty recipe for serving a crowd (picnics, potlucks, etc). You can grill the patties early in the day, rather than at the last minute when your guests are arriving.

No-More-Bottled Barbecue Sauce
Lauren Eberhard
Seneca, IL

Makes 2-2¹/2 cups sauce

1 cup finely chopped onions
¹/4 cup oil
6-oz. can tomato paste
¹/2 cup water
¹/4 cup brown sugar
¹/4 cup lemon juice (freshly squeezed juice is best)
3 Tbsp. Worcestershire sauce
2 Tbsp. prepared mustard
2 tsp. salt
¹/4 tsp. pepper

1. Combine ingredients in slow cooker.
2. Cover. Cook on low 3 hours.
3. Use on hamburgers, sausage, pork chops, ribs, steaks, chicken, turkey, or fish.

Note: Sauce will keep in refrigerator for up to 2 weeks.

Pizzaburgers
Deborah Swartz
Grottoes, VA

Makes 4-6 servings

1 lb. ground beef
¹/2 cup chopped onions
¹/4 tsp. salt
¹/8 tsp. pepper
8 ozs. pizza sauce
10³/4-oz. can cream of mushroom soup
2 cups shredded cheddar cheese

1. Brown ground beef and onion in skillet. Drain.
2. Add remaining ingredients. Mix well. Pour into slow cooker.
3. Cover. Cook on low 1-2 hours.
4. Serve on hamburger buns.

New Mexico Cheeseburgers
Colleen Konetzni
Rio Rancho, NM

Makes 8 servings

1 lb. ground beef, browned
6 potatoes, peeled and sliced
¹/2 cup chopped green chilies
1 onion, chopped
10³/4-oz. can cream of mushroom soup
2 cups cubed Velveeta cheese

1. Layer beef, potatoes, green chilies, and onions in slow cooker.
2. Spread soup over top.
3. Top with cheese.
4. Cover. Cook on high 1 hour. Reduce heat to low and cook 6-8 hours.

Menu Idea

New Mexico Cheeseburgers
Favorite Green Salad
Fresh Rolls

Yum-Yums

Evelyn L. Ward
Greeley, CO

Makes 12 servings

3 lbs. ground beef
2 onions, chopped
10¾-oz. can cream of chicken soup
1½ cups tomato juice
1 tsp. prepared mustard
1 tsp. Worcestershire sauce
1 tsp. salt
¼ tsp. pepper

1. Brown beef and onions in skillet. Drain.
2. Add remaining ingredients. Pour into slow cooker.
3. Cover. Cook on low 4-6 hours.
4. Serve on hamburger buns.

This is a great recipe for serving a crowd. A club I am a part of serves it when we do fund raisers. Our menu is Yum-yums, marinated bean salad, and strawberry short cake. We make the food in our homes and carry it to the meeting site.

Dianna's Barbecue

Lauren Eberhard
Seneca, IL

Makes 12 servings

4 lbs. ground beef, browned
24-oz. bottle ketchup
4 Tbsp. prepared mustard
2 Tbsp. vinegar
4 Tbsp. sugar
¾ cup water
1 tsp. pepper
1 Tbsp. paprika
1 cup chopped celery
1 cup chopped onion
sandwich rolls

1. Combine all ingredients except rolls in slow cooker.
2. Cover. Cook on high 1-2 hours or on low 4 hours.
3. Serve in sandwich rolls.

Chili Spaghetti

Clara Newswanger
Gordonville, PA

Makes 8-10 servings

½ cup diced onions
2 cups tomato juice
2 tsp. chili powder
1 tsp. salt
¾ cup grated mild cheese
1½ lbs. ground beef, browned
12-oz. dry spaghetti, cooked

1. Combine all ingredients in slow cooker.
2. Cover. Cook on low 4 hours. Check mixture about halfway through the cooking time. If it's becoming dry, stir in an additional cup of tomato juice.

Variations:

1. Add 8-oz. can sliced mushrooms to Step 1.

2. Use 2 Tbsp. chili powder instead of 2 tsp. chili powder for added flavor.

Dawn's Spaghetti and Meat Sauce

Dawn Day
Westminster, CA

Makes 6-8 servings

1 lb. ground beef
1 Tbsp. oil, if needed
1/2 lb. mushrooms, sliced
1 medium onion, chopped
3 garlic cloves, minced
1/2 tsp. dried oregano
1/2 tsp. salt
1/4 cup grated Parmesan or Romano cheese
6-oz. can tomato paste
2 15-oz. cans tomato sauce
15-oz. can chopped or crushed tomatoes

1. Brown ground beef in skillet, in oil if needed. Reserve drippings and transfer meat to slow cooker.
2. Saute mushrooms, onion, and garlic until onions are transparent. Add to slow cooker.
3. Add remaining ingredients to cooker. Mix well.
4. Cover. Cook on low 6 hours.
5. Serve with pasta and garlic bread.

Note: This recipe freezes well.

Quick and Easy Spaghetti

Beverly Getz
Warriors Mark, PA

Makes 8 servings

1 1/2 lbs. ground beef
2 onions, chopped
26-oz. jar spaghetti sauce with mushrooms
10 3/4-oz. can tomato soup
1 or 2 14.5-oz. cans stewed tomatoes
1 can mushrooms
1/2 tsp. garlic powder
1/2 tsp. garlic salt
1/2 tsp. minced dried garlic
1/2 tsp. onion salt
1/2 tsp. Italian seasoning
1 lb. spaghetti, cooked

1. Brown beef and onion in skillet. Pour into slow cooker.
2. Add remaining ingredients to cooker except spaghetti.
3. Cover. Cook on low 4 hours.
4. Serve over spaghetti.

Spaghetti Sauce for a Crowd

Sue Pennington
Bridgewater, VA

Makes 18 cups

1 lb. ground beef
1 lb. ground turkey
1 Tbsp. oil
5 15-oz. cans tomato sauce
3 6-oz. cans tomato paste
1 cup water
1/2 cup minced fresh parsley, or 3 Tbsp. dried parsley
1/2 cup minced fresh oregano, or 3 Tbsp. dried oregano
4 tsp. salt

1. Brown meat in oil in skillet. Place in 6-qt. slow cooker. (A 5-qt. cooker will work, but it will be brimful.)
2. Add remaining ingredients. Mix together thoroughly.
3. Cover. Cook on low 4-6 hours.

Notes:

1. Add 1 medium onion, chopped, and/or 3 cloves garlic, minced, to Step 1, browning along with the meat.

2. Add 1 can crushed tomatoes, or 2 cups cut-up fresh tomatoes, to Step 2 to add a fresh-tomato taste. (This will make your cooker even fuller, so you may want to switch to two 4- or 5-qt. cookers.)

3. Make the sauce without meat if you prefer.

4. Use as a pizza sauce, especially if you make it meatless.

5. Sauce can be refrigerated for a week or frozen up to 3 months.

Beef and Sausage Spaghetti Sauce

Sherri Grindle
Goshen, IN

Makes 10-12 servings

1 lb. ground beef
1 lb. Italian sausage, bulk, or cut in thin slices
1 large onion, chopped
3 Tbsp. oil, if needed
5 lbs. tomato puree, or 3 28-oz. cans
6 cloves garlic, minced
2 Tbsp. parsley
1 Tbsp. salt
1/4 rounded tsp. pepper
3 bay leaves
1 Tbsp. dried oregano
crushed red pepper, optional

1. Brown meat and onion in skillet in oil, unless they produce enough of their own drippings.
2. Combine all ingredients in slow cooker.
3. Cover. Cook on low 8 hours.
4. Serve over pasta.

Variation: Add 1 box spaghetti noodles 1 hour before serving and cook on high for last hour.

Hosting Idea

Keep the meal simple and do as much ahead as possible. People usually don't care so much what is served. They are just happy for a chance to sit and visit with each other.
—Sherri Grindle

Spaghetti Sauce with a Kick

Andrea O'Neil
Fairfield, CT

Makes 4-6 servings

1 lb. ground beef
1 onion, chopped
2 28-oz. cans crushed tomatoes
16-oz. can tomato sauce
1-lb. Italian sausage, cut in chunks
3 cloves garlic, crushed
1 Tbsp. Italian seasoning
2 tsp. dried basil
red pepper flakes to taste

1. Brown beef and onions in skillet. Drain and transfer to slow cooker.
2. Add remaining ingredients.
3. Cover. Cook on low 4-6 hours.
4. Serve over your favorite pasta.

Variation: Add 1-2 tsp. salt and 1-2 Tbsp. brown sugar or honey, if desired.

Slow Cooker Lasagna

Crystal Brunk
Singers Glen, VA

Makes 6-8 servings

1 lb. ground beef, browned
4-5 cups spaghetti sauce, depending upon how firm or how juicy you want the finished lasagna
24-oz. container cottage cheese
1 egg
8-10 lasagna noodles, uncooked
2-3 cups mozzarella cheese

1. Combine ground beef and spaghetti sauce.
2. Combine egg and cottage cheese.
3. Layer half of the ground beef mixture, the dry noodles, the cottage cheese mixture, and the mozzarella cheese in the slow cooker. Repeat layers.
4. Cover. Cook on high 4-5 hours or on low 6-8 hours.

Menu Idea

Slow Cooker Lasagna
Peas or Corn
Garlic Bread

Lazy Lasagna

Deborah Santiago
Lancaster, PA

Makes 6 servings

1 lb. ground beef, browned
32-oz. jar spaghetti sauce
8-oz. bag curly-edged noodles, cooked, or lasagna noodles cut up, cooked
16-oz. carton cottage cheese
8 ozs. shredded mozzarella cheese
Parmesan cheese to taste

1. Combine beef and spaghetti sauce.
2. Combine noodles, cottage cheese, and mozzarella cheese.
3. Layer one-third of the beef mixture, followed by half the noodle mixture in slow cooker. Repeat layers, ending with beef mixture. Sprinkle with Parmesan cheese.
4. Cover. Cook on low 3-4 hours.
5. Serve with salad and French bread.

Slow Cooker Almost Lasagna

Jeanette Oberholtzer
Manheim, PA

Makes 8-10 servings

1 box rotini or ziti, cooked
2 Tbsp. olive oil
2 28-oz. jars pasta sauce with tomato chunks
2 cups tomato juice
1/2 lb. ground beef
1/2 lb. bulk sausage, crumbled, or links cut into 1/4" slices
1 cup Parmesan cheese
1/2 cup Italian bread crumbs
1 egg
2 cups mozzarella cheese, divided
2 cups ricotta cheese
2 eggs
1 cup Parmesan cheese
1 1/2 tsp. parsley flakes
3/4 tsp. salt
1/4 tsp. pepper

1. In large bowl, toss pasta with olive oil. Add pasta sauce and tomato juice and mix well.
2. Brown beef and sausage together in skillet. Drain.
3. Add 1 cup Parmesan cheese, bread crumbs, 1 egg, and 1 cup mozzarella cheese to meat.
4. In separate bowl, beat together ricotta cheese, 2 eggs, 1 cup Parmesan cheese, parsley, salt, and pepper.
5. Pour half of pasta-sauce mixture into slow cooker. Spread entire ricotta mixture over pasta. Cover with remaining pasta-sauce mixture. Sprinkle with remaining 1 cup mozzarella cheese.
6. Cover. Cook on low 4-6 hours.

Egg Noodle Lasagna

Anna Stoltzfus
Honey Brook, PA

Makes 12-16 servings

6 1/2 cups wide egg noodles, cooked
3 Tbsp. butter or margarine
2 1/4 cups spaghetti sauce
1 1/2 lbs. ground beef, browned
6 ozs. Velveeta cheese, cubed
3 cups shredded mozzarella cheese

1. Toss butter with hot noodles.
2. Spread one-fourth of spaghetti sauce in slow cooker. Layer with one-third of noodles, beef, and cheeses. Repeat layers 2 more times.
3. Cover. Cook on low 4 hours, or until cheese is melted.

Meat Loaf Burgers

Lafaye M. Musser
Denver, PA

Makes 6 servings

1 large onion, sliced
1 rib celery, chopped
2 lbs. ground beef
1 tsp. salt
1 1/4 tsp. pepper
2 cups tomato juice
4 garlic cloves, minced
1 Tbsp. ketchup
1 tsp. Italian seasoning
1/2 tsp. salt
6 hamburger buns

1. Place onion and celery in slow cooker.
2. Combine beef, salt, and pepper. Shape into 6 patties. Place in slow cooker.

3. Combine tomato juice, garlic, ketchup, Italian seasoning, and salt. Pour over patties.

4. Cover. Cook on low 7-9 hours.

5. Serve on hamburger buns.

Barbecued Hamburgers

Martha Hershey
Ronks, PA

Makes 4 serving

1 lb. ground beef
1/4 cup chopped onions
3 Tbsp. ketchup
1 tsp. salt
1 egg, beaten
1/4 cup seasoned bread crumbs
18-oz. bottle of your favorite barbecue
    sauce

1. Combine beef, onions, ketchup, salt, egg, and bread crumbs. Form into 4 patties. Brown both sides lightly in skillet. Place in slow cooker.

2. Cover with barbecue sauce.

3. Cover. Bake on high 3 hours or low 6 hours.

We first had Barbecued Hamburgers at a 4-H picnic, and they have been a family favorite ever since.

Note: Mix the hamburger patties, brown them, and freeze them in advance, and you'll have little to do at the last minute.

Menu Idea

Barbecued Hamburgers
Baked Beans (pages 133-140)
Fresh Fruit, cut-up
Iced Tea

Hamburger-Potato Slow Cooker Dinner

Lafaye M. Musser
Denver, PA

Makes 6-8 servings

1 lb. ground beef
1 cup water
1/2 tsp. cream of tartar
6 medium potatoes, thinly sliced
1 onion, chopped
1/4 cup flour
1/2 tsp. salt
1/4 tsp. pepper
1 cup grated cheddar cheese, divided
2 Tbsp. butter or margarine
10 3/4-oz. can cream of mushroom soup

1. Brown ground beef in skillet, using oil if necessary.

2. In separate bowl, combine water and cream of tartar. Toss potatoes in water. Drain.

3. In another bowl, mix together onion, flour, salt, pepper, and half of cheese.

4. Place browned beef in bottom of cooker. Top with a layer of sliced potatoes. Add onion-cheese mixture.

5. Dot top with butter.

6. Pour soup over all.

7. Cover. Cook on low 7-9 hours or high 3-4 hours.

8. Sprinkle remaining cheese over top, 30 minutes before serving.

Variations:
1. Use cream of celery soup instead of cream of mushroom soup.
   —Mary Sommerfeld, Lancaster, PA

2. Use cream of chicken soup instead of cream of mushroom soup.
   —Yvonne Boettger, Harrisonburg, VA

1-2-3-4 Casserole

Betty K. Drescher
Quakertown, PA

Makes 8 servings

1 lb. ground beef
2 onions, sliced
3 carrots, thinly sliced
4 potatoes, thinly sliced
1/2 tsp. salt
1/8 tsp. pepper
1 cup cold water
1/2 tsp. cream of tartar
10 3/4-oz. can cream of mushroom soup
1/4 cup milk
1/2 tsp. salt
1/8 tsp. pepper

1. Layer in greased slow cooker: ground beef, onions, carrots, 1/2 tsp. salt, and 1/8 tsp. pepper.
2. Dissolve cream of tartar in water in bowl. Toss sliced potatoes with water. Drain.
3. Combine soup and milk. Toss with potatoes. Add remaining salt and pepper. Arrange potatoes in slow cooker.
4. Cover. Cook on low 7-9 hours.

Variations:
1. Substitute sour cream for the milk.

2. Top potatoes with 1/2 cup shredded cheese.

Cooker Casserole

Carol Eberly
Harrisonburg, VA

Makes 6-8 servings

2 cups grated carrots
1 medium-sized onion, sliced
4 cups grated raw potatoes
1 lb. ground beef, browned
1 tsp. salt
1/4 tsp. pepper
1 Tbsp. Worcestershire sauce
10 3/4-oz. can cream of mushroom soup

1. Layer carrots, onions, potatoes, and ground beef in slow cooker.
2. Combine salt, pepper, Worcestershire sauce, and soup in bowl. Pour over ground beef.
3. Cover. Cook on low 8-10 hours.

Hamburger Potato Casserole

Sue Pennington
Bridgewater, VA

Makes 6-10 servings

1 lb. ground beef
1 Tbsp. oil
6-8 potatoes, peeled and sliced
4-6 carrots, sliced
2 medium onions, sliced
1 cup peas
1 cup grated cheddar cheese
1 tsp. salt
1/4 tsp. pepper
10-oz. can cream of chicken soup

1. Brown ground beef in oil in skillet.
2. Layer half of beef, potatoes, carrots, onions, peas and cheese in cooker. Sprinkle with salt and pepper. Repeat layers.
3. Pour cream of chicken soup over top.
4. Cover. Cook on low 8-10 hours.

My husband came up with this recipe. Our family loves it and often requests it when I ask them what they want to eat.

Hamburger Casserole
Kelly Evenson
Pittsboro, NC

Makes 6-8 servings

2 large potatoes, sliced
2-3 medium carrots, sliced
1 cup frozen peas, thawed and drained
3 medium onions, sliced
2 celery ribs, sliced
garlic salt to taste
pepper to taste
salt to taste
1 lb. ground beef, browned and drained
10¾-oz. can tomato soup
1 soup can of water

1. Layer vegetables in order given into slow cooker.
2. Sprinkle each layer with garlic salt, pepper, and salt.
3. Place meat on top of celery.
4. Combine soup and water. Pour over all.
5. Cover. Cook on low 8 hours.
6. Serve with applesauce.

Wholesome Hamburger Dinner
Reba Rhodes
Bridgewater, VA

Makes 6-8 servings

1 lb. ground beef
1 tsp. salt
¼ tsp. pepper
1 cup sliced carrots
1 cup coarsely chopped celery
1 medium onion, sliced
1 cup green beans
2 tsp. sugar
2-3 cups tomato juice
½ lb. grated cheese

1. Brown ground beef in skillet. Place in bottom of slow cooker.
2. Layer remaining ingredients, except cheese, over ground beef in order given.
3. Cover. Cook on high 3-4 hours or low 5-6 hours.
4. Thirty minutes before the end of the cooking time, layer cheese on top. Cover and resume cooking.
5. Serve with cornbread.

Note: You can double all the vegetable amounts, if you wish. Increase cooking time to 5-6 hours on high or 9-11 hours on low, or until vegetables are as tender as you like.

Hosting Idea

If you wait until you have all your work done, you will never have company. They don't usually care about what's undone anyway.
—Reba Rhodes

Stuffed Baked Topping

Fannie Miller
Hutchinson, KS

Makes 12 servings

3 lbs. ground beef
1 cup chopped green peppers
1/2 cup chopped onions
6 Tbsp. butter
1/4 cup flour
3 cups milk
1/2 cup pimento, or chopped sweet red
    peppers
3/4 lb. cheddar cheese
3/4 lb. your favorite mild cheese
1/2 tsp. hot pepper sauce
1/4 tsp. dry mustard
salt to taste
12 baked potatoes

1. Brown ground beef, green peppers, and onions in butter. Transfer mixture to slow cooker, reserving drippings.
2. Stir flour into drippings. Slowly add milk. Cook until thickened.
3. Add pimento, cheeses, and seasonings. Pour over ingredients in slow cooker.
4. Cover. Heat on low.
5. Serve over baked potatoes, each one split open on an individual dinner plate.

Hosting Idea

When we have a large family gathering of 25 to 30 people, I like to butter our slow cooker, then mash the potatoes, and place them in the slow cooker on low. That saves me last-minute scurrying to mash them, and it keeps the potatoes warm until all are served.

—Mary Martins

Ground Beef Stew

Ruth Ann Hoover
New Holland, PA
Kim Stoltzfus
New Holland, PA

Makes 8-10 servings

1 lb. ground beef, browned
6 medium potatoes, peeled and cubed
16-oz. pkg. baby carrots
3 cups water
3 Tbsp. dry onion soup mix
1 garlic clove, minced
1 1/2 tsp. Italian seasoning
1-1 1/2 tsp. salt
1/2 tsp. garlic powder
1/4 tsp. pepper
10 3/4-oz. can tomato soup
6-oz. can Italian tomato paste

1. Combine all ingredients except tomato soup and paste in slow cooker.
2. Cover. Cook on high 3 1/2-4 hours.
3. Stir in soup and tomato paste.
4. Cover. Cook on high 1 hour more.

Variation: If you'd like to add color and more vegetables to the stew, stir in 1 1/2 cups frozen peas in Step 3.

Prompt

Mary Martins
Fairbank, IA

Makes 6-8 servings

4-6 medium-sized potatoes, sliced
1/2-3/4 cup minute rice
1 onion, sliced
1 1/2 lbs. ground beef
1 diced green pepper, optional
1 qt. tomatoes with juice
salt to taste
pepper to taste

1. Layer ingredients in order given in greased slow cooker. Salt and pepper each layer to taste.
2. Cover. Cook on high for 1 1/2-2 hours.

Variation: *You may substitute 1 qt. V-8 juice for the quart of tomatoes with juice.*

Cheeseburger Casserole

Erma Kauffman
Cochranville, PA

Makes 6 servings

1 lb. ground beef
1 small onion, chopped
1 tsp. salt
dash of pepper
1/2 cup bread crumbs
1 egg
tomato juice to moisten
4 1/2 cups mashed potatoes
   (leftover mashed potatoes work well)
9 slices American cheese

1. Combine beef, onions, salt, pepper, bread crumbs, egg, and tomato juice. Place one-third of mixture in slow cooker.
2. Spread with one-third of mashed potatoes and 3 slices cheese. Repeat 2 times.
3. Cover. Cook on low 3 hours.

Hamburger/Green Bean Dish

Hazel L. Propst
Oxford, PA

Makes 4-5 servings

1 lb. ground beef
1 onion, chopped
1 qt. string beans
10 3/4-oz. can tomato soup
3/4 tsp. salt
1/4 tsp. pepper
6-7 cups mashed potatoes
1 egg, beaten

1. Brown meat and onion in skillet. Stir in beans, soup, and seasonings. Pour into slow cooker.
2. Combine mashed potatoes with egg. Spread over meat mixture in slow cooker.
3. Cover. Cook on low 5-6 hours, or until beans are tender.

Meal-in-One
Melanie L. Thrower
McPherson, KS

Makes 6-8 servings

2 lbs. ground beef
1 onion, diced
1 green bell pepper, diced
1 tsp. salt
1/4 tsp. pepper
1 large bag frozen hash brown potatoes
16-oz. container sour cream
24-oz. container cottage cheese
1 cup Monterey Jack cheese, shredded

1. Brown ground beef, onion, and green pepper in skillet. Drain. Season with salt and pepper.
2. In slow cooker, layer one-third of the potatoes, meat, sour cream, and cottage cheese. Repeat twice.
3. Cover. Cook on low 4 hours, sprinkling Monterey Jack cheese over top during last hour.
4. Serve with red or green salsa.

Variation: For a cheesier dish, prepare another cup of shredded cheese and sprinkle 1/2 cup over the first layer of potatoes, meat, sour cream, and cottage cheese, and another 1/2 cup over the second layer of those ingredients.

Cedric's Casserole
Kathy Purcell
Dublin, OH

Makes 4-6 servings

1 medium onion, chopped
3 Tbsp. butter or margarine
1 lb. ground beef
1/2-3/4 tsp. salt
1/4 tsp. pepper
3 cups shredded cabbage
10 3/4-oz. can tomato soup

1. Saute onion in skillet in butter.
2. Add ground beef and brown. Season with salt and pepper.
3. Layer half of cabbage in slow cooker, followed by half of meat mixture. Repeat layers.
4. Pour soup over top.
5. Cover. Cook on low 3-4 hours.
6. Serve with garlic bread and canned fruit.

I grew up with this recipe and remember my mother serving it often. It makes a wonderful potluck take-a-long.

Beef and Macaroni

Esther J. Yoder
Hartville, OH

Makes 4-5 servings

1 lb. ground beef
1 small onion, chopped
half a green pepper, chopped
1 cup cooked macaroni
1/2 tsp. dried basil
1/2 tsp. dried thyme
1 tsp. Worcestershire sauce
1 tsp. salt
10³/4-oz. can cheddar cheese soup

1. Brown beef, onions, and green pepper in skillet. Pour off drippings and place meat and vegetables in slow cooker.
2. Combine all ingredients in cooker.
3. Cover. Cook on high 2-2½ hours, stirring once or twice.
4. Serve with broccoli and applesauce.

Plenty More in the Kitchen

Jean Robinson
Cinnaminson, NJ

Makes 12-16 servings

3 lbs. ground beef
1 cup chopped onions
1 Tbsp. oil
26-oz. jar tomato sauce or spaghetti sauce
1 tsp. salt
2 tsp. chili powder
1 tsp. pepper
2 Tbsp. dark brown sugar
16-oz. can whole-kernel corn
2 14½-oz. cans beef broth
8-oz. pkg. dry elbow macaroni
1 cup grated sharp cheese

1. Brown beef and onion in oil.
2. Combine all ingredients except cheese. Pour into slow cooker.
3. Cover. Cook on high 1 hour. Turn to low and cook 4 more hours.
4. Sprinkle with cheese and cook 10 minutes more.

Variation: You can change the balance of ingredients by using only 1-1½ lbs. ground beef and adding another 1/2-1 cup dry macaroni.

This is a tried and true recipe adapted from an old 1984 Pennsylvania Grange Cookbook. An easy meal to carry outside to the picnic table or a Little League game.

Menu Idea

Plenty More in the Kitchen
Garlic Bread
A Big Salad

Cheese and Pasta in a Pot

Cathy Boshart
Lebanon, PA

Makes 8 servings

2 lbs. ground beef
1 Tbsp. oil
2 medium onions, chopped
1 garlic clove, minced
14-oz. jar spaghetti sauce
16-oz. can stewed tomatoes
4-oz. can sliced mushrooms
8 ozs. dry shell macaroni, cooked al dente
1½ pints sour cream
½ lb. provolone cheese, sliced
½ lb. mozzarella cheese, sliced thin or
    shredded

1. Brown ground beef in oil in skillet. Drain off all but 2 Tbsp. drippings.
2. Add onions, garlic, spaghetti sauce, stewed tomatoes, and undrained mushrooms to drippings. Mix well. Simmer 20 minutes, or until onions are soft.
3. Pour half of macaroni into slow cooker. Cover with half the tomato/meat sauce. Spread half the sour cream over sauce. Top with provolone cheese. Repeat, ending with mozzarella cheese.
4. Cover. Cook on high 2 hours or low 3 hours.

Menu Idea

Cheese and Pasta in a Pot
Italian Bread with Garlic and Butter
    Spread
Tossed Salad
Angel Food Cake with Fruit Sauce

Hearty Rice Casserole

Dale Peterson
Rapid City, SD

Makes 12-16 servings

10¾-oz. can cream of mushroom soup
10¾-oz. can creamy onion soup
10¾-oz. can cream of chicken soup
1 cup water
1 lb. ground beef, browned
1 lb. pork sausage, browned
1 large onion, chopped
1 large green pepper, chopped
1½ cups long grain rice
shredded cheese, optional

1. Combine all ingredients except cheese in slow cooker. Mix well.
2. Cover. Cook on low 6-7 hours, sprinkling with cheese during last hour, if you wish.

Hamburger Rice Casserole
Shari Mast
Harrisonburg, VA

Makes 6-8 servings

1/2 lb. ground beef
1 onion, chopped
1 cup diced celery
1 tsp. dried basil
1 tsp. dried oregano
10³/4-oz. can cream of mushroom soup
1 soup can water
4 cups cooked rice
4-oz. can mushroom pieces, drained
Velveeta cheese slices

1. Brown ground beef, onion, and celery in skillet. Season with basil and oregano.
2. Combine soup and water in bowl.
3. In well greased slow cooker, layer half of rice, half of mushrooms, half of ground-beef mixture, and half of soup. Repeat layers.
4. Cover. Cook on high 4 hours.
5. Top with cheese 30 minutes before serving.
6. This casserole, served with cornbread and applesauce, makes a well-rounded meal that is quick and easy to prepare and well-received by children and adults.

Beef and Pepper Rice
Liz Ann Yoder
Hartville, OH

Makes 4-6 servings

1 lb. ground beef
2 green peppers, or 1 green and 1 red
   pepper, coarsely chopped
1 cup chopped onions
1 cup brown rice, uncooked
2 beef bouillon cubes, crushed
3 cups water
1 Tbsp. soy sauce

1. Brown beef in skillet. Drain.
2. Combine all ingredients in slow cooker. Mix well.
3. Cover. Cook on low 5-6 hours or on high 3 hours, or until liquid is absorbed.

Menu Idea

Beef and Pepper Rice
Applesauce
Lima Beans

Stuffed Green Peppers

Patricia Howard
Albuquerque, NM

Makes 6 servings

6 green peppers
1 lb. ground beef
1/4 cup chopped onions
1 tsp. salt
1/4 tsp. pepper
1 1/4 cups cooked rice
1 Tbsp. Worcestershire sauce
8-oz. can tomato sauce
1/4 cup beef broth

1. Cut stem ends from peppers. Carefully remove seeds and membrane without breaking pepper apart. Parboil in water for 5 minutes. Drain. Set aside.

2. Brown ground beef and onions in skillet. Drain off drippings. Place meat and onions in mixing bowl.

3. Add seasonings, rice, and Worcestershire sauce to meat and combine well. Stuff green peppers with mixture. Stand stuffed peppers upright in large slow cooker.

4. Mix together tomato sauce and beef broth. Pour over peppers.

5. Cover. Cook on low 5-7 hours.

Stuffed Peppers with Cheese

Rosaria Strachan
Fairfield, CT

Makes 6-8 servings

6-8 medium-sized green peppers
1-2 lbs. ground beef
1 onion, chopped and sauteed
salt to taste
pepper to taste
1 egg
1 1/2 cups cooked rice
15-oz. can tomato sauce, divided
1/2-3/4 cup shredded cheddar cheese

1. Remove caps and seeds from peppers, but keep them whole.

2. Combine ground beef, onion, salt, pepper, egg, rice, 1/3 can tomato sauce, and cheddar cheese. Stuff into peppers. Stand in large slow cooker, or two smaller cookers.

3. Cover with remaining tomato sauce.

4. Cover. Cook on low 8-10 hours.

Spanish Stuffed Peppers

Katrine Rose
Woodbridge, VA

Makes 4 servings

1 lb. ground beef
7-oz. pkg. Spanish rice mix
1 egg
1/4 cup chopped onions
4 medium-sized green bell peppers,
    halved lengthwise, cored, and seeded
28-oz. can tomatoes
10¾-oz. can tomato soup
1 cup water
shredded cheese, optional

1. Combine beef, rice mix (reserving seasoning packet), egg, and onions. Divide meat mixture among pepper halves.
2. Pour tomatoes into slow cooker. Arrange pepper halves over tomatoes.
3. Combine tomato soup, rice-mix seasoning packet, and water. Pour over peppers.
4. Cover. Cook on low 8-10 hours.
5. Twenty minutes before the end of the cooking time, top stuffed peppers with cheese.

Haystacks

Judy Buller
Bluffton, OH

Makes 10-12 servings

2 lbs. ground beef, browned
1 small onion, chopped
2 8-oz. cans tomato sauce
2 15-oz. cans chili beans with chili gravy,
    or red beans

2 10-oz. cans mild enchilada sauce,
    or mild salsa
1/2 tsp. chili powder
1 tsp. garlic salt
pepper to taste

Condiments:
raisins
chopped apples
shredded lettuce
chopped tomatoes
shredded cheese
corn chips
rice or baked potatoes

1. Combine beef, onion, tomato sauce, chili beans, enchilada sauce, chili powder, garlic salt, and pepper. Pour into slow cooker.
2. Cover. Bake on low 2-3 hours or high 1 hour.
3. Serve over baked potatoes or rice and add condiment of your choice on top.

Because this recipe offers such a wide choice of toppings, all diners are sure to find something they like. Haystacks are easy to serve buffet-style. The wide array of condiments sparks conversation—and becomes an adventure in eating. Members of my family like a little of each topping over the chili. Guests are often surprised to see how large their haystacks are when they're finished serving themselves. They frequently fill their entire plates! The atmosphere can be comfortable when everything is prepared ahead. And with this recipe, the serving time can vary.
Do the rice or baked potatoes in a second slow cooker.

Menu Idea

Haystacks
Rice or Baked Potatoes
Cut-Up Fresh Fruit
Light Dessert

Mexican Goulash

Sheila Plock
Boalsburg, PA

Makes 8-10 servings

1½-2 lbs. ground beef
2 onions, chopped
1 green pepper, chopped
½ cup celery, chopped
1 garlic clove, minced
28-oz. can whole tomatoes, cut up
6-oz. can tomato paste
4.25-oz. can sliced black olives, drained
14½-oz. can green beans, drained
15.25-oz. can Mexicorn, drained
15-oz. can dark red kidney beans
diced jalapeno peppers to taste
1 tsp. salt
¼ tsp. pepper
1 Tbsp. chili powder
3 dashes Tabasco sauce
grated cheddar cheese

1. Brown ground beef. Reserve drippings and transfer beef to slow cooker.
2. Saute onions, pepper, celery, and garlic in drippings in skillet. Transfer to slow cooker.
3. Add remaining ingredients. Mix well.
4. Cover. Cook on high 3-4 hours.
5. Sprinkle individual servings with grated cheese. Serve with tortilla chips.

Tortilla Bake

Kelly Evenson
Pittsboro, NC

Makes 6-8 servings

10¾-oz. can cheddar cheese soup
1½-oz. pkg. dry taco seasoning mix
8 corn tortillas
1½ lbs. ground beef, browned and drained
3 medium tomatoes, coarsely chopped
toppings: sour cream, grated cheese, thinly
    sliced green onions, cut-up bell peppers,
    diced avocado, shredded lettuce

1. Combine soup and taco seasoning.
2. Cut each tortilla into 6 wedges. Spoon one-quarter of ground beef into slow cooker. Top with one-quarter of all tortilla wedges. Spoon one-quarter of soup mixture on tortillas. Top with one-quarter of tomatoes. Repeat layers 3 times.
3. Cover. Cook on low 6-8 hours.
4. To serve, spoon onto plates and offer toppings as condiments.

Menu Idea

Tortilla Bake
Yellow Rice
Tortilla Chips and Salsa
Sherbet

Three-Bean Burrito Bake

Darla Sathre
Baxter, MN

Makes 6 servings

1 Tbsp. oil
1 onion, chopped
1 green bell pepper, chopped
2 garlic cloves, minced
16-oz. can pinto beans, drained
16-oz. can kidney beans, drained
15-oz. can black beans, drained
4-oz. can sliced black olives, drained
4-oz. can green chilies
2 15-oz. cans diced tomatoes
1 tsp. chili powder
1 tsp. ground cumin
6-8 6" flour tortillas
2 cups shredded Co-Jack cheese
sour cream

1. Saute onions, green peppers, and garlic in large skillet in oil.
2. Add beans, olives, chilies, tomatoes, chili powder, and cumin.
3. In greased slow cooker, layer ¾ cup vegetables, a tortilla, ⅓ cup cheese. Repeat layers until all those ingredients are used, ending with sauce.
4. Cover. Cook on low 8-10 hours.
5. Serve with dollops of sour cream on individual servings.

Taco Casserole

Marcia S. Myer
Manheim, PA

Makes 6 servings

1½ lbs. ground beef, browned
14½-oz. can diced tomatoes with chilies
10¾-oz. can cream of onion soup
1 pkg. dry taco seasoning mix
¼ cup water
6 corn tortillas cut in ½" strips
½ cup sour cream
1 cup shredded cheddar cheese
2 green onions, sliced, optional

1. Combine beef, tomatoes, soup, seasoning mix, and water in slow cooker.
2. Stir in tortilla strips.
3. Cover. Cook on low 7-8 hours.
4. Spread sour cream over casserole. Sprinkle with cheese.
5. Cover. Let stand 5 minutes until cheese melts.
6. Remove cover. Garnish with green onions. Allow to stand for 15 more minutes before serving.

Casserole Verde

Julia Fisher
New Carlisle, OH

Makes 6 servings

1 lb. ground beef
1 small onion, chopped
1/8 tsp. garlic powder
8-oz. can tomato sauce
1/3 cup chopped black olives
4-oz. can sliced mushrooms
8-oz. container sour cream
8-oz. container cottage cheese
4.25-oz. can chopped green chilies
12-oz. pkg. tortilla chips
8 ozs. Monterey Jack cheese, grated

1. Brown ground beef, onions, and garlic in skillet. Drain. Add tomato sauce, olives, and mushrooms.

2. In a separate bowl, combine sour cream, cottage cheese, and green chilies.

3. In slow cooker, layer a third of the chips, and half the ground beef mixture, half the sour cream mixture, and half the shredded cheese. Repeat all layers, except reserve last third of the chips to add just before serving.

4. Cover. Cook on low 4 hours.

5. Ten minutes before serving time, scatter reserved chips over top and continue cooking, uncovered.

Tiajuana Tacos

Helen Kenagy
Carlsbad, NM

Makes 6 servings

3 cups cooked chopped beef
1-lb. can refried beans
1/2 cup chopped onions
1/2 cup chopped green peppers
1/2 cup chopped ripe olives
8-oz. can tomato sauce
3 tsp. chili powder
1 Tbsp. Worcestershire sauce
1/2 tsp. garlic powder
1/4 tsp. pepper
1/4 tsp. paprika
1/8 tsp. celery salt
1/8 tsp. ground nutmeg
3/4 cup water
1 tsp. salt
1 cup crushed corn chips
6 taco shells
shredded lettuce
chopped tomatoes
grated cheddar cheese

1. Combine first 15 ingredients in slow cooker.

2. Cover. Cook on high 2 hours.

3. Just before serving, fold in corn chips.

4. Spoon mixture into taco shells. Top with lettuce, tomatoes, and cheese.

Pork
Main Dishes

Barbecued Ribs

Virginia Bender
Dover, DE

Makes 6 servings

4 lbs. pork ribs
1/2 cup brown sugar
12-oz. jar chili sauce
1/4 cup balsamic vinegar
2 Tbsp. Worcestershire sauce
2 Tbsp. Dijon mustard
1 tsp. hot sauce

1. Place ribs in slow cooker.
2. Combine remaining ingredients. Pour half of sauce over ribs.
3. Cover. Cook on low 8-10 hours.
4. Serve with remaining sauce.

Sweet and Sour Ribs

Cassandra Ly
Carlisle, PA

Makes 8-10 servings

3-4 lbs. boneless country-style pork ribs
20-oz. can pineapple tidbits
2 8-oz. cans tomato sauce
1/2 cup thinly sliced onions
1/2 cup thinly sliced green peppers
1/2 cup packed brown sugar
1/4 cup cider vinegar
1/4 cup tomato paste
2 Tbsp. Worcestershire sauce
1 garlic clove, minced
1 tsp. salt
1/2 tsp. pepper

1. Place ribs in slow cooker.
2. Combine remaining ingredients. Pour over ribs.
3. Cover. Cook on low 8-10 hours.
4. Serve over rice.

Country-Style Ribs and Sauerkraut

Rhonda Burgoon
Collingswood, NJ

Makes 4-6 servings

16-oz. bag sauerkraut, rinsed and drained
1 onion, diced
1 red-skinned apple, chopped
2-3 lbs. country-style pork ribs
1 cup beer

1. Combine sauerkraut, onion, and apple in bottom of slow cooker.
2. Layer ribs over sauerkraut.
3. Pour beer over ribs just before turning on cooker.
4. Cover. Cook on low 8-10 hours.
5. Serve with homemade cornbread and mashed potatoes, or serve deboned on a kaiser roll as a sandwich.

1-2-3 Barbecued Country Ribs

Barbara Walker
Sturgis, SD

Makes 4 servings

4 lbs. spareribs, or 3 lbs. country-style ribs, cut in serving-size pieces
18-oz. bottle prepared barbecue sauce

1. Pour a little sauce into bottom of slow cooker. Put in a layer of ribs, meaty side up. Cover with barbecue sauce.

2. Continue layering until all ribs are in the pot. Submerge them as much as possible in the sauce.
3. Cover. Cook on low 8-10 hours.

Note: No need to precook the ribs if they're lean. If they're fattier than you like, parboil in water in stockpot before placing in cooker, to cook off some of the grease.

Tender 'N Tangy Ribs

Sherri Grindle
Goshen, IN

Makes 2-3 servings

3/4-1 cup vinegar
1/2 cup ketchup
2 Tbsp. sugar
2 Tbsp. Worcestershire sauce
1 clove garlic, minced
1 tsp. ground mustard
1 tsp. paprika
1/2-1 tsp. salt
1/8 tsp. pepper
2 lbs. pork spareribs or country-style ribs
1 Tbsp. oil

1. Combine first nine ingredients in slow cooker.
2. Cut ribs into serving-size pieces. Brown in oil in skillet. Transfer to slow cooker.
3. Cover. Cook on low 4-6 hours.
4. Serve with baked potatoes and rice.

I often use this recipe if I am having company for Sunday lunch.

Barbara Jean's Whole Pork Tenderloin

Barbara Jean Fabel
Wausau, WI

Makes 6-8 servings

1/2 cup sliced celery
1/4 lb. fresh mushrooms, quartered
1 medium onion, sliced
1/4 cup melted butter
2 1 1/4-lb. pork tenderloins
1 Tbsp. butter
2 tsp. salt
1/4 tsp. pepper
1 Tbsp. butter
1/2 cup beef broth
1 Tbsp. flour

1. Placed celery, mushrooms, onion, and 1/4 cup melted butter in slow cooker.
2. Brown tenderloins in skillet in 1 Tbsp. butter. Layer over vegetables in slow cooker.
3. Sprinkle with salt and pepper.
4. Combine bouillon and flour until smooth. Pour over tenderloins.
5. Cover. Cook on high 3 hours or low 4-5 hours.

Autumn Harvest Pork Loin

Stacy Schmucker Stoltzfus
Enola, PA

Makes 4-6 servings

1 cup cider or apple juice
1 1/2-2-lb. pork loin
salt
pepper
2 large Granny Smith apples, peeled and sliced
1 1/2 whole butternut squashes, peeled and cubed
1/2 cup brown sugar
1/4 tsp. cinnamon
1/4 tsp. dried thyme
1/4 tsp. dried sage

1. Heat cider in hot skillet. Sear pork loin on all sides in cider.
2. Sprinkle meat with salt and pepper on all sides. Place in slow cooker, along with juices.
3. Combine apples and squash. Sprinkle with sugar and herbs. Stir. Place around pork loin.
4. Cover. Cook on low 5-6 hours.
5. Remove pork from cooker. Let stand 10-15 minutes. Slice into 1/2"-thick slices.
6. Serve topped with apples and squash.

Pork Roast

Lucille Amos
Greensboro, NC

Makes 6-8 servings

1 Boston butt roast
1 cup Worcestershire sauce
1 cup brown sugar

1. Place roast in greased slow cooker.
2. Pour Worcestershire sauce over roast.
3. Pat brown sugar on roast.
4. Cover. Cook on high 1 hour. Reduce heat to low for 8-10 hours.
5. Slice and serve topped with broth and drippings from cooker.

Pork Roast with Sauerkraut

Betty K. Drescher
Quakertown, PA

Makes 8-10 servings

3-4-lb. pork roast
32-oz. bag sauerkraut
2 apples, peeled and sliced
1 medium onion, sliced thin
14½-oz. can Italian tomatoes, drained and smashed

1. Place roast in slow cooker.
2. Add sauerkraut.
3. Layer apples and onion over roast.
4. Top with tomatoes.
5. Cover. Cook on low 7-9 hours, or until meat is tender.

Variation: If you like a brothy dish, add 1 cup water along with sauerkraut in Step 2.

No Fuss Sauerkraut

Vera M. Kuhns
Harrisonburg, VA

Makes 12 servings

3-lb. pork roast
3 2-lb. pkgs. sauerkraut (drain off juice from 1 pkg.)
2 apples, peeled and sliced
½ cup brown sugar
1 cup apple juice

1. Place meat in large slow cooker.
2. Place sauerkraut on top of meat.
3. Add apples and brown sugar. Add juice.
4. Cover. Cook on high 4-5 hours.
5. Serve with mashed potatoes.

Note: If your slow cooker isn't large enough to hold all the ingredients, cook one package of sauerkraut and half the apples, brown sugar, and apple juice in another cooker. Mix the ingredients of both cookers together before serving.

Flautas with Pork Filling

Donna Lantgen
Rapid City, SD

Makes 6-8 servings

1 lb. pork roast or chops, cubed
1/4 cup chopped onions
4-oz. can diced green chilies
7-oz. can green chile salsa or chile salsa
1 tsp. cocoa powder
16-oz. can chili

1. Brown cubed pork in skillet. Drain. Place in slow cooker.
2. Add remaining ingredients except chili.
3. Cover. Cook on low 2-3 hours.
4. Add chili. Cook 2-3 hours longer.
5. Serve on flour tortillas with guacamole dip.

Note: This is especially good on spinach-herb tortillas.

Pork Chops

Linda Sluiter
Schererville, IN

Makes 4 servings

4 boneless pork chops, 1" thick
1/2 tsp. dry mustard
1/4 cup flour
1/2 tsp. sugar
1 tsp. vinegar
1/2 cup water
1/2 cup ketchup
1/2 tsp. salt

1. Place pork chops in slow cooker.
2. Combine remaining ingredients and pour over pork chops.
3. Cover. Cook on high 2-3 hours, and then low 3-4 hours, or cook on low 8 hours.

Pork Chops Hong Kong

Marjorie Y. Guengerich
Harrisonburg, VA

Makes 6-8 servings

10-oz. bottle soy sauce
6-8 Tbsp. sugar
6-8 pork chops
10³/4-oz. can cream of mushroom soup

1. Combine soy sauce and sugar. Pour over pork chops. Marinate for 60 minutes.
2. Transfer pork chops to slow cooker.
3. Add soup.
4. Cover. Cook on low 6 hours or high 3 hours.

Barbecued Pork Chops
LaVerne A. Olson
Lititz, PA

Makes 6-8 servings

6-8 pork chops, lightly browned in skillet
1/2 cup ketchup
1 tsp. salt
1 tsp. celery seed
1/2 tsp. ground nutmeg
1/3 cup vinegar
1/2 cup water
1 bay leaf

1. Place pork chops in slow cooker.
2. Combine remaining ingredients. Pour over chops.
3. Cover. Cook on low 2-3 hours, or until chops are tender.
4. Remove bay leaf before serving.

Pork Chop Casserole
Nancy Wagner Graves
Manhattan, KS

Makes 4-6 servings

6-8 pork chops
salt to taste
pepper to taste
oil
2 medium potatoes, peeled and sliced
1 large onion, sliced
1 large green pepper, sliced
1/2 tsp. dried oregano
16-oz. can tomatoes

1. Season pork chops with salt and pepper. Brown in oil in skillet. Transfer to slow cooker.
2. Add remaining ingredients in order listed.
3. Cover. Cook on low 8-10 hours or on high 3-4 hours.

Pork Chop
Slow Cooker Casserole
Janice Crist
Quinter, KS

Makes 5 servings

5 pork chops
4-5 medium potatoes, quartered or sliced
10¾-oz. can cream of chicken soup
10¾-oz. can cream of celery soup
15-oz. can green beans, drained

1. Layer ingredients in slow cooker in order listed.
2. Cover. Cook on low 5-6 hours or on high 4 hours.

Pork Chops with Vegetables

LaVerne A. Olson
Lititz, PA

Makes 6 servings

6 boneless pork chops
2 Tbsp. butter or margarine
1½ cups sliced mushrooms
1 tsp. crushed rosemary
10¾-oz. can cream of mushroom soup
2 Tbsp. water
½-1 lb. green beans, cut in 2" pieces

1. Brown pork chops in skillet in 1 Tbsp. butter. Transfer to slow cooker.
2. Cook mushrooms and rosemary in 1 Tbsp. butter until just wilted. Add to chops.
3. Combine soup, rosemary, mushrooms, water, and beans. Pour over chops.
4. Cover. Cook on low 6-8 hours or on high 4 hours.
5. Serve over hot noodles.

Pork Chops on Rice

Hannah D. Burkholder
Bridgewater, VA

Makes 4 servings

½ cup brown rice
⅔ cup converted white rice
¼ cup butter or margarine
½ cup chopped onions
4-oz. can sliced mushrooms, drained
½ tsp. dried thyme
½ tsp. sage
½ tsp. salt
¼ tsp. black pepper
4 boneless pork chops, ¾"-1" thick
10½-oz. can beef consomme
2 Tbsp. Worcestershire sauce
½ tsp. dried thyme
½ tsp. paprika
¼ tsp. ground nutmeg

1. Saute white and brown rice in butter in skillet until rice is golden brown.
2. Remove from heat and stir in onions, mushrooms, thyme, sage, salt, and pepper. Pour into greased slow cooker.
3. Arrange chops over rice.
4. Combine consomme and Worcestershire sauce. Pour over chops.
5. Combine thyme, paprika, and nutmeg. Sprinkle over chops.
6. Cover. Cook on low 7-9 hours or on high 4-5 hours.

Baked Beans and Chops

John D. Allen
Rye, CO

Makes 6 servings

2 16½-oz. cans baked beans
6 rib pork chops, ½" thick
1½ tsp. prepared mustard
1½ Tbsp. brown sugar
1½ Tbsp. ketchup
6 onion slices, ¼" thick

1. Pour baked beans into bottom of greased slow cooker.
2. Layer pork chops over beans.
3. Spread mustard over pork chops. Sprinkle with brown sugar and drizzle with ketchup.
4. Top with onion slices.
5. Cover. Cook on high 4-6 hours.

Oxford Canal Chops Deluxe

Willard E. Roth
Elkhart, IN

Makes 6 servings

6 6-oz. boneless pork chops
¼ cup flour
1 tsp. powdered garlic
1 tsp. sea salt
1 tsp. black pepper
1 tsp. dried basil and/or dried oregano
2 Tbsp. oil
2 medium onions, sliced
1 cup burgundy wine
14½-oz. can beef broth
1 soup can water
6-oz. can tomato sauce
8 ozs. dried apricots
½ lb. fresh mushroom caps

1. Shake chops in bag with flour and seasonings.
2. Glaze onions in oil in medium hot skillet. Add chops and brown.
3. Pour extra flour over chops in skillet. In large bowl mix together wine, broth, water, and tomato sauce, then pour over meat. Bring to boil.
4. Remove chops from skillet and place in cooker. Layer in apricots and mushrooms. Pour broth over top.
5. Cover. Cook on high 4 hours or low 6 hours.
6. Serve with the Celtic speciality Bubble and Squeak—Irish potatoes mashed with green cabbage or brussels sprouts.

This was a hit when prepared in the tiny kitchen of a houseboat on the Oxford Canal and then shared by six friends.

Fruited Pork Chops

Jean Butzer
Batavia, NY

Makes 4 servings

4 pork chops
1/2 tsp. salt
dash of pepper
1 Tbsp. prepared mustard
2 Tbsp. wine vinegar
1/8 tsp. dried dill weed
17-oz. can fruit cocktail
2 Tbsp. cornstarch
2 Tbsp. water

1. Sprinkle chops with salt and pepper. Place in slow cooker.
2. Combine mustard, vinegar, and dill.
3. Drain fruit cocktail, reserving 1/2 cup syrup. Add 1/2 cup syrup to mustard mixture. Pour over chops.
4. Cover. Cook on low 4-6 hours, or until meat is tender.
5. Remove chops. Turn to high.
6. Dissolve cornstarch in water. Stir into slow cooker. Add fruit cocktail.
7. Cover. Cook on high 10-15 minutes. Spoon fruit sauce over chops.

Cherry Pork Chops

Jo Haberkamp
Fairbank, IA

Makes 6 servings

6 pork chops, each cut 3/4" thick
1 Tbsp. oil
salt
pepper
1 cup cherry pie filling
2 tsp. lemon juice
1/2 tsp. instant chicken bouillon granules
1/8 tsp. ground mace

1. Brown pork chops in oil in skillet. Sprinkle each chop with salt and pepper.
2. Combine remaining ingredients in slow cooker. Mix well.
3. Place browned pork chops on top of cherry mixture.
4. Cover. Cook on low 4-5 hours.
5. Place chops on platter. Spoon some of the cherry sauce on top. Pass remaining sauce and serve with rice or baked potatoes.

Pork Chops in Orange Sauce

Kelly Evenson
Pittsboro, NC

Makes 4 servings

4 thick, center-cut pork chops
salt to taste
pepper to taste
1 Tbsp. oil
1 orange
1/4 cup ketchup
3/4 cup orange juice
1 Tbsp. orange marmalade
1 Tbsp. cornstarch
1/4 cup water

1. Season pork chops on both sides with salt and pepper.
2. Brown chops lightly on both sides in skillet in oil. Transfer to slow cooker. Reserve 2 Tbsp. drippings and discard the rest.
3. Grate 1/2 tsp. orange zest from top or bottom of orange. Combine zest with ketchup, orange juice, and marmalade. Pour into skillet. Simmer 1 minute, stirring constantly. Pour over chops.
4. Cover. Cook on low 5-6 hours. Remove chops and keep warm.
5. Dissolve cornstarch in water. Stir into slow cooker until smooth. Cook on high 15 minutes, or until thickened.
6. Serve with orange sauce on top, along with slices of fresh orange.
7. Serve over noodles or rice with a green salad.

Apples, Sauerkraut, and Chops

Carol Sherwood
Batavia, NY

Makes 4 servings

4 pork chops, 1/2" thick, browned
1 onion, sliced and separated into rings
1/8 tsp. garlic flakes or powder
3 cups sauerkraut, drained
1 cup unpeeled apple slices
1 1/2 tsp. caraway seeds
1/4 tsp. salt
1/4 tsp. dried thyme
1/4 tsp. pepper
3/4 cup apple juice

1. Place half of onions, garlic flakes, sauerkraut, apple slices, and caraway seeds in slow cooker. Season with half the salt, thyme, and pepper.
2. Add pork chops.
3. Layer remaining ingredients in order given.
4. Pour apple juice over all.
5. Cover. Cook on low 6-8 hours or high 4 hours.

Pork Chops with Stuffing

Erma Kauffman
Cochranville, PA

Makes 2 servings

4 slices bread, cubed
1 egg
1/4 cup grated, or finely chopped, celery
1/4-1/2 tsp. salt
1/8 tsp. pepper
2 thickly cut pork chops
1 cup water

1. Combine bread cubes, eggs, celery, salt, and pepper.
2. Cut pork chops part way through, creating a pocket. Fill with stuffing.
3. Pour water into slow cooker. Add chops.
4. Cover. Cook on low 4-5 hours.

Pork Chops and Stuffing with Curry

Mary Martins
Fairbank, IA

Makes 3-4 servings

1 box stuffing mix
1 cup water
10 3/4-oz. can cream of mushroom soup
1 tsp., or more, curry powder,
    according to your taste preference
3-4 pork chops

1. Combine stuffing mix and water. Place half in bottom of slow cooker.

2. Combine soup and curry powder. Pour half over stuffing. Place pork chops on top.
3. Spread remaining stuffing over pork chops. Pour rest of soup on top.
4. Cover. Cook on low 6-7 hours.
5. Serve with a tossed salad and a cooked vegetable.

Autumn Pork Chops

Leesa Lesenski
Whately, MA

Makes 4-6 servings

4-6 boneless pork chops
2 cups apple juice
1/2 tsp. ground cinnamon

1. Place pork chops in slow cooker.
2. Cover with apple juice.
3. Sprinkle with cinnamon.
4. Cover. Cook on low 10 hours.

Menu Idea

Autumn Pork Chops
Rice or Potatoes
Applesauce

Italian Sausage

Lauren Eberhard
Seneca, IL

Makes 15 servings

5 lbs. Italian sausage in casing
4 large green peppers, sliced
3 large onions, sliced
1 or 2 garlic cloves, minced
28-oz. can tomato puree
14-oz. can tomato sauce
12-oz. can tomato paste
1 Tbsp. dried oregano
1 Tbsp. dried basil
½ tsp. garlic powder
1½ tsp. salt
2 tsp. sugar

1. Cut sausage into 4" or 5" pieces and brown on all sides in batches in skillet.
2. Saute peppers, onions, and garlic in drippings.
3. Combine tomato puree, sauce, and paste in bowl. Add seasonings and sugar.
4. Layer half of sausage, onions, and peppers in 6-qt. slow cooker, or in 2 4-qt. cookers. Cover with half the tomato mixture. Repeat layers.
5. Cover. Cook on high 1 hour and low 5-6 hours.
6. Serve over pasta, or dip mixture with a straining spoon onto Italian sandwich rolls.

Dawn's Sausage and Peppers

Dawn Day
Westminster, CA

Makes 8-10 servings

3 medium onions, sliced
1 sweet red pepper, sliced
1 sweet green pepper, sliced
1 sweet yellow pepper, sliced
4 garlic cloves, minced
1 Tbsp. oil
28 oz.-can chopped tomatoes
1 tsp. salt
½ tsp. red crushed pepper
2-3 lbs. sweet Italian sausage,
    cut into 3" pieces

1. Saute onions, peppers, and garlic in oil in skillet. When just softened, place in slow cooker.
2. Add tomatoes, salt, and crushed red pepper. Mix well.
3. Add sausage links.
4. Cover. Cook on low 6 hours.
5. Serve on rolls, or over pasta or baked potatoes.

Variation: For a thicker sauce, stir in 3 Tbsp. ClearJell during the last 15 minutes of the cooking time.

Savory Sausage Sandwiches
Mary Jane Musser
Manheim, PA

Makes 8 servings

2 lbs. fresh sausage, cut into bun-length
   pieces
2 pkgs. dry spaghetti sauce mix
12-oz. can tomato paste
3 cups water
1/2 cup brown sugar
1/4 cup vinegar
8 Italian or hot dog rolls
grated cheese

1. Cook sausage in skillet in water for 10
minutes. Drain. Place in slow cooker.
2. Combine remaining ingredients. Simmer
5 minutes in saucepan. Pour over sausage.
3. Cover. Cook on high 3 hours or low 6
hours.
4. Serve in rolls topped with grated cheese.

*Variation: Use 1 qt. spaghetti sauce, either
homemade or bought, instead of sauce mix,
tomato paste, and water.*

Sausage and Sauerkraut
Eileen Lehman
Kidron, OH

Makes 12 servings

2-3 lbs. fresh sausage, cut in 3"-lengths, or
   removed from casings
3 32-oz. cans sauerkraut

1. Brown sausage in skillet.
2. Combine sausage and sauerkraut in slow
cooker.
3. Cover. Cook on low 4-8 hours.
4. Serve with mashed potatoes, a jello salad,
and pumpkin pie.

*It is traditional to serve sauerkraut on New
Year's Day in Kidron.*

Brats and Spuds
Kathi Rogge
Alexandria, IN

Makes 6 servings

5-6 bratwurst links, cut into 1" pieces
5 medium-sized potatoes, peeled and
   cubed
27-oz. can sauerkraut, rinsed and drained
1 medium tart apple, chopped
1 small onion, chopped
1/4 cup packed brown sugar
1/2 tsp. salt

1. Brown bratwurst on all sides in skillet.
2. Combine remaining ingredients in slow
cooker. Stir in bratwurst and pan drippings.
3. Cover. Cook on high 4-6 hours, or until
potatoes and apples are tender.

*Variation: Add a small amount of caraway seeds
or crisp bacon pieces, just before serving.*

Sausage-Potato Slow Cooker Dinner

Deborah Swartz
Grottoes, VA

Makes 6-8 servings

1 cup water
1/2 tsp. cream of tartar
6 medium potatoes, thinly sliced
3/4 lb. sausage, casings removed and
    browned
1 onion, chopped
1/4 cup flour
salt to taste
pepper to taste
1 1/2 cups grated cheddar cheese, divided
2 Tbsp. butter or margarine
10 3/4-oz. can cream of mushroom soup

1. Combine water and cream of tartar. Toss sliced potatoes in water. Drain.

2. Layer potatoes, sausage, onion, flour, a sprinkling of salt and pepper, and half of cheddar cheese in slow cooker. Repeat layers until ingredients are used.

3. Dot butter over top. Pour soup over all.

4. Cover. Cook on low 7-9 hours or on high 3-4 hours.

5. Sprinkle reserved cheese over top just before serving.

Sausage and Scalloped Potatoes

Carolyn Baer
Conrath, WI

Makes 5 servings

2 1/2 lbs. potatoes, sliced 1/4" thick
1 lb. fully cooked smoked sausage links,
    sliced 1/2" thick
2 medium onions, chopped
10 3/4-oz. can cheddar cheese soup
10 3/4-oz. can cream of celery soup

1. Layer one-third of potatoes, one-third of sausage, one-third of onions, one-third of cheddar cheese soup, and one-third of celery soup into slow cooker. Repeat 2 times.

2. Cover. Cook on low 10 hours or high 5 hours.

I like to prepare this delicious dish when I will be gone for the day, but know I will have guests for the evening meal. When I get home, the meat and potatoes are already cooked. I simply have to heat the peas, fix a salad, and slice the dessert.

Sausage and Sweet Potatoes

Ruth Hershey
Paradise, PA

Makes 4-6 servings

1 lb. bulk sausage, browned in skillet
2 sweet potatoes, peeled and sliced
3 apples, peeled and sliced
2 Tbsp. brown sugar
1 Tbsp. flour
1/4 tsp. ground cinnamon
1/4 tsp. salt
1/4 cup water

1. Layer sausage, sweet potatoes, and apples in slow cooker.
2. Combine remaining ingredients and pour over ingredients in slow cooker.
3. Cover. Cook on low 8-10 hours or high 4 hours.

Golden Autumn Stew

Naomi E. Fast
Hesston, KS

Makes 8-10 servings

2 cups cubed Yukon gold potatoes
2 cups cubed, peeled sweet potatoes
2 cups cubed, peeled butternut squash
1 cup cubed, peeled rutabaga
1 cup diced carrots
1 cup sliced celery
1 lb. smoked sausage
2 cups apple juice or cider
1 tart apple, thinly sliced
salt to taste
pepper to taste
1 Tbsp. sugar or honey

1. Combine vegetables in slow cooker.
2. Place ring of sausage on top.
3. Add apple juice and apple slices.
4. Cover. Cook on high 2 hours and on low 4 hours, or until vegetables are tender. Do not stir.
5. To serve, remove sausage ring. Season with salt, pepper, and sugar as desired. Place vegetables in bowl. Slice meat into rings and place on top.
6. Serve with hot baking-powder biscuits and honey, and a green salad or cole slaw.

Don't omit the rutabaga! Get acquainted with its rich uniqueness. It will surprise and please your taste buds.

Harvest Kielbasa

Christ Kaczynski
Schenectady, NY

Makes 6 servings

2 lbs. smoked kielbasa
3 cups unsweetened applesauce
1/2 cup brown sugar
3 medium onions, sliced

1. Slice kielbasa into 1/4" slices. Brown in skillet. Drain.
2. Combine applesauce and brown sugar.
3. Layer kielbasa, onions, and applesauce mixture in slow cooker.
4. Cover. Cook on low 4-8 hours.

The longer it cooks, the better the flavor.

Keilbasa Stew

Fannie Miller
Hutchinson, KS

Makes 6-8 servings

6 strips of bacon
1 onion, chopped
1-1½ lbs. smoked, fully cooked kielbasa,
   thinly sliced
2 15½-oz. cans Great Northern beans
2 8-oz. cans tomato sauce
4-oz. can chopped green chilies
2 medium carrots, thinly sliced
1 medium green pepper, chopped
½ tsp. Italian seasoning
½ tsp. dried thyme
½ tsp. black pepper

1. Fry bacon in skillet until crisp. Crumble bacon and place in large slow cooker. Add onions and sausage to drippings in skillet. Cook until onions are soft.
2. Transfer onions and sausage to slow cooker.
3. Add all remaining ingredients to cooker and stir together well.
4. Cover. Cook on low 8-10 hours, or until vegetables are tender.

Rice and Beans— and Sausage

Marcia S. Myer
Manheim, PA

Makes 8 servings

3 celery ribs, chopped
1 onion, chopped
2 garlic cloves, minced
1¾ cups tomato juice
2 16-oz. cans kidney beans, drained
¾ tsp. dried oregano
¾ tsp. dried thyme
¼ tsp. red pepper flakes
¼ tsp. pepper
½ lb. (or more) fully cooked smoked
   turkey sausage, or kielbasa, cut into
   ¼" slices
4 cups cooked rice
shredded cheese, optional

1. Combine all ingredients except rice and shredded cheese in slow cooker.
2. Cover. Cook on low 4-6 hours.
3. Serve over rice. Garnish with shredded cheese, if you wish.

Hosting Idea

My mother always had a small centerpiece, usually flowers, on the table. I learned how important that is.

Two other tips from Mother. If you don't have a lot of food, serve it in a pretty dish. If all you have for tea is peanut butter sandwiches, cut them in fancy geometric shapes.

—Sharon Miller

Election Lunch

Alix Nancy Botsford
Seminole, OK

Makes 6-12 servings

2-3 Tbsp. olive oil
1 large onion, chopped
1 lb. sausage, cut into thin slices, or
casings removed and crumbled
1 rib celery, sliced
1 Tbsp. Worcestershire sauce
1 1/2 tsp. dry mustard
1/4 cup honey
10-oz. can tomatoes with green chili
peppers
1-lb. can lima or butter beans, drained,
with liquid reserved
1-lb. can red kidney beans, drained, with
liquid reserved
1-lb. can garbanzo beans, drained, with
liquid reserved

1. Brown onion and sausage in oil.
2. Combine ingredients in 6-qt. slow cooker,
or divide between 2 4-qt. cookers and stir to
combine. Add reserved juice from lima,
kidney, and garbanzo beans if there's enough
room in the cookers.
3. Cover. Cook on low 2-4 hours.

*I mixed up this hearty stew the night before
Election Day and took it to the voting site the
next morning. I plugged it in, and all day long we
could smell the stew cooking. I work at a very
sparsely populated, country poling place and
ended up giving out the recipe and little water-cup
samples to many voters!*

*I have four different sizes of slow cookers. One
is very tiny, with only an on and off switch, for
keeping cheese sauce hot. One I use for heating
gravy. Another I often use to keep mashed
potatoes warm.*

Menu Idea

Election Lunch
Toast Fingers
(Toast all the slices in a loaf of
whole-grain bread. Let cool.
Butter and toast a second time.
Cut twice-toasted bread into strips.)
Your Favorite Salad

Chili Casserole

Sharon Miller
Holmesville, OH

Makes 6 servings

1 lb. bulk pork sausage, browned
2 cups water
15 1/2-oz. can chili beans
14 1/2-oz. can diced tomatoes
3/4 cup brown rice
1/4 cup chopped onions
1 Tbsp. chili powder
1 tsp. Worcestershire sauce
1 tsp. prepared mustard
3/4 tsp. salt
1/8 tsp. garlic powder
1 cup shredded cheddar cheese

1. Combine all ingredients except cheese in
slow cooker.
2. Cover. Cook on low 7 hours.
3. Stir in cheese during last 10 minutes of
cooking time.

Sausage Pasta Stew

Betty K. Drescher
Quakertown, PA 18951

Makes 8 servings

1 lb. Italian sausage, casings removed
4 cups water
26-oz. jar meatless spaghetti sauce
16-oz. can kidney beans, rinsed and
   drained
1 medium yellow summer squash, cut in
   1" pieces
2 medium carrots, cut in ¼" slices
1 medium red or green sweet pepper,
   diced
⅓ cup chopped onions
1½ cups uncooked spiral pasta
1 cup frozen peas
1 tsp. sugar
½ tsp. salt
¼ tsp. pepper

1. Saute sausage in skillet until no longer
pink. Drain and place in slow cooker.
2. Add water, spaghetti sauce, kidney beans,
squash, carrots, pepper, and onions. Mix well.
3. Cover. Cook on low 7-9 hours, or until
vegetables are tender.
4. Add remaining ingredients. Mix well.
5. Cover. Cook on high 15-20 minutes until
pasta is tender.

*Note: Add 1 Tbsp. tapioca in Step 5 if you like a
thicker stew.*

Pizza Rigatoni

Tina Snyder
Manheim, PA

Makes 6-8 servings

1½ lbs. bulk sausage
3 cups rigatoni, lightly cooked
4 cups shredded mozzarella cheese
10¾-oz. can cream of mushroom soup
1 small onion, sliced
15-oz. can pizza sauce
8-oz. can pizza sauce
3½-oz. pkg. sliced pepperoni
6-oz. can sliced ripe olives

1. Cook and drain sausage. Place half in
4-qt., or larger, slow cooker.
2. Layer half of pasta, cheese, soup, onion,
pizza sauce, pepperoni, and olives over
sausage. Repeat layers.
3. Cover. Cook on low 4 hours.

*Note: If your store doesn't carry 8-oz. cans pizza
sauce, substitute an 8-oz. can tomato sauce with
basil, garlic, and oregano.*

Crockpot Pizza

Sharon Miller
Holmesville, OH

Makes 6 servings

1½ lbs. bulk sausage
1 small onion, chopped
1-lb. pkg. pasta or noodles, uncooked
28-oz. jar spaghetti sauce
16-oz. can tomato sauce
¾ cup water
4-oz. can mushrooms, drained
16-oz. pkg. shredded mozzarella cheese
8-oz. pkg. pepperoni, chopped

1. Brown sausage and onion in skillet. Drain. Place one-third of mixture in cooker.
2. Layer in one-third of uncooked pasta.
3. Combine spaghetti sauce, tomato sauce, water, and mushrooms in bowl. Ladle one-third of that mixture over noodles.
4. Repeat the above layers 2 more times.
5. Top with pepperoni. Top that with shredded cheese.
6. Cover. Cook on low 6-8 hours.

Ham in Foil

Jeanette Oberholtzer
Manheim, PA
Vicki Dinkel
Sharon Springs, KS
Janet Roggie
Lowville, NY

Makes 8 servings

½ cup water
3-4-lb. precooked ham
liquid smoke

1. Pour water into slow cooker.
2. Sprinkle ham with liquid smoke. Wrap in foil. Place in slow cooker.
3. Cover. Cook on high 1 hour, then on low 6 hours.
4. Cut into thick chunks or ½" slices and serve.

Glazed Ham in a Bag

Eleanor J. Ferreira
North Chelmsford, MA

Makes 12 servings

5-lb. cooked ham
3 Tbsp. orange juice
1 Tbsp. Dijon mustard

1. Rinse meat. Place in cooking bag.
2. Combine orange juice and mustard. Spread over ham.
3. Seal bag with twist tie. Poke 4 holes in top of bag. Place in slow cooker.
4. Cover. Cook on low 6-8 hours.
5. To serve, remove ham from bag, reserving juices. Slice ham and spoon juices over. Serve additional juice alongside in small bowl.

Cheesy Potatoes and Ham

Beth Maurer
Harrisonburg, VA

Makes 4-6 servings

6 cups sliced, peeled potatoes
2½ cups cooked ham, cubed
1½ cups shredded cheddar cheese
10¾-oz. can cream of mushroom soup
½ cup milk

1. In slow cooker, layer one-third of potatoes, of ham, and of cheese. Repeat two more times.
2. Combine soup and milk. Pour over ingredients in slow cooker.
3. Cover. Cook on high 1 hour. Reduce to low for 6-8 hours, or just until potatoes are soft.

Ham, Bean, and Potato Dish

Hazel L. Propst
Oxford, PA

Makes 6-8 servings

8-10 small potatoes
3-4 cans string beans, undrained
ham hock or leftover ham
salt to taste
pepper to taste

1. Place potatoes in bottom of slow cooker.
2. Alternate layers of beans and ham over potatoes. Sprinkle with salt and pepper.
3. Cover. Cook on low 8 hours if using ham hock; 6 hours if using leftover ham.

Creamy Ham Topping (for baked potatoes)

Judy Buller
Bluffton, OH

Makes 6 servings

¼ cup butter or margarine
¼ cup flour
2 cups milk
¼ cup half-and-half
1 Tbsp. chopped parsley
1 Tbsp. chicken bouillon granules
½ tsp. Italian seasoning
2 cups diced cooked ham
¼ cup Romano cheese, grated
1 cup sliced mushrooms
baked potatoes
shredded cheese
sour cream

1. Melt butter in saucepan. Stir in flour. Add milk and half-and-half.
2. Stir in remaining ingredients (except baked potatoes, shredded cheese, and sour cream). Pour into slow cooker.
3. Cover. Cook on low 1-2 hours.
4. Serve over baked potatoes. Top with shredded cheese and sour cream.

Ham and Lima Beans

Charlotte Shaffer
East Earl, PA

Makes 6 servings

1 lb. dry lima beans
1 onion, chopped
1 bell pepper, chopped
1 tsp. dry mustard
1 tsp. salt
1 tsp. pepper
1/2 lb. ham, finely cubed
1 cup water
10 3/4-oz. can tomato soup

1. Cover beans with water. Soak 8 hours. Drain.
2. Combine ingredients in slow cooker.
3. Cover. Cook on low 7 hours or high 4 hours.
4. If mixture begins to dry out, add 1/2 cup water or more and stir well.
5. This is delicious served with hot cornbread.

Ham and Hash Browns

Evelyn Page
Riverton, WY
Anna Stoltzfus
Honey Brook, PA

Makes 6-8 servings

28-oz. pkg. frozen hash brown potatoes
2 1/2 cups cubed cooked ham
2-oz. jar pimentos, drained and chopped
10 3/4-oz. can cheddar cheese soup
3/4 cup half-and-half, or milk
dash of pepper
salt to taste

1. Combine potatoes, ham, and pimentos in slow cooker.
2. Combine soup, half-and-half, and seasonings. Pour over potatoes.
3. Cover. Cook on low 6-8 hours. (If you turn the cooker on when you go to bed, you'll have a wonderfully tasty breakfast in the morning.)

Variation: Add a 4-oz. can of mushrooms, drained, or 1/4 lb. sliced fresh mushrooms, to Step 1.

Black Beans with Ham

Colleen Heatwole
Burton, MI

Makes 8-10 servings

4 cups dry black beans
1-2 cups diced ham
1 tsp. salt, optional
1 tsp. cumin
1/2-1 cup minced onion
2 garlic cloves, minced
3 bay leaves
1 qt. diced tomatoes
1 Tbsp. brown sugar

1. Cover black beans with water and soak for 8 hours, or over night. Drain and pour beans into slow cooker.
2. Add all remaining ingredients and stir well. Cover with water.
3. Cover cooker. Cook on low 10-12 hours.
4. Serve over rice.

This is our favorite black bean recipe. We make it frequently in the winter.

Ham 'n Cabbage Stew

Dede Peterson
Rapid City, SD

Makes 4-5 servings

1/2 lb. cooked ham, cubed
1/2 cup diced onions
1 garlic clove, minced
4-oz. can sliced mushrooms
4 cups shredded cabbage
2 cups sliced carrots
1/4 tsp. pepper
1/4 tsp. caraway seeds
2/3 cup beef broth
1 Tbsp. cornstarch
2 Tbsp. water

1. Combine all ingredients except cornstarch and water in slow cooker.
2. Cover. Cook on low 4-6 hours.
3. Mix cornstarch into water until smooth. Stir into slow cooker during last hour to thicken slightly.

Hosting Idea

Get your guests to help. Plan in advance where each dish of food should be placed on the serving table. Write the name of each food, including any special notations such as "sugar-free," "low-fat," etc., on a small piece of stiff paper that can be folded and stood, tent-fashion, where that food should be placed. Stand those signs in their positions on the serving table. Now anyone can help carry food to the table. When the dish is put in its spot, its sign should stand in front of it, so guests will know what they are choosing.

— Dolores Kratz

Ham and Corn Slow Cooker Casserole

Vicki Dinkel
Sharon Springs, KS

Makes 8 servings

1/2 cup butter or margarine
1 small green pepper, chopped
1 medium onion, chopped
1/2 cup flour
1/2 tsp. paprika
1/2 tsp. salt
1/2 tsp. pepper
1/4 tsp. dried thyme
1 tsp. dry mustard
4 cups milk
8-oz. can cream-style corn
2 cups diced, slightly cooked potatoes
4 cups diced cooked ham
1 cup shredded cheddar cheese

1. Saute green pepper and onion in butter in skillet.
2. Stir in flour and seasonings.
3. Gradually stir in milk and cook until thickened. Pour into slow cooker.
4. Stir in remaining ingredients.
5. Cover. Cook on low 8 hours or high 4 hours.

Cheesy Ham and Broccoli

Dolores Kratz
Souderton, PA

Makes 6 servings

1 bunch fresh broccoli
1¹/2 cups chopped ham
³/4 cup uncooked rice
4-oz. can mushrooms, drained
1 small onion, chopped
10³/4-oz. can cheddar cheese soup
³/4 cup water
¹/4 cup half-and-half, or milk
dash of pepper
¹/2-1 can chow mein noodles

1. Cut broccoli into pieces and steam for 4 minutes in microwave. Place in slow cooker.
2. Add remaining ingredients except noodles. Mix well.
3. Sprinkle with noodles.
4. Cover. Cook on low 6-7 hours.
5. Serve with tossed salad or applesauce.

Broccoli Casserole

Rebecca Meyerkorth
Wamego, KS

Makes 4 servings

16-oz. pkg. frozen broccoli cuts, thawed and drained
2-3 cups cubed, cooked ham
10³/4-oz. can cream of mushroom soup
4 ozs. of your favorite mild cheese, cubed
1 cup milk
1 cup instant rice, uncooked
1 rib celery, chopped
1 small onion, chopped

1. Combine broccoli and ham in slow cooker.
2. Combine soup, cheese, milk, rice, celery, and onion. Stir into broccoli.
3. Cover. Cook on low 4-5 hours.

Casserole in the Cooker

Ruth Ann Hoover
New Holland, PA

Makes 4 servings

16-oz. pkg. frozen broccoli, thawed and drained
3 cups cubed fully cooked ham
10³/4-oz. can cream of mushroom soup
8-oz. jar processed cheese sauce
1 cup milk
1 cup instant rice
1 celery rib, chopped
1 small onion, chopped

1. Combine broccoli and ham in slow cooker.
2. Combine remaining ingredients. Stir into broccoli/ham mixture.
3. Cover. Cook on low 4-5 hours.

Ham and Broccoli

Dede Peterson
Rapid City, SD

Makes 6-8 servings

3/4 lb. fresh broccoli, chopped,
　 or 10-oz. pkg. frozen chopped broccoli
10³/4-oz. can cream of mushroom soup
8-oz. jar processed cheese sauce
2¹/2 cups milk
1¹/4 cups long-grain rice, uncooked
1 rib celery, sliced
1/8 tsp. pepper
3 cups cooked and cubed ham
8-oz. can water chestnuts, drained and
　 sliced
1/2 tsp. paprika

　1. Combine all ingredients except ham, water chestnuts, and paprika in slow cooker.
　2. Cover. Cook on high 3-4 hours.
　3. Stir in ham and water chestnuts. Cook 15-20 minutes, until heated through. Let stand 10 minutes before serving.
　4. Sprinkle with paprika before serving.

Schnitz und Knepp

Jean Robinson
Cinnaminson, NJ

Makes 6 servings

Snitz:
1 qt. dried sweet apples
3 lbs. ham slices, cut into 2″ cubes
2 Tbsp. brown sugar
1 cinnamon stick

Knepp (Dumplings):
2 cups flour
4 tsp. baking powder
1 egg, well beaten
3 Tbsp. melted butter
scant 1/2 cup milk
1 tsp. salt
1/4 tsp. pepper

　1. Cover apples with water in large bowl and let soak for a few hours.
　2. Place ham in slow cooker. Cover with water.
　3. Cover cooker. Cook on high 2 hours.
　4. Add apples and water in which they have been soaking.
　5. Add brown sugar and cinnamon stick. Mix until dissolved.
　6. Cover. Cook on low 3 hours.
　7. Combine dumpling ingredients in bowl. Drop into hot liquid in cooker by tablespoonfuls. Turn to high. Cover. Do not lift lid for 15 minutes.
　8. Serve piping hot on a large platter. A celery-carrot jello salad rounds out the meal well.

This was my grandmother's recipe and she had no slow cooker. Schnitz und Knepp cooked on the back of the woodstove till the quilting was done. I was allowed to drop in the dumplings.

Ham with Sweet Potatoes and Oranges

Esther Becker
Gordonville, PA

Makes 4 servings

2-3 sweet potatoes, peeled and sliced
    1/4" thick
1 large ham slice
3 seedless oranges, peeled and sliced
3 Tbsp. orange juice concentrate
3 Tbsp. honey
1/2 cup brown sugar
2 Tbsp. cornstarch

1. Place sweet potatoes in slow cooker.
2. Arrange ham and orange slices on top.
3. Combine remaining ingredients. Drizzle over ham and oranges.
4. Cover. Cook on low 7-8 hours.
5. Delicious served with lime jello salad.

Southwest Hominy

Reita F. Yoder
Carlsbad, NM

Makes 12-14 servings

4 20-oz. cans hominy, drained
10³/4-oz. can cream of mushroom soup
10³/4-oz. can cream of chicken soup
1 cup diced green chilies
1/2 lb. Velveeta cheese, cubed
1 lb. hot dogs or ham, diced

1. Combine all ingredients in slow cooker.
2. Cover. Cook on low 2-4 hours. Stir before serving.

Underground Ham and Cheese

Carol Sommers
Millersburg, OH

Makes 12-16 servings

4 cups cooked ham, cut into chunks
4 Tbsp. butter or margarine
1/2 cup chopped onions
1 Tbsp. Worcestershire sauce
2 10³/4-oz. cans cream of mushroom soup
1 cup milk
2 cups Velveeta cheese, cubed
4 qts. mashed potatoes
1 pt. sour cream
browned and crumbled bacon

1. Combine ham, butter, onions, and Worcestershire sauce in saucepan. Cook until onions are tender. Place in large slow cooker, or divide between 2 4- or 5-qt. cookers.
2. In saucepan, heat together soup, milk, and cheese until cheese melts. Pour into cooker(s).
3. Combine potatoes and sour cream. Spread over mixture in slow cooker(s).
4. Sprinkle with bacon.
5. Cover. Cook on low 3-4 hours, or until cheese mixture comes to top when done (hence, the name "underground").

91

Verenike Casserole

Jennifer Yoder Sommers
Harrisonburg, VA 22802

Makes 8-10 servings

24 ozs. cottage cheese
3 eggs
1 tsp. salt
1/2 tsp. pepper
1 cup sour cream
2 cups evaporated milk
2 cups cubed cooked ham
7-9 dry lasagna noodles

1. Combine all ingredients except noodles.
2. Place half of creamy ham mixture in bottom of cooker. Add uncooked noodles. Cover with remaining half of creamy ham sauce. Be sure noodles are fully submerged in sauce.
3. Cover. Cook on low 5-6 hours.
4. Serve with green salad, peas, and zwiebach or bread.

This is an easy way to make the traditional Russian Mennonite dish—verenike, or cheese pockets. Its great taste makes up for its appearance!

Shepherd's Pie

Melanie Thrower
McPherson, KS

Makes 3-4 servings

1 lb. ground pork
1 Tbsp. vinegar
1 tsp. salt
1/4 tsp. hot pepper
1 tsp. paprika
1/4 tsp. dried oregano
1/4 tsp. black pepper
1 tsp. chili powder
1 small onion, chopped
15-oz. can corn, drained
3 large potatoes
1/4 cup milk
1 tsp. butter
1/4 tsp. salt
dash of pepper
shredded cheese

1. Combine pork, vinegar, and spices. Cook in skillet until brown. Add onion and cook until onions begin to glaze. Spread in bottom of slow cooker.
2. Spread corn over meat.
3. Boil potatoes until soft. Mash with milk, butter, 1/4 tsp. salt, and dash of pepper. Spread over meat and corn.
4. Cover. Cook on low 3 hours. Sprinkle top with cheese a few minutes before serving.

Variation: You can substitute ground beef for the pork.

This is my 9-year-old son's favorite dish.

Ham Balls

Jo Haberkamp
Fairbank, IA

Makes 12-16 servings

Ham Balls:
3 eggs
3 cups crushed graham crackers
2 cups milk
1 tsp. salt
1 tsp. onion salt
1/4 tsp. pepper
2 lbs. ground ham
1 1/2 lbs. ground beef
1 1/2 lbs. ground pork

Topping:
1/2 cup ketchup
1/4 cup water
1 cup brown sugar
1/4 cup plus 2 Tbsp. vinegar
1/2 tsp. dry mustard

1. Beat eggs slightly in large bowl. Add graham crackers, milk, salt, onion salt, pepper, and ground meats. Mix well.
2. Form into 24 balls, using 1/2 cup measuring cup for each ball.
3. Combine topping ingredients.
4. Layer meat balls and topping in greased slow cooker.
5. Cover. Cook on high 1 hour. Reduce heat to low and cook 3-4 hours more.

Ham Balls

Deborah Swartz
Grottoes, VA

Makes 24 large meatballs or 8 servings

Ham Balls:
1 1/2 lbs. ground pork
1 1/2 lbs. ground ham
1 1/4 cups cracker crumbs
1/4 tsp. salt
1/8 tsp. pepper
1 cup milk
2 eggs, beaten

Syrup:
1 1/2 cups brown sugar
1/2 cup vinegar
1/2 cup water
1 Tbsp. prepared mustard

1. Combine ham ball ingredients. Shape into 24 meatballs. Place in 9" x 13" pan.
2. Combine syrup ingredients. Pour over meatballs.
3. Bake at 350° for 10 minutes. Remove from oven. Place meatballs in slow cooker. Pour syrup over top.
4. Cover. Cook on high 3 1/4 hours.

Ham Loaf or Balls

Michelle Strite
Goshen, IN

Makes 8-10 servings

Ham Loaf or Balls:
1 lb. ground ham
1 lb. ground pork or ground beef
1 cup soft bread crumbs
2 eggs, slightly beaten
1 cup milk
2 Tbsp. minced onions
1¼ tsp. salt
⅛ tsp. pepper

Glaze:
¾ cup brown sugar
1 tsp. dry mustard
1 Tbsp. cornstarch
¼ cup vinegar
½ cup water

1. Combine ham loaf or balls ingredients. Form into loaf or balls and place in slow cooker.

2. Combine dry ingredients for glaze in bowl. Mix in vinegar and water until smooth. Pour into saucepan. Cook until slightly thickened. Pour over meat.

3. Cover. Cook on high 4-6 hours.

Variations:
1. For a firmer loaf, or balls, use dry bread crumbs instead of soft. Use only ¾ cup milk instead of 1 cup.

2. Form meat mixture into 1" balls. Brown lightly by baking on cookie sheet in 400° for 5-10 minutes. Place balls in slow cooker. Pour cooked glaze over balls, cover, and cook on high 2-4 hours.

—Julia A. Fisher, New Carlisle, OH

Menu Idea

Ham Loaf
Garlic Mashed Potatoes (page 204),
   or Hash Brown Potato Casserole
   (page 211)
Apple Crisp

Barbecue Sandwiches

Sherry L. Lapp
Lancaster, PA

Makes 6-8 sandwiches

1½ lbs. cubed pork
1 lb. stewing beef, cubed
6-oz. can tomato paste
¼ cup vinegar
½ cup brown sugar
1 tsp. salt
1 Tbsp. chili powder
1 large onion, chopped
1 green pepper, chopped

1. Combine ingredients in slow cooker.
2. Cover. Cook on low 8 hours.
3. Shred meat with fork before serving on rolls.
4. Bring to the table with creamy cole slaw.

Pork Barbecue

Barbara L. McGinnis
Jupiter, FL

Makes 6 servings

3-4-lb. pork loin
salt to taste
pepper to taste
2 cups cider vinegar
2 tsp. sugar
½ cup ketchup
crushed red pepper to taste
Tabasco sauce to taste
sandwich rolls

1. Sprinkle pork with salt and pepper. Place in slow cooker.
2. Pour vinegar over meat. Sprinkle sugar on top.
3. Cover. Cook on low 8 hours.
4. Remove pork from cooker and shred meat.
5. In bowl mix together ketchup, red pepper, Tabasco sauce, and ½ cup vinegar-sugar drippings. Stir in shredded meat.
6. Serve on sandwich rolls with cole slaw.

Variation: To increase the tang, add 1 tsp. dry mustard in Step 5. Use ¼ cup ketchup and ¼ cup orange juice, instead of ½ cup ketchup.

Frankwiches

Esther Mast
East Petersburg, PA

Makes 16-18 servings

2 10¾-oz. cans cheddar cheese soup
½ cup finely chopped onions
½ cup sweet pickle relish
4 tsp. prepared mustard
2 lbs. hot dogs, thinly sliced
8-oz. container sour cream

1. Combine soup, onions, relish, and mustard. Stir in sliced hot dogs.
2. Cover. Cook on low 4 hours.
3. Stir in sour cream.
4. Cover. Cook on high 10-15 minutes, stirring occasionally.
5. Serve over toasted English muffin halves or squares of hot cornbread.

Notes: Instead of using this as sandwich filling you can serve it over rice as a main dish. Add a green vegetable and a jello salad and you have a easy, refreshing, quick meal!

This will also bring smiles to the faces of your grandchildren! Add a relish tray and some chips, and you have a quick summer meal on the patio. Top it off with frozen popsicles.

Zesty Wieners

Lisa F. Good
Harrisonburg, VA

Makes 6-8 servings

1 dozen hot dogs
1/2 cup chopped onions
1 tsp. butter
1 tsp. pepper
2 Tbsp. sugar
2 tsp. prepared mustard
1 cup ketchup
3 Tbsp. Worcestershire sauce

1. Place hot dogs in slow cooker.
2. Saute onions in butter in skillet until almost tender.
3. Add remaining ingredients. Pour over hot dogs in slow cooker.
4. Cover. Cook on low 4 hours.

Menu Idea

Zesty Wieners
Macaroni and Cheese (pages 145-146)
Creamed Lima Beans

Bandito Chili Dogs

Sue Graber
Eureka, IL

Makes 10 servings

1 lb. hot dogs
2 15-oz. cans chili, with or without beans
10 3/4-oz. can condensed cheddar cheese soup
4-oz. can chopped green chilies
10 hot dog buns
1 medium onion, chopped
1-2 cups corn chips, coarsely crushed
1 cup shredded cheddar cheese

1. Place hot dogs in slow cooker.
2. Combine chili, soup, and green chilies. Pour over hot dogs.
3. Cover. Cook on low 3-3 1/2 hours.
4. Serve hot dogs in buns. Top with chili mixture, onion, corn chips, and cheese.

This is a fun recipe for after a football game or outside activity. The main part of your meal is ready when you get home.

Menu Idea

Bandito Chili Dogs
Applesauce
Carrot and Celery Sticks, Cauliflower and Broccoli Crudites
Cookies

Hot Dogs and Noodles

Dolores Kratz
Souderton, PA

Makes 6 servings

8-oz. pkg. medium egg noodles, cooked
    and drained
1¼ cups grated Parmesan cheese
1 cup milk
¼ cup butter or margarine, melted
1 Tbsp. flour
¼ tsp. salt
1-lb. pkg. hot dogs, sliced
¼ cup packed brown sugar
¼ cup mayonnaise
2 Tbsp. prepared mustard

1. Place noodles, cheese, milk, butter, flour, and salt in slow cooker. Mix well.
2. Combine hot dogs with remaining ingredients. Spoon evenly over noodles.
3. Cover. Cook on low 5-6 hours.

Super-Bowl Little Smokies

Mary Sommerfeld
Lancaster, PA
Alicia Denlinger
Lancaster, PA

Makes 9-10 main-dish servings,
or 15-20 appetizer servings

3 1-lb. pkgs. Little Smokies
8-oz. bottle Catalina dressing
splash of liquid smoke

1. Combine all ingredients in slow cooker.
2. Cover. Cook on low 2 hours.
3. Use toothpicks to serve.

These are always a hit at parties, whether it's Christmas, New Year's, or the Super Bowl. They are good any time that you'd like to serve food beyond dessert, but you don't want to have a sit-down meal.

Menu Idea

Super-Bowl Little Smokies
Raw Veggies and Dip
Fruit Tray
Cheese Cubes and Crackers
Brownies and Ice Cream

Cranberry Franks

Loretta Krahn
Mountain Lake, MN

Makes 15-20 servings

2 pkgs. cocktail wieners or little smoked
  sausages
16-oz. can jellied cranberry sauce
1 cup ketchup
3 Tbsp. brown sugar
1 Tbsp. lemon juice

  1. Combine all ingredients in slow cooker.
  2. Cover. Cook on high 1-2 hours.

Great picnic, potluck, or buffet food.

Crockpot Smokies

Dede Peterson
Rapid City, SD

Makes 8-10 servings

2 lbs. Little Smokies
18-oz. bottle barbecue sauce (your choice
  of flavors)

  1. Put Little Smokies in slow cooker.
  2. Cover with barbecue sauce.
  3. Cover. Cook on low 3-4 hours.

Hosting Idea

When you're going to host a party, plan to spread your counter or long table with lots of slow cookers. Borrow them ahead of time from your neighbors and friends.

Early in the day of your get-together, line up as many slow cookers as needed and get the foods started—the corn, sweet potatoes, baked pineapple, mashed potatoes, meats, appetizer, soup. When your guests arrive, you have no last-minute fixin's to do.

Remove the slow cookers' lids, add long-handled utensils, and invite your guests to help themselves.

—Dolores Kratz

Chicken Main Dishes

Sunday Roast Chicken

Ruth A. Feister
Narvon, PA

Makes 4-5 servings

Seasoning Mix:
1 Tbsp. salt
2 tsp. paprika
1½ tsp. onion powder
1½ tsp. garlic powder
1½ tsp. dried basil
1 tsp. dry mustard
1 tsp. cumin
2 tsp. pepper
½ tsp. dried thyme
½ tsp. savory

2 Tbsp. butter
2 cups chopped onions
1 cup chopped green pepper
1 roasting chicken
¼ cup flour
1-2 cups chicken stock

1. Combine seasoning mix ingredients in small bowl.
2. Melt butter over high heat in skillet. When butter starts to sizzle, add chopped onions and peppers, and 3 Tbsp. seasoning mix. Cook until onions are golden brown. Cool.
3. Stuff cavity of chicken with cooled vegetables.
4. Sprinkle outside of chicken with 1 Tbsp. seasoning mix. Rub in well.
5. Place chicken in large slow cooker.
6. Cover. Cook on low 6 hours.
7. Empty vegetable stuffing and juices into saucepan. Whisk in flour and 1 cup stock. Cook over high heat until thickened. Add more stock if you prefer a thinner gravy.

The first time I served this dish was when we had family visiting us from Mississippi. We had a wonderful time sitting around a large table sharing many laughs and catching up on the years since our last visit.

Menu Idea

Sunday Roast Chicken
Mashed Potatoes (pages 204-206)
Green Beans Almondine

Old-Fashioned Stewed Chicken

Bonnie Goering
Bridgewater, VA

Makes 6-8 servings

3-4-lb. chicken, cut up
1 small onion, cut into wedges
1 rib celery, sliced
1 carrot, sliced
1 Tbsp. chopped fresh parsley
   (1 tsp. dried)
1 Tbsp. chopped fresh thyme (1 tsp. dried)
1 Tbsp. chopped fresh rosemary
   (1 tsp. dried)
3 tsp. salt
1/4 tsp. pepper
3-4 cups hot water

1. Place chicken in slow cooker. Add remaining ingredients.
2. Cover. Cook on low 8 hours.
3. Use broth as a base to make gravy. Debone chicken and set aside. Thicken broth with flour-water paste. When bubbly and thickened, stir chicken pieces into gravy.
4. Serve with mashed potatoes or noodles and creamed peas.

I cook every Thursday afternoon for a 93-year-old woman who lives by herself. She taught me how to cook with fresh herbs from her garden. I've found they make food taste so much better that I've started an herb garden. And I dry some herbs to use during the winter.

One-Pot Easy Chicken

Jean Robinson
Cinnaminson, NJ

Makes 6 servings

6-8 potatoes, quartered
1-2 large onions, sliced
3-5 carrots, cubed
5-lbs. chicken, skin removed (quarters or
   legs and thighs work well)
1 small onion, chopped
1 tsp. black pepper
1 Tbsp. whole cloves
1 Tbsp. garlic salt
1 Tbsp. chopped fresh oregano
1 tsp. dried rosemary
1/2 cup lemon juice or chicken broth

1. Layer potatoes, sliced onions, and carrots in bottom of slow cooker.
2. Rinse and pat chicken dry. In bowl mix together chopped onions, pepper, cloves, and garlic salt. Dredge chicken in seasonings. Place in cooker over vegetables. Spoon any remaining seasonings over chicken.
3. Sprinkle with oregano and rosemary. Pour lemon juice over chicken.
4. Cover. Cook on low 6 hours.

This is a lifesaver when the grandchildren come for a weekend. I get to play with them, and dinner is timed and ready when we are.

Menu Idea

One-Pot Easy Chicken
Celery and Carrot Sticks
Green Beans
Jello Salad

Chicken Cacciatore with Spaghetti

Phyllis Pellman Good
Lancaster, PA

Makes 4-5 servings

2 onions, sliced
2½-3 lbs. chicken legs
2 garlic cloves, minced
16-oz. can stewed tomatoes
8-oz. can tomato sauce
1 tsp. salt
¼ tsp. pepper
1-2 tsp. dried oregano
½ tsp. dried basil
1 bay leaf
¼ cup white wine

1. Place onions in bottom of slow cooker.
2. Lay chicken legs over onions.
3. Combine remeaining ingredients. Pour over chicken.
4. Cover. Cook on low 6-6½ hours.
5. Remove bay leaf. Serve over hot buttered spaghetti, linguini, or fettucini.

Chicken Cacciatore

Eleanor J. Ferreira
North Chelmsford, MA

Makes 8 servings

2 chickens, cut into pieces
1 cup flour
2 tsp. salt
½ tsp. pepper
olive oil
2 4-oz. cans sliced mushrooms
3 medium onions, sliced
2 celery ribs, chopped
4 large green peppers, cut into 1" strips
28-oz. can tomatoes
28-oz. can tomato puree
½ tsp. dried basil
½ tsp. dried oregano
½ tsp. salt
¼ tsp. pepper
½ tsp. dried parsley

1. Shake chicken pieces, one at a time, in bag with flour, salt, and pepper. When well coated, brown chicken pieces on both sides in skillet in oil. Place chicken in large slow cooker or two medium-sized cookers, reserving drippings.
2. Saute mushrooms, onions, celery, and peppers in drippings from chicken. Spread over chicken.
3. Mix remaining ingredients together in bowl and pour over chicken and vegetables.
4. Cover. Cook on low 7-8 hours.
5. Serve over hot spaghetti.

Chicken and Sausage Cacciatore

Joyce Kaut
Rochester, NY

Makes 4-6 servings

1 large green pepper, sliced in 1″ strips
1 cup sliced mushrooms
1 medium onion, sliced in rings
1 lb. skinless, boneless chicken breasts, browned
1 lb. Italian sausage, browned
½ tsp. dried oregano
½ tsp. dried basil
1½ cups Italian-style tomato sauce

1. Layer vegetables in slow cooker.
2. Top with meat.
3. Sprinkle with oregano and basil.
4. Top with tomato sauce.
5. Cover. Cook on low 8 hours.
6. Remove cover during last 30 minutes of cooking time to allow sauce to cook-off and thicken.
7. Serve over cooked spiral pasta.

Menu Idea

Chicken and Sausage Cacciatore
Spiral Pasta
Stewed Tomatoes
Crusty Bread

Con Pollo

Dorothy Van Deest
Memphis, TN

Makes 4-6 servings

3-4-lb. whole chicken
salt to taste
pepper to taste
paprika to taste
garlic salt to taste
6-oz. can tomato paste
½ cup beer
3-oz. jar stuffed olives with liquid

1. Wash chicken. Sprinkle all over with salt, pepper, paprika, and garlic salt. Place in slow cooker.
2. Combine tomato paste and beer. Pour over chicken. Add olives.
3. Cover. Cook on low 8-10 hours or high 3-4 hours.
4. Serve over rice or noodles, along with salad and cornbread, and sherbet for dessert.

This is chicken with a Spanish flair. This easy supper is quick, too, by slow-cooker standards, if you use the high temperature. Let your slow cooker be the chef.

Basil Chicken

Sarah Niessen
Akron, PA

Makes 4-6 servings

1 lb. baby carrots
2 medium onions, sliced
1-2 cups celery slices and leaves
3-lb. chicken

½ cup chicken broth,
   or white cooking wine
2 tsp. salt
½ tsp. black pepper
1 tsp. dried basil

1. Place carrots, onions, and celery in bottom of slow cooker.
2. Add chicken.
3. Pour broth over chicken.
4. Sprinkle with salt, pepper, and basil.
5. Cover. Cook on low 7-10 hours, or until chicken and vegetables are tender.

Curry

Dawn Ranck
Harrisonburg, VA

Makes 6-8 servings

28-oz. can tomatoes
4 whole chicken breasts, cut in half
1 onion, chopped
half a green pepper, chopped
2 carrots, chopped
2 ribs celery, chopped
1-2 Tbsp. curry
1 tsp. turmeric
½ tsp. salt
¼ tsp. pepper
1 Tbsp. sugar
1 chicken bouillon cube dissolved in
   ¼ cup hot water

1. Combine all ingredients in slow cooker.
2. Cover. Cook on high 2-3 hours or on low 5-6 hours.

Dad's Spicy Chicken Curry

Tom & Sue Ruth
Lancaster, PA

Makes 8 servings

4 lbs. chicken pieces, with bones
water
2 onions, diced
10-oz. pkg. frozen chopped spinach,
   thawed and squeezed dry
1 cup plain yogurt
2-3 diced red potatoes
3 tsp. salt
1 tsp. garlic powder
1 tsp. ground ginger
1 tsp. ground cumin
1 tsp. ground coriander
1 tsp. pepper
1 tsp. ground cloves
1 tsp. ground cardamom
1 tsp. ground cinnamon
½ tsp. chili powder
1 tsp. red pepper flakes
3 tsp. turmeric

1. Place chicken in large slow cooker. Cover with water.
2. Cover. Cook on high 2 hours, or until tender.
3. Drain chicken. Remove from slow cooker. Cool briefly and cut/shred into small pieces. Return to slow cooker.
4. Add remaining ingredients.
5. Cover. Cook on low 4-6 hours, or until potatoes are tender.
6. Serve on rice. Accompany with fresh mango slices or mango chutney.

Variation: Substitute 5 tsp. curry powder for the garlic, ginger, cumin, coriander, and pepper.

Delicious Chicken with Curried Cream Sauce

Jennifer J. Gehman
Harrisburg, PA

Makes 4-6 servings

4-6 boneless, skinless, chicken breasts or
   legs and thighs
oil
salt to taste
pepper to taste
10³/4-oz. can cream of chicken soup
1/2 cup mayonnaise
1-2 Tbsp. curry powder
1/2 tsp. salt
1/8 tsp. pepper
1 lb. fresh, or 15-oz. can, asparagus spears
1/2-1 cup shredded cheddar cheese

1. Brown chicken on all sides in skillet in oil. Season with salt and pepper. Place in slow cooker.

2. Combine soup, mayonnaise, curry powder, salt, and pepper. Pour over chicken.

3. Cover. Cook on high 3 hours or on low 5 hours.

4. If using fresh asparagus, steam lightly until just-tender. If using canned asparagus, heat. Drain asparagus and place in bottom of serving dish.

5. Cover asparagus with chicken. Sprinkle with cheese.

6. Serve with egg noodles or white rice. Add another cooked vegetable, along with fruit salad, applesauce, or mandarin oranges, as side dishes.

Curried Chicken

Marlene Bogard
Newton, KS

Makes 5 servings

2¹/2-3¹/2-lb. fryer chicken, cut up
salt to taste
pepper to taste
1 Tbsp. curry powder
1 garlic clove, crushed or minced
1 Tbsp. melted butter
1/2 cup chicken broth, or 1 chicken
   bouillon cube dissolved in 1/2 cup water
2 Tbsp. onion, chopped fine
29-oz. can cling peaches
1/2 cup pitted prunes
3 Tbsp. cornstarch
3 Tbsp. cold water

1. Sprinkle chicken with salt and pepper. Place in slow cooker.

2. Combine curry, garlic, butter, broth, and onions in bowl.

3. Drain peaches, reserving syrup. Add 1/2 cup syrup to curry mixture. Pour over chicken.

4. Cover. Cook on low 4-6 hours. Remove chicken from pot. Turn on high.

5. Stir in prunes.

6. Dissolve cornstarch in cold water. Stir into pot.

7. Cover. Cook on high 10 minutes, or until thickened. Add peaches. Add cooked chicken.

8. Serve over rice. Offer peanuts, shredded coconut, and fresh pineapple chunks as condiments.

Garlic Lime Chicken

Loretta Krahn
Mountain Lake, MN

Makes 5 servings

5 chicken breast halves
1/2 cup soy sauce
1/4-1/3 cup lime juice, according to your
taste preference
1 Tbsp. Worcestershire sauce
2 garlic cloves, minced,
or 1 tsp. garlic powder
1/2 tsp. dry mustard
1/2 tsp. ground pepper

1. Place chicken in slow cooker.
2. Combine remaining ingredients and pour over chicken.
3. Cover. Cook on high 4-6 hours or on low 6-8 hours.

Herbed Chicken

LaVerne A. Olson
Lititz, PA

Makes 8 serving

4 whole chicken breasts, halved
10 3/4-oz. can cream of mushroom or
chicken soup
1/4 cup soy sauce
1/4 cup oil
1/4 cup wine vinegar
3/4 cup water
1/2 tsp. minced garlic
1 tsp. ground ginger
1/2 tsp. dried oregano
1 Tbsp. brown sugar

1. Place chicken in slow cooker.
2. Combine remaining ingredients. Pour over chicken.
3. Cover. Cook on low 2-2 1/2 hours. Uncover and cook 15 minutes more.
Serve with rice.

A favorite with the whole family, even grandchildren. The gravy is delicious.

Teriyaki Chicken

Colleen Konetzni
Rio Rancho, NM

Makes 6 servings

6-8 skinless chicken thighs
1/2 cup soy sauce
2 Tbsp. brown sugar
2 Tbsp. grated fresh ginger
2 garlic cloves, minced

1. Wash and dry chicken. Place in slow cooker.
2. Combine remaining ingredients. Pour over chicken.
3. Cover. Cook on high 1 hour. Reduce heat to low and cook 6-7 hours.
4. Serve over rice with a fresh salad.

Easy Chicken

Ruth Liebelt
Rapid City, SD

Makes 6-8 servings

8-10 chicken wings or legs and thighs
½ cup soy sauce
½ cup sugar
½ tsp. Tabasco sauce
pinch of ground ginger

1. Place chicken in greased slow cooker.
2. Combine remaining ingredients and pour over chicken.
3. Cover. Cook on low 8 hours.
4. Serve with cooked rice, rolls, and salad.

Barbecued Chicken

Gladys Longacre
Susquehanna, PA

Makes 4-6 servings

3-4 lbs. boneless, skinless, chicken breasts
oil
1 onion, chopped
¼ cup chopped green pepper
1 cup ketchup
1-2 Tbsp. hickory-smoked barbecue sauce
1 Tbsp. prepared mustard
1 Tbsp. Worcestershire sauce
1 Tbsp. lemon juice
2 Tbsp. vinegar
3 Tbsp. brown sugar
¼ cup water
½ tsp. salt
⅛ tsp. pepper

1. Lightly brown chicken in oil in skillet. Place in slow cooker.
2. Layer onions and green pepper over chicken.
3. Combine remaining ingredients and pour over chicken.
4. Cover. Cook on low 6 hours or high 3½-4 hours.
5. Serve chicken and sauce over cooked rice.

Barbecued Chicken

Joanne Kennedy
Plattsburgh, NY

Makes 4 servings

2 whole boneless, skinless chicken breasts, cubed
1 medium onion, sliced
1 green pepper, sliced
1 cup chopped celery
2 Tbsp. Worcestershire sauce
2 Tbsp. brown sugar
1½ cups ketchup
1½ cups water
½ tsp. pepper

1. Combine all ingredients in slow cooker.
2. Cover. Cook on low 8 hours or high 4 hours.
3. Serve over rice with a tossed salad.

106

Chicken Stew with Peppers and Pineapples

Judi Manos
West Islip, NY

Makes 4 servings

1 lb. boneless, skinless chicken breasts, cut
in 1 1/2" cubes
4 medium carrots, sliced into 1" pieces
1/2 cup chicken broth
2 Tbsp. gingerroot, chopped
1 Tbsp. brown sugar
2 Tbsp. soy sauce
1/2 tsp. ground allspice
1/2 tsp. red pepper sauce
8-oz. can pineapple chunks, drained
(reserve juice)
1 Tbsp. cornstarch
1 medium sweet green pepper,
cut in 1" pieces

1. Combine chicken, carrots, chicken broth,
gingerroot, sugar, soy sauce, allspice, and red
pepper sauce in slow cooker.
2. Cover. Cook on low 7-8 hours or on high
3-4 hours.
3. Combine pineapple juice and cornstarch
until smooth. Stir into chicken mixture. Add
pineapple and green pepper.
4. Cover. Cook on high 15 minutes, or until
slightly thickened.
5. Serve over cooked rice.

*Variation: Add 1 cut-up fresh tomato 30 minutes
before end of cooking time.*

Maui Chicken

John D. Allen
Rye, CO

Makes 6 servings

6 boneless chicken breast halves
2 Tbsp. oil
14 1/2-oz. can chicken broth
20-oz. can pineapple chunks
1/4 cup vinegar
2 Tbsp. brown sugar
2 tsp. soy sauce
1 garlic clove, minced
1 medium green bell pepper, chopped
3 Tbsp. cornstarch
1/4 cup water

1. Brown chicken in oil. Transfer chicken to
slow cooker.
2. Combine remaining ingredients. Pour
over chicken.
3. Cover. Cook on high 4-6 hours.
4. Serve over rice.

Chicken in a Hurry

Yvonne Boettger
Harrisonburg, VA

Makes 4-5 servings

2½-3 lbs. skinless chicken drumsticks
½ cup ketchup
¼ cup water
¼ cup brown sugar
1 pkg. dry onion soup mix

1. Arrange chicken in slow cooker.
2. Combine remaining ingredients. Pour over chicken.
3. Cover. Cook on high 4-5 hours or low 7-8 hours.

Tender Barbecued Chicken

Betty Stoltzfus
Honeybrook, PA

Makes 4-6 servings

3-4 lb. broiler chicken
1 medium onion, thinly sliced
1 medium lemon, thinly sliced
18-oz. bottle barbecue sauce
¾ cup cola-flavored soda

1. Place chicken in slow cooker.
2. Top with onion and lemon.
3. Combine barbecue sauce and cola. Pour into slow cooker.
4. Cover. Cook on low 8-10 hours, or until chicken juices run clear.
5. Cut into serving-sized pieces and serve with barbecue sauce. Slice any leftovers and use in sandwiches.

Spicy Sweet Chicken

Carolyn Baer
Conrath, WI

Makes 4 servings

2½-3 lbs. chicken breasts, thighs, and/or legs, skinned
1 Tbsp. oil
16-oz. can whole cranberry sauce
¼ cup spicy-sweet Catalina salad dressing
2 Tbsp. dry onion soup mix
1 Tbsp. cornstarch

1. Rinse chicken. Pat dry. Brown in hot oil in skillet. Place in slow cooker.
2. Combine half of cranberry sauce, and all of salad dressing and soup mix. Pour over chicken.
3. Cover. Cook on low 6 hours or high 3 hours.
4. Stir cornstarch into remaining cranberry sauce. Stir into chicken mixture.
5. Turn slow cooker to high. Cover and cook 30-45 minutes more, or until thickened and bubbly.
6. Serve over cooked noodles or rice.

Aloha Chicken Cosmopolitan

Dianna Milhizer
Brighton, MI

Makes 12 servings

**5 lbs. boneless, skinless chicken breasts,
cut into strips or cubed
dash of salt
1 cup frozen orange juice
1 cup coconut milk
1 cup soy sauce
¼ cup sesame oil**

1. Lightly salt chicken and then refrigerate for 30 minutes.
2. Drain chicken of any juices that have gathered and combine with other ingredients in large slow cooker.
3. Cover. Cook on low 6 hours.
4. Serve with white rice.

Blue Ribbon Cranberry Chicken

Marjorie Y. Guengerich
Harrisonburg, VA

Makes 4-6 servings

**2½-3-lb. chicken, cut up
16-oz. can whole cranberry sauce
8-oz. bottle Russian salad dressing
1 pkg. dry onion soup mix**

1. Rinse chicken. Pat dry with paper towel. Place in slow cooker.
2. Combine cranberry sauce, salad dressing, and soup mix. Pour over chicken.
3. Cover and chill 1-8 hours, or overnight.

4. Cover. Cook on high 4 hours or on low 6-8 hours.
5. Serve over rice or noodles.

Chicken with Applesauce

Kelly Evenson
Pittsboro, NC

Makes 4 servings

**4 boneless, skinless chicken breast halves
salt to taste
pepper to taste
4-5 Tbsp. oil
2 cups applesauce
¼ cup barbecue sauce
½ tsp. poultry seasoning
2 tsp. honey
½ tsp. lemon juice**

1. Season chicken with salt and pepper. Brown in oil for 5 minutes per side.
2. Cut up chicken into 1" chunks and transfer to slow cooker.
3. Combine remaining ingredients. Pour over chicken and mix together well.
4. Cover. Cook on high 2-3 hours, or until chicken is tender.
5. Serve over rice or noodles.

Saucy Apricot Chicken

Anna Stoltzfus
Honey Brook, PA

Makes 6 servings

6 boneless, skinless chicken breast halves
2 12-oz. jars apricot preserves
1 pkg. dry onion soup mix

1. Place chicken in slow cooker.
2. Combine preserves and onion soup mix in separate bowl. Spoon over chicken.
3. Cover. Cook on low 4-5 hours.
4. Serve over rice.

Chicken ala Orange

Carlene Horne
Bedford, NH

Makes 8 servings

8 boneless, skinless chicken breast halves
1/2 cup chopped onion
12-oz. jar orange marmalade
1/2 cup Russian dressing
1 Tbsp. dried parsley, or to taste

1. Place chicken and onion in slow cooker.
2. Combine marmalade and dressing. Pour over chicken.
3. Sprinkle with parsley.
4. Cover. Cook on low 4-6 hours.
5. Serve with rice.

Scrumptious Chicken

Kathi Rogge
Alexandria, IN

Makes 8 servings

8 skinned chicken breast halves
10¾-oz. can cream of mushroom, or
   cream of chicken soup
16 ozs. sour cream
1 pkg. dry onion soup mix
fresh basil or oregano, chopped

1. Place chicken in slow cooker.
2. Combine all remaining ingredients except fresh herbs. Pour over chicken.
3. Cover. Cook on low 6 hours. (If convenient for you, stir after 3 hours of cooking.)
4. Sprinkle with fresh herbs just before serving.
5. Serve with brown and wild rice, mixed, or couscous.

Variations:
1. Cut up 4 lightly cooked chicken breast halves. Place in slow cooker.

2. Add 8 ozs. sour cream, 1 pkg. dry onion soup mix, and a 10¾-oz. can cream of mushroom soup. Mix together well.

3. Cover and cook on low 3-4 hours.

4. Serve over rice or noodles.
   —Sherry Conyers, McPherson, KS

Menu Idea

Scrumptious Chicken
Brown and Wild Rice, mixed
Mexican Corn or Seasoned Green Beans
Chilled Fruit Salad

3. Cover. Cook on low 8 hours.
4. Serve over croissants split in half. Sprinkle with paprika and parsley.

Creamy Chicken Breasts
Judy Buller
Bluffton, OH

Makes 6-8 servings

6-8 chicken breast halves
salt to taste
pepper to taste
paprika to taste
10³/4-oz. can cream of mushroom soup
1/2 cup sour cream

1. Season chicken breasts with salt, pepper, and paprika. Place in slow cooker.
2. Combine mushroom soup and sour cream. Pour over chicken.
3. Cover. Cook on low 6 hours.
4. Serve with rice, noodles, or mashed potatoes.

Miriam's Chicken
Arlene Leaman Kliewer
Lakewood, CO

Makes 6 servings

4 chicken breast halves, cut up into
    1" chunks and uncooked
8-oz. pkg. cream cheese, cubed
2 10³/4-oz. cans cream soup (your
    favorite—or a combination of your
    favorites)
6 croissants
paprika
fresh parsley, minced

1. Place chicken in slow cooker.
2. Combine cream cheese and soups. Pour over chicken. Stir.

Elegant Chicken with Gravy
Leesa Lesenski
South Deerfield, MA

Makes 6 serving

6 boneless chicken breast halves
10³/4-oz. can cream of broccoli, or broccoli
    cheese, soup
10³/4-oz. can cream of chicken soup
1/2 cup white wine
4-oz. can sliced mushrooms, undrained,
    optional

1. Place chicken breasts in slow cooker.
2. In bowl mix together soups, wine, and mushroom slices. Pour over chicken.
3. Cover. Cook on high 3 hours or on low 6 hours, or until chicken is tender but not dry.
4. Serve over rice or noodles.

111

Janie's Chicken a La King

Lafaye M. Musser
Denver, PA

Makes 4 servings

10³/4-oz. can cream of chicken soup
3 Tbsp. flour
1/2 tsp. salt
1/4 tsp. pepper
dash cayenne pepper
1 lb. boneless chicken, uncooked and cut
    in pieces
1 rib celery, chopped
1/2 cup chopped green pepper
1/4 cup chopped onions
9-oz. bag frozen peas, thawed

1. Combine soup, flour, salt, pepper, and cayenne pepper in slow cooker.
2. Stir in chicken, celery, green pepper, and onion.
3. Cover. Cook on low 7-8 hours.
4. Stir in peas.
5. Cover. Cook 30 minutes longer.
6. Serve in pastry cups or over rice, waffles, or toast.

Savory Chicken

Shari Mast
Harrisonburg, VA

Makes 8-10 servings

4 boneless, skinless chicken breast halves
4 skinless chicken quarters
10³/4-oz. can cream of chicken soup
1 Tbsp. water
1/4 cup chopped sweet red peppers
1 Tbsp. chopped fresh parsley,
    or 1 tsp. dried parsley
1 Tbsp. lemon juice
1/2 tsp. paprika

1. Layer chicken in slow cooker.
2. Combine remaining ingredients and pour over chicken.
3. Cover. Cook on high 4-5 hours.

Savory Chicken, Meal #2

leftover chicken and broth from first
    Savory Chicken Meal
2 carrots
1 rib celery
2 medium-sized onions
2 Tbsp. flour or cornstarch
1/4 cup cold water

1. For a second Savory Chicken Meal, pick leftover chicken off bone. Set aside.
2. Return remaining broth to slow cooker and stir in thinly sliced carrots and celery and onions cut up in chunks. Cook 3-4 hours on high.
3. In separate bowl, mix flour or cornstarch with cold water. When smooth, stir into hot broth.
4. Stir in cut-up chicken. Heat 15-20 minutes, or until broth thickens and chicken is hot.
5. Serve over rice or pasta.

Creamy Chicken and Vegetables

Dawn M. Propst
Levittown, PA

Makes 4 servings

10³/4-oz. can cream of mushroom soup,
    divided
4 boneless, skinless chicken breast halves
16-oz. pkg. frozen vegetable medley
    (broccoli, cauliflower, and carrots),
    thawed and drained
1/2 tsp. salt
1/8-1/4 tsp. pepper
1 cup shredded cheddar cheese, divided

1. Pour small amount of soup in bottom of slow cooker.

2. Add chicken breasts, vegetables, and seasonings.

3. Mix in 1/2 cup cheddar cheese. Cover with remaining soup.

4. Cover. Cook on low 5-6 hours, or until vegetables are cooked and chicken is no longer pink.

5. Sprinkle with remaining cheese 10-15 minutes before serving.

Szechwan-Style Chicken and Broccoli

Jane Meiser
Harrisonburg, VA

Makes 4 servings

2 whole boneless, skinless chicken or
    turkey breasts
oil
1/2 cup picante sauce
2 Tbsp. soy sauce
1/2 tsp. sugar
1/2 Tbsp. quick-cooking tapioca
1 medium onion, chopped
2 garlic cloves, minced
1/2 tsp. ground ginger
2 cups broccoli florets
1 medium red pepper, cut into pieces

1. Cut chicken into 1" cubes and brown lightly in oil in skillet. Place in slow cooker.

2. Stir in remaining ingredients.

3. Cover. Cook on high 1-1½ hours or on low 2-3 hours.

Creamy Chicken and Noodles

Rhonda Burgoon
Collingswood, NJ

Makes 4-6 servings

2 cups sliced carrots
1½ cups chopped onions
1 cup sliced celery
2 Tbsp. snipped fresh parsley
bay leaf
3 medium-sized chicken legs and thighs
   (about 2 lbs.)
2 10¾-oz. cans cream of chicken soup
½ cup water
1 tsp. dried thyme
1 tsp. salt
¼ tsp. pepper
1 cup peas
10 ozs. wide noodles, cooked

1. Place carrots, onions, celery, parsley, and bay leaf in bottom of slow cooker.
2. Place chicken on top of vegetables.
3. Combine soup, water, thyme, salt, and pepper. Pour over chicken and vegetables.
4. Cover. Cook on low 8-9 hours or high 4-4½ hours.
5. Remove chicken from slow cooker. Cool slightly. Remove from bones, cut into bite-sized pieces and return to slow cooker.
6. Remove and discard bay leaf.
7. Stir peas into mixture in slow cooker. Allow to cook for 5-10 more minutes.
8. Pour over cooked noodles. Toss gently to combine.
9. Serve with crusty bread and a salad.

Chicken Alfredo

Dawn M. Propst
Levittown, PA

Makes 4-6 servings

16-oz. jar Alfredo sauce
4-6 boneless, skinless chicken breast
   halves
8 ozs. dry noodles, cooked
4-oz. can mushroom pieces and stems,
   drained
1 cup shredded mozzarella cheese,
   or ½ cup grated Parmesan cheese

1. Pour about one-third of Alfredo sauce in bottom of slow cooker.
2. Add chicken and cover with remaining sauce.
3. Cover. Cook on low 8 hours.
4. Fifteen minutes before serving, add noodles and mushrooms, mixing well. Sprinkle top with cheese. Dish is ready to serve when cheese is melted.
5. Serve with green salad and Italian bread.

Gourmet Chicken Breasts

Sharon Swartz Lambert
Dayton, VA
Deborah Santiago
Lancaster, PA

Makes 4-6 servings

6-8 slices dried beef
4-6 boneless, skinless chicken breast
  halves
2-3 slices bacon, cut in half lengthwise
10³/₄-oz. cream of mushroom soup
8-oz. carton sour cream
1/2 cup flour

1. Line bottom of slow cooker with dried beef.
2. Roll up each chicken breast half and wrap with a half-slice of bacon. Place in slow cooker.
3. Combine remaining ingredients in bowl. Pour over breasts.
4. Cover. Cook on low 6-8 hours.
5. Serve with cooked noodles, rice, or mashed potatoes.

Creamy Nutmeg Chicken

Amber Swarey
Donalds, SC

Makes 6 servings

6 boneless chicken breast halves
oil
1/4 cup chopped onions
1/4 cup minced parsley
2 10³/₄-oz. cans cream of mushroom soup
1/2 cup sour cream
1/2 cup milk

1 Tbsp. ground nutmeg
1/4 tsp. sage
1/4 tsp. dried thyme
1/4 tsp. crushed rosemary

1. Brown chicken in skillet in oil. Reserve drippings and place chicken in slow cooker.
2. Saute onions and parsley in drippings until onions are tender.
3. Stir in remaining ingredients. Mix well. Pour over chicken.
4. Cover. Cook on low 3 hours, or until juices run clear.
5. Serve over mashed or fried potatoes, or rice.

Slow Cooker
Creamy Chicken Italian

Sherri Grindle
Goshen, IN

Makes 6 servings

8 boneless, skinless chicken breast halves
1 pkg. dry Italian salad dressing mix
1/4 cup water
8-oz. pkg. cream cheese, softened
10³/₄-oz. can cream of chicken soup
4-oz. can mushrooms, drained

1. Place chicken in greased slow cooker.
2. Combine salad dressing and water. Pour over chicken.
3. Cover. Cook on low 4-5 hours.
4. In saucepan, combine cream cheese and soup. Heat slightly to melt cream cheese. Stir in mushrooms. Pour over chicken.
5. Cover. Cook 1 additional hour on low.
6. Serve over noodles or rice.

Variation: Add frozen vegetables along with the mushrooms.

Mushroom Chicken in Sour Cream Sauce

Lavina Hochstedler
Grand Blanc, MI
Joyce Shackelford
Green Bay, WI

Makes 6 servings

1 1/2 tsp. salt
1/4 tsp. pepper
1/2 tsp. paprika
1/4 tsp. lemon pepper
1 tsp. garlic powder
6 skinless, bone-in chicken breast halves
10 3/4-oz. can cream of mushroom soup
8-oz. container sour cream
1/2 cup dry white wine or chicken broth
1/2 lb. fresh mushrooms, sliced

1. Combine salt, pepper, paprika, lemon pepper, and garlic powder. Rub over chicken. Place in slow cooker.
2. Combine soup, sour cream, and wine or broth. Stir in mushrooms. Pour over chicken.
3. Cover. Cook on low 6-8 hours or high 5 hours.
4. Serve over potatoes, rice, or couscous. Delicious accompanied with broccoli-cauliflower salad and applesauce.

Oriental Chicken Cashew Dish

Dorothy Horst
Tiskilwa, IL

Makes 6 servings

14-oz. can bean sprouts, drained
3 Tbsp. butter or margarine, melted
4 green onions, chopped
4-oz. can mushroom pieces
10 3/4-oz. can cream of mushroom soup
1 cup sliced celery
12 1/2-oz. can chunk chicken breast, or 1 cup cooked chicken cubed
1 Tbsp. soy sauce
1 cup cashew nuts

1. Combine all ingredients except nuts in slow cooker.
2. Cover. Cook on low 4-9 hours or on high 2-3 hours.
3. Stir in cashew nuts before serving.
4. Serve over rice.

Menu Idea

Oriental Chicken Cashew Dish
Rice
Egg Rolls, accompanied by Fish Sauce
Hot Jasmine or Lotus Tea

I teach English as a Second Language to Vietnamese women. Occasionally they invite us to join them for dinner on Vietnamese New Year. We enjoy the fellowship and Vietnamese traditions immensely. They always have a "Lucky Tree," a tree with yellow flowers which blooms in Vietnam on New Year's. They decorate the tree by hanging red envelopes in it. Each contains a money gift; one is given to each unmarried person present, including the babies.

Chicken Azteca

Katrine Rose
Woodbridge, VA

Makes 10-12 servings

2 15-oz. cans black beans, drained
4 cups frozen corn kernels
2 garlic cloves, minced
3/4 tsp. ground cumin
2 cups chunky salsa, divided
10 skinless, boneless chicken breast halves
2 8-oz. pkgs. cream cheese, cubed
cooked rice
shredded cheddar cheese

1. Combine beans, corn, garlic, cumin, and half of salsa in slow cooker.
2. Arrange chicken breasts over top. Pour remaining salsa over top.
3. Cover. Cook on high 2-3 hours or on low 4-6 hours.
4. Remove chicken and cut into bite-sized pieces. Return to cooker.
5. Stir in cream cheese. Cook on high until cream cheese melts.
6. Spoon chicken and sauce over cooked rice. Top with shredded cheese.

Tamale Chicken

Jeanne Allen
Rye, CO

Makes 6 servings

1 medium onion, chopped
4-oz. can chopped green chilies
2 Tbsp. oil
10 3/4-oz. can cream of chicken soup
2 cups sour cream
1 cup sliced ripe olives
1 cup chopped stewed tomatoes
2 cups shredded cheddar cheese
8 chicken breast halves, cooked and chopped
16-oz. can beef tamales, chopped
1 tsp. chili powder
1 tsp. garlic powder
1 tsp. pepper
1/2 cup shredded cheddar cheese

1. Saute onion and chilies in oil in skillet.
2. Combine all ingredients except 1/2 cup shredded cheese. Pour into slow cooker.
3. Top with remaining cheese.
4. Cover. Cook on high 3-4 hours.
5. Pass chopped fresh tomatoes, shredded lettuce, sour cream, salsa, and or guacamole so guests can top their Tamale Chicken with these condiments.

Tex-Mex Chicken and Rice

Kelly Evenson
Pittsboro, NC

Makes 8 servings

1 cup converted uncooked white rice
28-oz. can diced peeled tomatoes
6-oz. can tomato paste
3 cups hot water
1 pkg. dry taco seasoning mix
4 whole boneless, skinless chicken breasts,
    uncooked and cut into 1/2" cubes
2 medium onions, chopped
1 green pepper, chopped
4-oz. can diced green chilies
1 tsp. garlic powder
1/2 tsp. pepper

1. Combine all ingredients except chilies
and seasonings in large slow cooker.
2. Cover. Cook on low 4-4 1/2 hours, or until
rice is tender and chicken is cooked.
3. Stir in green chilies and seasonings and
serve.
4. Serve with mixed green leafy salad and
refried beans.

Red Pepper Chicken

Sue Graber
Eureka, IL

Makes 4 servings

4 boneless, skinless chicken breast halves
15-oz. can black beans, drained
12-oz. jar roasted red peppers, undrained
14 1/2-oz. can Mexican stewed tomatoes,
    undrained
1 large onion, chopped
1/2 tsp. salt
pepper to taste
hot cooked rice

1. Place chicken in slow cooker.
2. Combine beans, red peppers, stewed
tomatoes, onion, salt, and pepper. Pour over
chicken.
3. Cover. Cook on low 4-6 hours, or until
chicken is no longer pink.
4. Serve over rice.

Chicken Gumbo

Virginia Bender
Dover, DE

Makes 6-8 servings

1 large onion, chopped
3-4 garlic cloves, minced
1 green pepper, diced
2 cups okra, sliced
2 cups tomatoes, chopped
4 cups chicken broth
1 lb. chicken breast, cut into 1" pieces
2 tsp. Old Bay Seasoning

1. Combine all ingredients in slow cooker.
2. Cover. Cook on low 8-10 hours or high 3-4 hours.
3. Serve over rice.

Chicken and Seafood Gumbo

Dianna Milhizer
Brighton, MI

Makes 12 servings

1 cup chopped celery
1 cup chopped onions
1/2 cup chopped green peppers
1/4 cup olive oil
1/4 cup, plus 1 Tbsp., flour
6 cups chicken stock
2 lbs. chicken, cut up
3 bay leaves
1 1/2 cups sliced okra
12-oz. can diced tomatoes
1 tsp. Tabasco sauce
salt to taste
pepper to taste
1 lb. ready-to-eat shrimp
1/2 cup snipped fresh parsley

1. Saute celery, onions, and peppers in oil. Blend in flour and chicken stock until smooth. Cook 5 minutes. Pour into slow cooker.
2. Add remaining ingredients except seafood and parsley.
3. Cover. Cook on low 10-12 hours.
4. One hour before serving add shrimp and parsley.
5. Remove bay leaves before serving.
6. Serve with white rice.

Chicken Rice Special

Jeanne Allen
Rye, CO

Makes 6-8 servings

6 chicken breast halves, cooked and
   chopped (save 4 cups broth)
1 lb. pork or turkey sausage, browned
half a large sweet green pepper, chopped
1 medium onion, chopped
4 ribs celery, chopped
1 cup rice, uncooked
2-oz. pkg. dry noodle-soup mix
1/2 cup sliced almonds
1-2 oz. jar pimentos, chopped

1. Combine all ingredients except almonds and pimentos in slow cooker.
2. Top with almonds and pimentos.
3. Cover. Cook on high 4-6 hours, or until rice is done and liquid has been absorbed.
4. Stir up 1 hour before serving.

Company Casserole
Vera Schmucker
Goshen, IN

Makes 4-6 servings

1¼ cups uncooked rice
½ cup (1 stick) butter, melted
3 cups chicken broth
3-4 cups cut-up cooked chicken breast
2 4-oz. cans sliced mushrooms, drained
⅓ cup soy sauce
12-oz. pkg. shelled frozen shrimp
8 green onions, chopped, 2 Tbsp. reserved
⅔ cup slivered almonds

1. Combine rice and butter in slow cooker. Stir to coat rice well.
2. Add remaining ingredients except almonds and 2 Tbsp. green onions.
3. Cover. Cook on low 6-8 hours or on high 3-4 hours, until rice is tender.
4. Sprinkle almonds and green onions over top before serving.
5. Serve with green beans, tossed salad, and fruit salad.

Chicken Broccoli Rice Casserole
Gloria Julien
Gladstone, MI

Makes 4-6 servings

1 onion, chopped
3 Tbsp. oil
2-3 cups uncooked chicken, cut in 1" pieces
10¾-oz. can cream of chicken soup
12-oz. can evaporated milk
2 cups cubed Velveeta cheese
3 cups cooked rice
2 cups frozen broccoli cuts, thawed
¼ tsp. pepper
4-oz. can mushrooms, drained

1. Saute onion in oil in skillet.
2. Add chicken and saute until no longer pink.
3. Combine all ingredients in slow cooker.
4. Cover. Cook on low 2-3 hours.

Notes:
1. This is an ideal dish for people who are not big meat-eaters.

2. This is good carry-in for potluck or fellowship meals. I put the ingredients together the night before.

Menu Idea

Chicken Broccoli Rice Casserole
Baked Beans (pages 133-140)
Salad of your choice
Homemade Bread

Baked Chicken and Rice
Fannie Miller
Hutchinson, KS

Makes 10-12 servings

2 cups dry instant rice
10³/4-oz. can cream of chicken soup
10³/4-oz. can cream of mushroom soup
10³/4-oz. can cream of celery soup
1/2 cup butter or margarine
1 soup can water
10 skinless chicken breast halves,
    or 1 chicken, cut into 10-12 pieces
1 pkg. dry onion soup mix

1. Place rice in large slow cooker.
2. Combine soups, butter, and water. Pour half over rice.
3. Lay chicken over rice. Pour remaining soup mixture over chicken.
4. Sprinkle with dry onion soup mix.
5. Cover. Cook on low 4-6 hours, or until chicken is done but not dry, and rice is tender but not mushy.

Chicken Pasta
Evelyn L. Ward
Greeley, CO

Makes 4 servings

1¹/2-lb. boneless chicken breast
1 large zucchini, diced
1 pkg. chicken gravy mix
2 Tbsp. water
2 Tbsp. evaporated milk or cream
1 large tomato, chopped
4 cups cooked macaroni
8 ozs. smoked Gouda cheese, grated

1. Cut chicken into 1" cubes. Place in slow cooker.
2. Add zucchini, gravy mix, and water, and stir together.
3. Cover. Cook on low 6 hours.
4. Add milk and tomato. Cook an additional 20 minutes.
5. Stir in pasta. Top with cheese. Serve immediately.

Comforting Chicken Stuffing
Ruth Liebelt
Rapid City, SD
Esther J. Yoder
Hartville, OH

Makes 4-6 servings

2 6-oz. boxes stuffing mix
1-2 cups cooked, diced chicken
10³/4-oz. can cream of chicken soup
1/3 cup water or milk
1/2 tsp. salt, optional
1/8-1/4 tsp. pepper, optional
4 Tbsp. (1/4 cup) butter or margarine,
    melted, optional

1. Prepare stuffing mix per package instructions. Spread in bottom of greased slow cooker.
2. Combine chicken, soup, water, and seasonings, if desired. Spread over stuffing. Top with melted butter, if you want.
3. Cover. Cook on low 4-6 hours or on high 2¹/2-3 hours. Loosen edges once or twice, or at least just before serving.
4. Delicious served with cole slaw and mixed fruit.

Chicken Dressing

Lydia A. Yoder
London, ON

Makes 20 servings

¾ cup butter or margarine
1 cup chopped onions
2 cups chopped celery
2 Tbsp. parsley flakes
1½ tsp. salt
½ tsp. pepper
3½-4 cups chicken broth
12-14 cups dried bread cubes
4 cups cut-up chicken
2 eggs, beaten
1 tsp. baking powder

1. Saute onion and celery in butter in skillet.
2. Combine seasonings and broth. Mix with bread cubes in large bowl.
3. Fold in chicken and sauteed onions and celery.
4. Add eggs and baking powder.
5. Lightly pack into large slow cooker.
6. Cover. Cook on low 3-4 hours.
7. Serve with turkey or chicken, mashed potatoes, a vegetable, and lettuce salad.

Note: The longer the dressing cooks, the drier it will become. Keep that in mind if you do not care for moist stuffing.

Chicken and Stuffing Dinner

Trudy Kutter
Corfu, NY

Makes 4-6 servings

4-6 skinless chicken breast halves
10¾-oz. can cream of chicken or celery soup
4-6 potatoes, peeled and sliced
6-oz. pkg. stuffing mix
1¼ cups water
2 Tbsp. melted butter
1-1½ cups frozen green beans, thawed

1. Place chicken in slow cooker.
2. Spoon soup over chicken.
3. Top with potatoes.
4. Combine stuffing mix, water, and butter. Spoon over potatoes.
5. Cover. Cook on low 6 hours.
6. Sprinkle green beans over stuffing.
7. Cover. Cook on low 45-60 minutes, or until beans are just tender.
8. Serve with a salad.

Chicken and Dumplings

Bonnie Miller
Louisville, OH

Makes 4 servings

2 lbs. boneless, skinless chicken breasts
1¾ cups chicken broth
2 chicken bouillon cubes
2 tsp. salt
1 tsp. pepper
1 tsp. poultry seasoning
2 celery ribs, cut into 1" pieces
6 small carrots, cut into 1" chunks

Biscuits:
2 cups buttermilk biscuit mix
1/2 cup, plus 1 Tbsp., milk
1 tsp. parsley

1. Place chicken in slow cooker.
2. Dissolve bouillon in both. Add to chicken.
3. Add salt, pepper, and poultry seasoning.
4. Spread celery and carrots over top.
5. Cover. Cook on low 6-8 hours or high 3 - 3½ hours.
6. Combine biscuit ingredients until just moistened. Drop by spoonfuls over steaming chicken.
7. Cover. Cook on high 35 minutes. Do not remove cover while dumplings are cooking. Serve immediately.

Menu Idea

Chicken and Dumplings
Cole Slaw
Baked Apples (page 221)
Cookies

Scalloped Chicken
Brenda Joy Sonnie
Newton, PA

Makes 4-6 servings

4 cups cooked chicken
1 box stuffing mix for chicken
2 eggs
1 cup water
1½ cups milk
1 cup frozen peas

1. Combine chicken and dry stuffing mix. Place in slow cooker.
2. Beat together eggs, water, and milk. Pour over chicken and stuffing.

3. Cover. Cook on high 2-3 hours. Add frozen peas during last hour of cooking.

Variation: For more flavor use chicken broth instead of water.

Hot Chicken Sandwiches
Glenna Fay Bergey
Lebanon, OR

Makes 6-8 servings

1 large chicken
1 cup water

1. Place chicken in slow cooker. Add water.
2. Cover. Cook on low 6-7 hours.
3. Debone chicken. Mix cut-up chicken with broth.
4. Spoon into dinner rolls with straining spoon to make small hot sandwiches. Top with your favorite condiments.

Note: This is also a great way to prepare a chicken for soups or casseroles. Save the broth if you're making soup.

Menu Idea

Hot Chicken Sandwiches
Carrot and Celery Sticks
Pickles and Olives
Chips

Chicken Wings Colorado

Nancy Rexrode Clark
Woodstock, MD

Makes 6-8 servings

1½ cups sugar
¼ tsp. salt
1 chicken bouillon cube
1 cup cider vinegar
½ cup ketchup
2 Tbsp. soy sauce
12-16 chicken wings
¼ cup cornstarch
½ cup cold water
red hot sauce to taste, optional

1. Combine sugar, salt, bouillon cube, vinegar, ketchup, and soy sauce and bring to boil in slow cooker.

2. Add chicken wings, pushing them down into the sauce.

3. Cover. Cook on low 6-7 hours.

4. Combine cornstarch and cold water. Add to slow cooker.

5. Cover. Cook on high until liquid thickens, about 30 minutes.

6. Season with red hot sauce, or let each diner add to his or her own serving.

Levi's Sesame Chicken Wings

Shirley Unternahrer Hinh
Wayland, IA

*Makes 16 appetizer servings,
or 6-8 main-dish servings*

3 lbs. chicken wings
salt to taste
pepper to taste
1¾ cups honey
1 cup soy sauce
½ cup ketchup
2 Tbsp. canola oil
2 Tbsp. sesame oil
2 garlic cloves, minced
toasted sesame seeds

1. Rinse wings. Cut at joint. Sprinkle with salt and pepper. Place on broiler pan.

2. Broil 5 inches from top, 10 minutes on each side. Place chicken in slow cooker.

3. Combine remaining ingredients except sesame seeds. Pour over chicken.

4. Cover. Cook on low 5 hours or high 2½ hours.

5. Sprinkle sesame seeds over top just before serving.

6. Serve as appetizer, or with white or brown rice and shredded lettuce to turn this appetizer into a meal.

My husband and his co-workers have a "pot-luck-lunch" at work. I think this is a nice way to break the monotony of the week or month. And it gives them a chance to share. What better way to keep it ready than a slow cooker!

Turkey Main Dishes

Slow Cooker Turkey Breast

Liz Ann Yoder
Hartville, OH

Makes 8-10 servings

6-lb. turkey breast
2 tsp. oil
salt to taste
pepper to taste
1 medium onion, quartered
4 garlic cloves, peeled
1/2 cup water

1. Rinse turkey and pat dry with paper towels.

2. Rub oil over turkey. Sprinkle with salt and pepper. Place, meaty side up, in large slow cooker.

3. Place onion and garlic around sides of cooker.

4. Cover. Cook on low 9-10 hours, or until meat thermometer stuck in meaty part of breast registers 170°.

5. Remove from slow cooker and let stand 10 minutes before slicing.

6. Serve with mashed potatoes, cranberry salad, and corn or green beans.

Variations:

1. Add carrot chunks and chopped celery to Step 3 to add more flavor to the turkey broth.

2. Reserve broth for soups, or thicken with flour-water paste and serve as gravy over sliced turkey.

3. Freeze broth in pint-sized containers for future use.

4. Debone turkey and freeze in pint-sized containers for future use. Or freeze any leftover turkey after serving the meal described above.

Turkey Breast with Orange Sauce

Jean Butzer
Batavia, NY

Makes 4-6 servings

1 large onion, chopped
3 garlic cloves, minced
1 tsp. dried rosemary
1/2 tsp. pepper
2-3-lb. boneless, skinless turkey breast
1 1/2 cups orange juice

1. Place onions in slow cooker.
2. Combine garlic, rosemary, and pepper.
3. Make gashes in turkey, about 3/4 of the way through at 2" intervals. Stuff with herb mixture. Place turkey in slow cooker.
4. Pour juice over turkey.
5. Cover. Cook on low 7-8 hours, or until turkey is no longer pink in center.

This very easy, impressive-looking and -tasting recipe is perfect for company.

Turkey Crockpot

Arlene Leaman Kliewer
Lakewood, CO

Makes 8 servings

5-lb. turkey breast
1 pkg. dry onion soup mix
16-oz. can whole cranberry sauce

1. Place turkey in slow cooker.
2. Combine soup mix and cranberry sauce. Spread over turkey.
3. Cover. Cook on low 8 hours.

Easy Turkey Breast

Susan Stephani Smith
Monument, CO

Makes 12 servings

1 Jenny O'Turkey Breast — with bone in and with gravy packet
salt

1. Wash frozen breast and sprinkle with salt.
2. Place turkey, gravy packet up, in slow cooker that's large enough to be covered when the turkey breast is in it.
3. Cover. Cook turkey on low 6-7 hours, or until tender, removing gravy packet when the turkey is partially thawed.(Keep packet in refrigerator.)
4. Make gravy according to directions on packet. Warm before serving.

Stuffed Turkey Breast

Jean Butzer
Batavia, NY

Makes 8 servings

¼ cup butter, melted
1 small onion, finely chopped
½ cup finely chopped celery
2½-oz. pkg. croutons with real bacon bits
1 cup chicken broth
2 Tbsp. fresh minced parsley
½ tsp. poultry seasoning
1 whole uncooked turkey breast,
   or 2 halves (about 5 lbs.)
salt to taste
pepper to taste
24" x 26" piece of cheesecloth for each
   breast half
dry white wine

1. Combine butter, onion, celery, croutons, broth, parsley, and poultry seasoning.
2. Cut turkey breast in thick slices from breastbone to rib cage, leaving slices attached to bone (crosswise across breast).
3. Sprinkle turkey with salt and pepper.
4. Soak cheesecloth in wine. Place turkey on cheesecloth. Stuff bread mixture into slits between turkey slices. Fold one end of cheesecloth over the other to cover meat. Place on metal rack or trivet in 5- or 6-qt. slow cooker.
5. Cover. Cook on low 7-9 hours or until tender. Pour additional wine over turkey during cooking.
6. Remove from pot and remove cheesecloth immediately. If browner breast is preferred, remove from pot and brown in 400° oven for 15-20 minutes. Let stand 10 minutes before slicing through and serving.
7. Thicken the drippings, if you wish, for gravy. Mix together 3 Tbsp. cornstarch and ¼ cup cold water. When smooth, stir into broth (with turkey removed from cooker).

Turn cooker to high and stir until cornstarch paste is dissolved. Allow to cook for about 10 minutes, until broth is thickened and smooth.

Slow Cooker Turkey and Dressing

Carol Sherwood
Batavia, NY

Makes 4-6 servings

8-oz. pkg., or 2 6-oz. pkgs., stuffing mix
½ cup hot water
2 Tbsp. butter, softened
1 onion, chopped
½ cup chopped celery
¼ cup sweetened, dried cranberries
3-lb. boneless turkey breast
¼ tsp. dried basil
½ tsp. salt
½ tsp. pepper

1. Spread dry stuffing mix in greased slow cooker.
2. Add water, butter, onion, celery, and cranberries. Mix well.
3. Sprinkle turkey breast with basil, salt, and pepper. Place over stuffing mixture.
4. Cover. Cook on low 5-6 hours, or until turkey is done but not dry.
5. Remove turkey. Slice and set aside.
6. Gently stir stuffing and allow to sit for 5 minutes before serving.
7. Place stuffing on platter, topped with sliced turkey.

Zucchini and Turkey Dish

Dolores Kratz
Souderton, PA

Makes 6 servings

3 cups zucchini, sliced
1 small onion, chopped
1/4 tsp. salt
1 cup cubed cooked turkey
2 fresh tomatoes, sliced,
    or 14½-oz. can diced tomatoes
1/2 tsp. dried oregano
1 tsp. dried basil
1/4 cup grated Parmesan cheese
1/2 cup shredded provolone cheese
3/4 cup Pepperidge Farms stuffing

1. Combine zucchini, onion, salt, turkey, tomatoes, oregano, and basil in slow cooker. Mix well.
2. Top with cheeses and stuffing.
3. Cover. Cook on low 8-9 hours.

Slow-Cooked Turkey Dinner

Miriam Nolt
New Holland, PA

Makes 4-6 servings

1 onion, diced
6 small red potatoes, quartered
2 cups sliced carrots
1½-2 lbs. boneless, skinless turkey thighs
1/4 cup flour
2 Tbsp. dry onion soup mix
10¾-oz. can cream of mushroom soup
2/3 cup chicken broth or water

1. Place vegetables in bottom of slow cooker.
2. Place turkey thighs over vegetables.
3. Combine remaining ingredients. Pour over turkey.
4. Cover. Cook on high 30 minutes. Reduce heat to low and cook 7 hours.

Barbecued Turkey Legs

Barbara Walker
Sturgis, SC

Makes 4-6 servings

4 turkey drumsticks
1-2 tsp. salt
1/4-1/2 tsp. pepper
1/3 cup molasses
1/4 cup vinegar
1/2 cup ketchup
3 Tbsp. Worcestershire sauce
3/4 tsp. hickory smoke
2 Tbsp. instant minced onion

1. Sprinkle turkey with salt and pepper. Place in slow cooker.
2. Combine remaining ingredients. Pour over turkey.
3. Cover. Cook on low 5-7 hours.

Barbecued Turkey Cutlets

Maricarol Magill
Freehold, NJ

Makes 6-8 servings

6-8 (1 1/2-2 lbs.) turkey cutlets
1/4 cup molasses
1/4 cup cider vinegar
1/4 cup ketchup
3 Tbsp. Worcestershire sauce
1 tsp. garlic salt
3 Tbsp. chopped onion
2 Tbsp. brown sugar
1/4 tsp. pepper

1. Place turkey cutlets in slow cooker.
2. Combine remaining ingredients. Pour over turkey.
3. Cover. Cook on low 4 hours.
4. Serve over white or brown rice.

Turkey and Sweet Potato Casserole

Michele Ruvola
Selden, NY

Makes 4 servings

3 medium sweet potatoes, peeled and cut into 2" pieces
10-oz. pkg. frozen cut green beans
2 lbs. turkey cutlets
12-oz. jar home-style turkey gravy
2 Tbsp. flour
1 tsp. parsley flakes
1/4-1/2 tsp. dried rosemary leaves, crumbled
1/8 tsp. pepper

1. Layer sweet potatoes, green beans, and turkey in slow cooker.
2. Combine remaining ingredients until smooth. Pour over mixture in slow cooker.
3. Cover. Cook on low 8-10 hours.
4. Remove turkey and vegetables and keep warm. Stir sauce. Serve with sauce over meat and vegetables, or with sauce in a gravy boat.
5. Serve with biscuits and cranberry sauce.

Turkey Barbecue

Marcia S. Myer
Manheim, PA

Makes 8 servings

2 lbs. chopped cooked turkey
1 1/4 cups ketchup
1 tsp. dry mustard
4 tsp. vinegar
4 tsp. Worcestershire sauce
2 Tbsp. sugar
1 tsp. onion salt
8 hamburger buns

1. Combine all ingredients in slow cooker.
2. Cover. Cook on low 3-4 hours.
3. Serve on hamburger buns.

Note: You can make the turkey by putting 2 lbs. uncooked turkey tenderloins in slow cooker, adding 1/2 cup water, and cooking the meat on low for 6 hours, or until juices run clear.

Turkey Sloppy Joes

Marla Folkerts
Holland, OH

Makes 6 servings

1 red onion, chopped
1 sweet pepper, chopped
1 1/2 lbs. boneless turkey, finely chopped
1 cup chili sauce or ketchup
1/4 tsp. salt
1 garlic clove, minced
1 tsp. Dijon-style mustard
1/8 tsp. pepper
thickly sliced homemade bread,
    or 6 sandwich rolls

1. Place onion, sweet pepper, and turkey in slow cooker.
2. Combine chili sauce, salt, garlic, mustard, and pepper. Pour over turkey mixture. Mix well.
3. Cover. Cook on low 4 1/2-6 hours.
4. Serve on homemade bread or sandwich rolls.

Turkey Loaf and Potatoes

Lizzie Weaver
Ephrata, PA

Makes 6-7 servings

2 lbs. ground turkey
1½ cups soft bread crumbs, or oatmeal
2 eggs, slightly beaten
1 small onion, chopped
1 tsp. salt
1 tsp. dry mustard
¼ cup ketchup
¼ cup evaporated milk
6 medium-sized potatoes, quartered

1. Combine all ingredients except potatoes. Form into loaf to fit in slow cooker.
2. Tear 4 strips of aluminum foil, each 18" x 2". Position them in the slow cooker, spoke-fashion, with the ends sticking out over the edges of the cooker to act as handles. Place loaf down in the cooker, centered over the foil strips.
3. Place potatoes around meat.
4. Cover. Cook on high 4-5 hours, or until potatoes are soft.
5. Serve with gravy, green vegetable, and cole slaw.

Savory Turkey Meatballs in Italian Sauce

Marla Folkerts
Holland, OH

Makes 8 servings

28-oz. can crushed tomatoes
1 Tbsp. red wine vinegar
1 medium onion, finely chopped
2 garlic cloves, minced
¼ tsp. Italian herb seasoning
1 tsp. dried basil
1 lb. ground turkey
⅛ tsp. garlic powder
⅛ tsp. black pepper
⅓ cup dried parsley
2 egg whites
¼ tsp. dried minced onion
⅓ cup quick oats
¼ cup grated Parmesan cheese
¼ cup flour
oil

1. Combine tomatoes, vinegar, onions, garlic, Italian seasonings, and basil in slow cooker. Turn to low.
2. Combine remaining ingredients, except flour and oil. Form into 1" balls. Dredge each ball in flour. Brown in oil in skillet over medium heat. Transfer to slow cooker. Stir into sauce.
3. Cover. Cook on low 6-8 hours.
4. Serve over pasta or rice.

Note: The meatballs and sauce freeze well.

Tricia's Cranberry Turkey Meatballs

Shirley Unternahrer Hinh
Wayland, IA

Makes 12 servings

16-oz. can jelled cranberry sauce
1/2 cup ketchup or barbecue sauce
1 egg
1 lb. ground turkey
half a small onion, chopped
1 tsp. salt
1/4 tsp. black pepper
1-2 tsp. grated orange peel, optional

1. Combine cranberry sauce and ketchup in slow cooker.
2. Cover. Cook on high until sauce is mixed.
3. Combine remaining ingredients. Shape into 24 balls.
4. Cook over medium heat in skillet for 8-10 minutes, or just until browned. Add to sauce in slow cooker.
5. Cover. Cook on low 3 hours.
6. Serve with rice and a steamed vegetable.

Turkey Meatballs and Gravy

Betty Sue Good
Broadway, VA

Makes 8 servings

2 eggs, beaten
3/4 cup bread crumbs
1/2 cup finely chopped onions
1/2 cup finely chopped celery
2 Tbsp. chopped fresh parsley
1/4 tsp. pepper
1/8 tsp. garlic powder
1 tsp. salt
2 lbs. ground raw turkey
1 1/2 Tbsp. cooking oil
10 3/4-oz. can cream of mushroom soup
1 cup water
7/8-oz. pkg. turkey gravy mix
1/2 tsp. dried thyme
2 bay leaves

1. Combine eggs, bread crumbs, onions, celery, parsley, pepper, garlic powder, salt, and meat. Shape into 1 1/2" balls.
2. Brown meat balls in oil in skillet. Drain meatballs and transfer to slow cooker.
3. Combine soup, water, dry gravy mix, thyme, and bay leaves. Pour over meatballs.
4. Cover. Cook on low 6-8 hours or high 3-4 hours. Discard bay leaves before serving.
5. Serve over mashed potatoes or buttered noodles.

Meat and Bean Main Dishes

"Famous" Baked Beans

Katrine Rose
Woodbridge, VA

Makes 10 servings

1 lb. ground beef
1/4 cup minced onions
1 cup ketchup
4 15-oz. cans pork and beans
1 cup brown sugar
2 Tbsp. liquid smoke
1 Tbsp. Worcestershire sauce

1. Brown beef and onions in skillet. Drain. Spoon meat and onions into slow cooker.
2. Add remaining ingredients and stir well.
3. Cover. Cook on high 3 hours or on low 5-6 hours.

There are many worthy baked bean recipes, but these are both easy and absolutely delicious. The secret to this recipe is the liquid smoke. I get many requests for this recipe, and some friends have added the word "famous" to its name.

Esther's Barbecued Beans

Esther J. Yoder
Hartville, OH

Makes 10 servings

1 lb. ground beef
1/2 cup chopped onions
1/2 tsp. salt
1/4 tsp. pepper
28-oz. can pork and beans (your favorite variety)
1/2 cup ketchup
1 Tbsp. Worcestershire sauce
1 Tbsp. vinegar
1/4 tsp. Tabasco sauce

1. Brown beef and onions together in skillet. Drain.
2. Combine all ingredients in slow cooker.
3. Cover. Cook on high 2-3 hours, stirring once or twice.
4. Serve with fresh raw vegetables and canned peaches.

Note: These beans' flavor gets better on the second and third days.

Dollywood Cowboy Beans
Reba Rhodes
Bridgewater, VA

Makes 8 servings

1 lb. ground beef
1 large onion, finely chopped
1 small green bell pepper, finely chopped
28-oz. can pork and beans
1½ cups ketchup
1 tsp. vinegar
3 Tbsp. brown sugar
2 tsp. prepared mustard
2 tsp. salt
1 tsp. pepper

1. Brown ground beef, onion, and bell pepper in skillet. Transfer to slow cooker.
2. Combine all ingredients in slow cooker. Mix well.
3. Cover. Cook on low 1-2 hours.

This travels well to a potluck or a picnic.

Hamburger Beans
Joanne Kennedy
Plattsburgh, NY

Makes 6 servings

1 lb. ground beef
1 onion, chopped
2 15-oz. cans pork and beans
15-oz. can butter beans, drained
15-oz. can kidney beans, drained
½ tsp. garlic powder
1 cup ketchup
¾ cup molasses
½ cup brown sugar

1. Brown ground beef and onion in skillet. Drain and transfer beef and onion into slow cooker.
2. Add remaining ingredients. Mix well.
3. Cover. Cook on low 6-7 hours.

One-Pot Dinner
Vicki Dinkel
Sharon Springs, KS

Makes 4 servings

½-1 lb. ground beef, according to your preference
½ lb. bacon, cut in pieces
1 cup chopped onions
2 31-oz. cans pork and beans
16-oz. can kidney beans, drained
1 cup ketchup
16-oz. can butter beans, drained
¼ cup brown sugar
1 Tbsp. liquid smoke
3 Tbsp. white vinegar
1 tsp. salt
dash of pepper

1. Brown ground beef in skillet. Drain off drippings. Place beef in slow cooker.
2. Brown bacon and onions in skillet. Drain off drippings. Add bacon and onions to slow cooker.
3. Stir remaining ingredients into cooker.
4. Cover. Cook on low 5-9 hours or high 3 hours.

Calico Beans
Mary Rogers
Waseca, MN

Makes 12-15 servings

1 lb. bacon
1 lb. ground beef
1/2 cup chopped onions
1/2 cup chopped celery
1/2 cup ketchup
1 Tbsp. prepared mustard
16-oz. can kidney beans, undrained
16-oz. can Great Northern beans, undrained
1/2 cup brown sugar
1 Tbsp. vinegar
16-oz. can butter beans, undrained
28-oz. can Bush's Baked Beans

1. Cut bacon in small pieces. Brown in skillet. Drain.
2. Brown ground beef in skillet and drain, reserving drippings.
3. Saute onions and celery in drippings until soft.
4. Combine all ingredients in slow cooker.
5. Cover. Simmer on low 3-4 hours.

This is a favorite dish that we serve at neighborhood and family gatherings any time of the year. Our children especially enjoy it.

Calico Beans
Alice Miller
Stuarts Draft, VA

Makes 10-12 servings

1/2 lb. ground beef
1/2 lb. bacon, chopped
1/2 cup chopped onions
1/2 cup ketchup
3/4 cup brown sugar
1/4 cup sugar
2 Tbsp. vinegar
1 tsp. dry mustard
1 tsp. salt
16-oz. can pork and beans, undrained
16-oz. can red kidney beans, undrained
16-oz. can yellow limas, undrained
16-oz. can navy beans, undrained

1. Brown ground beef, bacon, and onions together in skillet. Drain off all but 2 Tbsp. drippings. Spoon meat and onions into slow cooker.
2. Stir ketchup, brown sugar, sugar, vinegar, mustard, and salt into drippings. Mix together well. Add to slow cooker.
3. Pour beans into slow cooker and combine all ingredients thoroughly.
4. Cover. Cook on high 3-4 hours.
5. Serve over rice, or take to a picnic as is.

Cowboy Beans

Sharon Timpe
Mequon, WI

Makes 10-12 servings

6 slices bacon, cut in pieces
½ cup onions, chopped
1 garlic clove, minced
16-oz. can baked beans
16-oz. can kidney beans, drained
15-oz. can butter beans or pinto beans,
   drained
2 Tbsp. dill pickle relish or chopped dill
   pickles
⅓ cup chili sauce or ketchup
2 tsp. Worcestershire sauce
½ cup brown sugar
⅛ tsp. hot pepper sauce, optional

1. Lightly brown bacon, onions, and garlic in skillet. Drain.
2. Combine all ingredients in slow cooker. Mix well.
3. Cover. Cook on low 5-7 hours or high 3-4 hours.

Trio Bean Casserole

Stacy Schmucker Stoltzfus
Enola, PA

Makes 4-6 servings

16-oz. can kidney beans, drained
16-oz. can green beans, drained
16-oz. can pork and beans with tomato
   sauce
½ cup chopped onions
½ cup brown sugar
½ cup ketchup

1 Tbsp. vinegar
1 tsp. prepared mustard
1 lb. bacon, fried and crumbled,
   or 1 lb. cooked ham, cubed
1 Tbsp. barbecue sauce

1. Combine all ingredients in slow cooker. Stir well.
2. Cover. Cook on high 2 hours or low 3-4 hours.

Menu Idea

Trio Bean Casserole
White Rice
Cornbread
Raw Veggies with Dip

Deb's Baked Beans

Deborah Swartz
Grottoes, VA

Makes 4-6 servings

4 slices bacon, fried and drained
2 Tbsp. reserved drippings
½ cup chopped onions
2 15-oz. cans pork and beans
½ tsp. salt, optional
2 Tbsp. brown sugar
1 Tbsp. Worcestershire sauce
1 tsp. prepared mustard

1. Fry bacon in skillet until crisp. Reserve 2 Tbsp. drippings. Crumble bacon.
2. Cook onions in bacon drippings.
3. Combine all ingredients in slow cooker.
4. Cover. Cook on high 1½-2 hours.

Lotsa-Beans Pot

Dorothy Van Deest
Memphis, TN

Makes 15-20 servings

8 bacon strips, diced
2 onions, thinly sliced
1 cup packed brown sugar
¹/2 cup cider vinegar
1 tsp. salt
1 tsp. ground mustard
¹/2 tsp. garlic powder
28-oz. can baked beans
16-oz. can kidney beans, rinsed and drained
15¹/2-oz. can pinto beans, rinsed and drained
15-oz. can lima beans, rinsed and drained
15¹/2-oz. can black-eyed peas, rinsed and rained

1. Cook bacon in skillet until crisp. Remove to paper towels.
2. Drain, reserving 2 Tbsp. drippings.
3. Saute onions in drippings until tender.
4. Add brown sugar, vinegar, salt, mustard, and garlic powder to skillet. Bring to boil.
5. Combine beans and peas in slow cooker. Add onion mixture and bacon. Mix well.
6. Cover. Cook on high 3-4 hours.

This hearty bean concoction tastes especially yummy when the gang comes in from a Saturday afternoon of raking leaves. Keep it warm to hot and serve it from the pot.

Menu Idea

Lotsa-Beans Pot
Herby Garlic Bread
Cheese Cubes
Pickles and Celery

Auntie Ginny's Baked Beans

Becky Harder
Monument, CO

Makes 8 servings

4 slices bacon, diced
28-oz. can pork and beans
1 tsp. dark molasses
1 Tbsp. brown sugar
1 cup dates, cut up
1 medium onion, chopped

1. Partially fry bacon. Drain.
2. Combine ingredients in slow cooker.
3. Cover. Cook on low 4-5 hours.

Note: There are many varieties of canned baked beans available. Choose a flavor that fits your guests—from vegetarian (you'll want to leave out the bacon above if this is important to your diners) to country-style to onion.

Written down at the bottom of this recipe was this note: "Harder picnic—1974." Notations such as that one help us remember special family get-togethers or reunions. This recipe was shared almost 20 years ago as we gathered cousins and aunts together in our hometown. Today no one from our family lives in the hometown and we cousins are scattered over six states, but one way to enjoy fond memories is to record dates or events on recipes we share with each other.

Menu Idea

Grilled Chicken
Aunt Ginny's Baked Beans
Chips
Fresh Vegetables, cut-up
Fresh Fruit, cut-up
S'mores

Creole Black Beans

Joyce Kaut
Rochester, NY

Makes 6-8 servings

1 1/2-2 lbs. smoked sausage,
   sliced in 1/2" pieces, browned
3 15-oz. cans black beans, drained
1 1/2 cups chopped onions
1 1/2 cups chopped green peppers
1 1/2 cups chopped celery
4 garlic cloves, minced
2 tsp. dried thyme
1 1/2 tsp. dried oregano
1 1/2 tsp. pepper
1 chicken bouillon cube
3 bay leaves
8-oz. can tomato sauce
1 cup water

1. Combine all ingredients in slow cooker.
2. Cover. Cook on low 8 hours or on high 4 hours.
3. Remove bay leaves.
4. Serve over rice, with a salad and fresh fruit for dessert.

Variation: You may substitute a 14.5-oz. can of stewed tomatoes for the tomato sauce.

Pizza Beans

Kelly Evenson
Pittsboro, NC

Makes 6 servings

16-oz. can pinto beans, drained
16-oz. can kidney beans, drained
2.25-oz. can ripe olives sliced, drained
28-oz. can stewed or whole tomatoes
3/4 lb. bulk Italian sausage
1 Tbsp. oil
1 green pepper, chopped
1 medium onion, chopped
1 garlic clove, minced
1 tsp. salt
1 tsp. dried oregano
1 tsp. dried basil
Parmesan cheese

1. Combine beans, olives, and tomatoes in slow cooker.
2. Brown sausage in oil in skillet. Drain, reserving drippings. Transfer sausage to slow cooker.
3. Saute green pepper in drippings 1 minute, stirring constantly. Add onions and continue stirring until onions start to become translucent. Add garlic and cook 1 more minute. Transfer to slow cooker.
4. Stir in seasonings.
5. Cover. Cook on low 7-9 hours.
6. To serve, sprinkle with Parmesan cheese.

Variation: For a thicker soup, 20 minutes before serving remove 1/4 cup liquid from cooker and add 1 Tbsp. cornstarch. Stir until dissolved. Return to soup. Cook on high for 15 minutes, or until thickened.

Pioneer Beans
Kay Magruder
Seminole, OK

Makes 4-6 servings

1 lb. dry lima beans
1 bunch green onions, chopped
3 beef bouillon cubes
6 cups water
1 lb. smoked sausage
1/2 tsp. garlic powder
3/4 tsp. Tabasco sauce

1. Combine all ingredients in slow cooker. Mix well.
2. Cover. Cook on high 8-9 hours, or until beans are soft but not mushy.
3. Serve with home-baked bread and butter.

Dawn's Special Beans
Dawn Day
Westminster, CA

Makes 8-10 servings

16-oz. can kidney beans
16-oz. can small white beans
16-oz. can butter beans
16-oz. can small red beans
1 cup chopped onions
2 tsp. dry mustard
1/2 tsp. hickory-smoke flavoring
1/2 cup dark brown sugar
1/2 cup honey
1 cup barbecue sauce
2 Tbsp. apple cider vinegar

1. Combine all ingredients in slow cooker.
2. Cover. Cook on low 6 hours.

3. Serve with hot dogs, hamburgers, and any other picnic food. These beans are also great for a potluck.

Note: If you like soupy beans, do not drain the beans before adding them to the cooker. If you prefer a drier outcome, drain all beans before pouring into cooker.

Partytime Beans
Beatrice Martin
Goshen, IN

Makes 14-16 servings

1 1/2 cups ketchup
1 onion, chopped
1 green pepper, chopped
1 sweet red pepper, chopped
1/2 cup water
1/2 cup packed brown sugar
2 bay leaves
2-3 tsp. cider vinegar
1 tsp. ground mustard
1/8 tsp. pepper
16-oz. can kidney beans, rinsed and drained
15 1/2-oz. can Great Northern beans, rinsed and drained
15-oz. can lima beans, rinsed and drained
15-oz. can black beans, rinsed and drained
15 1/2-oz. can black-eyed peas, rinsed and drained

1. Combine first 10 ingredients in slow cooker. Mix well.
2. Add remaining ingredients. Mix well.
3. Cover. Cook on low 5-7 hours, or until onion and peppers are tender.
4. Remove bay leaves before serving.
5. Serve with grilled hamburgers, tossed salad or veggie tray, chips, fruit, and cookies.

Slow Cooker Kidney Beans

Jeanette Oberholtzer
Manheim, PA

Makes 12 servings

2 30-oz. cans kidney beans, rinsed and
   drained
28-oz. can diced tomatoes, drained
2 medium-sized red bell peppers, chopped
1 cup ketchup
1/2 cup brown sugar
1/4 cup honey
1/4 cup molasses
1 Tbsp. Worcestershire sauce
1 tsp. dry mustard
2 medium red apples, cored, cut into
   pieces

1. Combine all ingredients, except apples,
in slow cooker.
2. Cover. Cook on low 4-5 hours.
3. Stir in apples.
4. Cover. Cook 2 more hours.

Tasty, meatless eating!

Red Beans and Pasta

Naomi E. Fast
Hesston, KS

Makes 6-8 servings

3 15-oz. cans chicken, or vegetable, broth
1/2 tsp. ground cumin
1 Tbsp. chili powder
1 garlic clove, minced
8 ozs. uncooked spiral pasta
half a large green pepper, diced
half a large red pepper, diced
1 medium onion, diced
15-oz. can red beans, rinsed and drained
chopped fresh parsley
chopped fresh cilantro

1. Combine broth, cumin, chili powder, and
garlic in slow cooker.
2. Cover. Cook on high until mixture comes
to boil.
3. Add pasta, vegetables, and beans. Stir
together well.
4. Cover. Cook on low 3-4 hours.
5. Add parsley or cilantro before serving.

Menu Idea

Red Beans and Pasta
Cheese Cubes of many kinds
Crusty Multi-Grain Bread
Fresh Fruit Salad

Hosting Idea

Use name cards at plates with Bible
verses on backs of cards. Have all at the
table read their verses. That can take
the place of grace.

Other Main Dish Favorites

Lamb Stew

Dottie Schmidt
Kansas City, MO

Makes 6 servings

2 lbs. lamb, cubed
1/2 tsp. sugar
2 Tbsp. oil
2 tsp. salt
1/4 tsp. pepper
1/4 cup flour
2 cups water
3/4 cup red cooking wine
1/4 tsp. powdered garlic
2 tsp. Worcestershire sauce
6-8 carrots, sliced
4 small onions, quartered
4 ribs celery, sliced
3 medium potatoes, diced

1. Sprinkle lamb with sugar. Brown in oil in skillet.
2. Remove lamb and place in cooker, reserving drippings. Stir salt, pepper, and flour into drippings until smooth. Stir in water and wine, until smooth, stirring until broth simmers and thickens.
3. Pour into cooker. Add remaining ingredients and stir until well mixed.
4. Cover. Cook on low 8-10 hours.
5. Serve with crusty bread.

Lamb Chops

Shirley Sears
Tiskilwa, IL

Makes 6-8 servings

1 medium onion, sliced
1 tsp. dried oregano
1/2 tsp. dried thyme
1/2 tsp. garlic powder
1/4 tsp. salt
1/8 tsp. pepper
8 loin lamb chops (1 3/4-2 lbs.)
2 garlic cloves, minced
1/4 cup water

1. Place onion in slow cooker.
2. Combine oregano, thyme, garlic powder, salt, and pepper. Rub over lamb chops. Place in slow cooker. Top with garlic. Pour water down along side of cooker, so as not to disturb the rub on the chops.
3. Cover. Cook on low 4-6 hours.

Venison Roast

Colleen Heatwole
Burton, MI

Makes 6-8 servings

3-4-lb. venison roast
1/4 cup vinegar
2 garlic cloves, minced
2 Tbsp. salt
1/2 cup chopped onions
15-oz. can tomato sauce
1 Tbsp. ground mustard
1 pkg. brown gravy mix
1/2 tsp. salt
1/4 cup water

1. Place venison in deep bowl. Combine vinegar, garlic, and salt. Pour over venison. Add enough cold water to cover venison. Marinate for at least 8 hours in refrigerator.
2. Rinse and drain venison. Place in slow cooker.
3. Combine remaining ingredients and pour over venison.
4. Cover. Cook on low 10-12 hours.
5. Serve with a green salad, potatoes, and rolls to make a complete meal.

Note: The sauce on this roast works well for any meat.

This is an easy meal to have for a Saturday dinner with guests or extended family. There is usually a lot of sauce, so make plenty of potatoes, noodles, or rice.

Venison in Sauce

Anona M. Teel
Bangar, PA

Makes 12 sandwiches

3-4-lb. venison roast
1/2 cup vinegar
2 garlic cloves, minced
2 Tbsp. salt
cold water
oil
large onion, sliced
half a green pepper, sliced
2 ribs celery, sliced
1-2 garlic cloves, minced
1 1/2-2 tsp. salt
1/4 tsp. pepper
1/2 tsp. dried oregano
1/4 cup ketchup
1 cup tomato juice

1. Combine vinegar, garlic cloves, and 2 Tbsp. salt. Pour over venison. Add water until meat is covered. Marinate 6-8 hours.

2. Cut meat into pieces. Brown in oil in skillet. Place in slow cooker.

3. Mix remaining ingredients together; then pour into cooker. Stir in meat.

4. Cover. Cook on low 8-10 hours.

5. Using two forks, pull the meat apart and then stir it through the sauce.

6. Serve on sandwich rolls, or over rice or pasta.

Beef-Venison Barbecue

Gladys Longacre
Susquehanna, PA

Makes 8 servings

1½ lbs. ground beef
½ lb. ground venison
oil, if needed
1 onion, chopped
½ cup chopped green peppers
1 garlic clove, minced
1 tsp. salt
¼ tsp. pepper
½ tsp. dried thyme
1 tsp. dried oregano
1 tsp. dried basil
¼ cup brown sugar
¼ cup vinegar
1 Tbsp. dry mustard
1 cup ketchup
½-1 Tbsp. hickory-smoked barbecue sauce
8 hamburger rolls

1. Brown meat in skillet, in oil if needed. Place in slow cooker.

2. Add remaining ingredients. Mix well.

3. Cover. Cook on high 1 hour or low 2-3 hours.

4. Serve barbecue in hamburger rolls.

Note: This recipe can be made in larger quantities to freeze and then reheat when needed.

This barbecue recipe was made in large quantities and served at the concession stand for our farm machinery sale in 1987. They used ice cream dippers to scoop the meat into the sandwich rolls.

Company Seafood Pasta

Jennifer Yoder Sommers
Harrisonburg, VA

Makes 4-6 servings

2 cups sour cream
3 cups shredded Monterey Jack cheese
2 Tbsp. butter or margarine, melted
½ lb. crabmeat, or imitation flaked crabmeat
⅛ tsp. pepper
½ lb. bay scallops, lightly cooked
1 lb. medium shrimp, cooked and peeled

1. Combine sour cream, cheese and butter in slow cooker.

2. Stir in remaining ingredients.

3. Cover. Cook on low 1-2 hours.

4. Serve immediately over linguine. Garnish with fresh parsley.

Curried Shrimp

Charlotte Shaffer
East Earl, PA

Makes 4-5 servings

1 small onion, chopped
2 cups cooked shrimp
1 tsp. curry powder
10¾-oz. can cream of mushroom soup
1 cup sour cream

1. Combine all ingredients except sour cream in slow cooker.
2. Cover. Cook on low 4-6 hours.
3. Ten minutes before serving, stir in sour cream.
4. Serve over rice or puff pastry.

Variation: Add another ½ tsp. curry for some added flavor.

Tuna Noodle Casserole

Ruth Hofstetter
Versailles, Missouri

Makes 8 servings

2½ cups dry noodles
1 tsp. salt
½ cup finely chopped onion
6- or 12-oz. can tuna, according to your taste preference
10¾-oz. can cream of mushroom soup
half a soup can of water
¼ cup almonds, optional
½ cup shredded Swiss or sharp cheddar cheese
1 cup frozen peas

1. Combine all ingredients in slow cooker, except peas.
2. Cover. Cook on high 2-3 hours or on low 6-8 hours, stirring occasionally.
3. Twenty minutes before end of cooking time, stir in peas and reduce heat to low if cooking on high.

Oriental Shrimp Casserole

Sharon Wantland
Menomonee Falls, WI

Makes 10 servings

4 cups cooked rice
2 cups cooked or canned shrimp
1 cup cooked or canned chicken
1-lb. can (2 cups) Chinese vegetables
10¾-oz. can cream of celery soup
½ cup milk
½ cup chopped green peppers
1 Tbsp. soy sauce
can of Chinese noodles

1. Combine all ingredients except noodles in slow cooker.
2. Cover. Cook on low 45 minutes.
3. Top with noodles just before serving.

1. Combine macaroni, butter, a
2. Layer cheese over top.
3. Pour in milk.
4. Cover. Cook on high 3-4 hours, or until macaroni are soft.

Macaroni and Cheese

Sherry L. Lapp
Lancaster, PA

Makes 8 servings

8-oz. pkg. elbow macaroni,
    cooked al dente
13-oz. can evaporated milk
1 cup whole milk
¼ cup butter, melted
2 large eggs, slightly beaten
4 cups grated sharp cheddar cheese,
    divided
¼-½ tsp. salt, according to your taste
    preferences
⅛ tsp. white pepper
¼ cup grated Parmesan cheese

1. In slow cooker, combine lightly cooked macaroni, evaporated milk, whole milk, melted butter, eggs, 3 cups cheddar cheese, salt, and pepper.
2. Top with remaining cheddar and Parmesan cheeses.
3. Cover. Cook on low 3 hours.

Crockpot Macaroni

Lisa F. Good
Harrisonburg, VA

Makes 6 servings

1½ cups dry macaroni
3 Tbsp. butter
1 tsp. salt
½ lb. Velveeta cheese, sliced
1 qt. milk

Slow and Easy Macaroni and Cheese

Janice Muller
Derwood, MD

Makes 6-8 servings

1 lb. dry macaroni
½ cup butter or margarine
2 eggs
12-oz. can evaporated milk
10¾-oz. can cheddar cheese soup
1 cup milk
4 cups shredded cheddar cheese, divided
⅛ tsp. paprika

1. Cook macaroni al dente. Drain and pour hot macaroni into slow cooker.
2. Slice butter into chunks and add to macaroni. Stir until melted.
3. Combine, eggs, evaporated milk, soup, and milk. Add 3 cups cheese. Pour over macaroni and mix well.
4. Cover. Cook on low 4 hours. Sprinkle with remaining cheese. Cook 15 minutes until cheese melts.
5. Sprinkle with paprika before serving.

Variation: Add 12-oz. can drained tuna to Step 3.

Macaroni and Cheese
Leona Yoder
Hartville, OH

Makes 8-10 servings

2-3 Tbsp. butter or margarine
1 qt. milk
1 lb. mild cheese, grated, or Velveeta
   cheese, cubed
1/2 tsp. salt
1/8 tsp. pepper
1 lb. macaroni, cooked al dente and rinsed

1. Melt margarine in large saucepan. Add milk. Heat slowly but do not boil.
2. When very hot, stir in cheese, salt, and pepper. Stir until cheese is melted.
3. Stir in macaroni.
4. Pour into greased slow cooker.
5. Cover. Cook on high 15 minutes, then on low 30 minutes.

This recipe is an oven-saver.

Fifty-sixty children eat this delightedly—in fact, it's one of their favorite meals—at the day school where I cook.

Menu Idea

Macaroni and Cheese
Lil' Smokie Sausages,
Applesauce
Fresh Veggies with Dip
Steamed Green Beans

Macaroni and Cheese
Arlene Groff
Lewistown, PA

Makes 5 servings

8 cups cooked macaroni
1 1/4 cups milk
1 lb. (1/2 block) Velveeta cheese, cubed
1/4 cup melted butter

1. Place macaroni in greased slow cooker.
2. Layer cheese over top. Pour milk and butter over all.
3. Cover. Cook on low 4 hours, stirring once halfway through cooking time.

Easy Stuffed Shells
Rebecca Plank Leichty
Harrisonburg, VA

Makes 4-6 servings

20-oz. bag frozen stuffed shells
15-oz. can marinara or spaghetti sauce
15-oz. can green beans, drained

1. Place shells around edge of greased slow cooker.
2. Cover with marinara sauce.
3. Pour green beans in center.
4. Cover. Cook on low 8 hours or on high 3 hours.
5. Serve with garlic toast and salad.

Variation: Reverse Steps 2 and 3. Double the amount of marinara sauce and pour over both the shells and the beans.

Cheese Souffle Casserole

Vicki Dinkel
Sharon Spring, KS

Makes 4 servings

14 slices fresh bread, crusts removed,
  divided
3 cups grated sharp cheese, divided
2 Tbsp. butter or margarine, melted,
  divided
6 eggs
3 cups milk, scalded
2 tsp. Worcestershire sauce
1/2 tsp. salt
paprika

1. Tear bread into small pieces. Place half in well-greased slow cooker. Add half the grated cheese and half the butter. Repeat layers.

2. Beat together eggs, milk, Worcestershire sauce, and salt. Pour over bread and cheese. Sprinkle top with paprika.

3. Cover. Cook on low 4-6 hours.

Arroz Con Queso

Nadine L. Martinitz
Salina, KS

Makes 6-8 servings

14.5-oz. can whole tomatoes, mashed
15-oz. can Mexican style beans, undrained
1 1/2 cups uncooked long grain rice
1 cup grated Monterey Jack cheese
1 large onion, finely chopped
1 cup cottage cheese
4.25-oz. can chopped green chili peppers,
  drained
1 Tbsp. oil
3 garlic cloves, minced
1 tsp. salt
1 cup grated Monterey Jack cheese

1. Combine all ingredients except final cup of cheese. Pour into well greased slow cooker.

2. Cover. Cook on low 6-9 hours.

3. Sprinkle with remaining cheese before serving.

4. Serve with salsa.

Minestra Di Ceci

Jeanette Oberholtzer
Manheim, PA

Makes 4-6 servings

1 lb. dry chickpeas
1 sprig fresh rosemary
10 leaves fresh sage
2 Tbsp. salt
1-2 large garlic cloves, minced
olive oil
1 cup small dry pasta, your choice of
    shape, or dry penne

1. Wash chickpeas. Place in slow cooker. Soak for 8 hours in full pot of water, along with rosemary, sage, and salt.
2. Drain water. Remove herbs.
3. Refill slow cooker with water to 1" above peas.
4. Cover. Cook on low 5 hours.
5. Saute garlic in olive oil in skillet until clear.
6. Puree half of peas, along with several cups of broth from cooker, in blender. Return puree to slow cooker. Add garlic and oil.
7. Boil pasta in saucepan until al dente, about 5 minutes. Drain. Add to beans.
8. Cover. Cook on high 30-60 minutes, or until pasta is tender and heated through, but not mushy.

Variation: Add 1/2 tsp. black pepper to Step 1, if you like.

Easy Wheatberries

Elaine Vigoda

Rochester, NY
Makes 4-6 servings

1 cup wheatberries
1 cup couscous, or small pasta like orzo
14 1/2-oz. can broth
1/2-1 broth can of water
1/2 cup dried craisins

1. Cover wheatberries with water and soak 2 hours before cooking. Drain. Spoon wheatberries into slow cooker.
2. Combine with remaining ingredients in slow cooker.
3. Cover. Cook on low until liquid is absorbed and berries are soft, about 2 hours.

Notes:
1. If craisins are unavailable, use raisins.

2. This is a satisfying vegetarian main dish, if you use vegetable broth.

Soups

 Meatless

Black Bean Soup

Sue Tjon
Austin, TX

Makes 6 servings

1-lb. bag black beans
2 10-oz. cans rotel tomatoes
1 medium onion, chopped
1 medium green bell pepper, chopped
1 Tbsp. minced garlic
14½-oz. can chicken or vegetable broth
water
Cajun seasoning to taste

1. Cover beans with water and soak for 8 hours or overnight. Drain well. Place beans in slow cooker.
2. Add tomatoes, onions, pepper, garlic, and chicken or vegetable broth. Add water just to cover beans. Add Cajun seasoning.
3. Cover. Cook on high 8 hours. Mash some of the beans before serving for a thicker consistency.
4. Serve over rice or in black bean tacos.

Note: Leftovers freeze well.

 Meatless

Many-Bean Soup

Trudy Kutter
Corfu, NY

Makes 12 servings

20-oz. pkg. dried 15-bean soup mix, or 2¼ cups dried beans
5 14½-oz. cans chicken or vegetable broth
2 cups chopped carrots
1½ cups chopped celery
1 cup chopped onions
2 Tbsp. tomato paste
1 tsp. Italian seasoning
½ tsp. pepper
14½-oz. can diced tomatoes

1. Combine all ingredients except tomatoes in slow cooker.
2. Cover. Cook on low 8-10 hours, or until beans are tender.
3. Stir in tomatoes.
4. Cover. Cook on high 10-20 minutes, or until soup is heated through.
5. Serve with bread and salad.

Crockpot Bean Soup

Betty B. Dennison
Grove City, PA

Makes 6 servings

3 15-oz. cans pinto beans, undrained
3 15-oz. cans Great Northern beans,
   undrained
4 cups chicken or vegetable broth
3 potatoes, peeled and chopped
4 carrots, sliced
2 celery ribs, sliced
1 large onion, chopped
1 green pepper, chopped
1 sweet red pepper, chopped, optional
2 garlic cloves, minced
1 tsp. salt, or to taste
1/4 tsp. pepper, or to taste
1 bay leaf, optional
1/2 tsp. liquid barbecue smoke, optional

1. Empty beans into 6-qt. slow cooker,
or divide ingredients between
2 4- or 5-qt. cookers.
2. Cover. Cook on low while preparing
vegetables.
3. Cook broth and vegetables in stockpot
until vegetables are tender-crisp. Transfer to
slow cooker.
4. Add remaining ingredients and mix well.
5. Cover. Cook on low 4-5 hours.
6. Serve with tossed salad, Italian bread or
cornbread.

Note:
*1. You can add the broth and vegetables to the
cooker without cooking them in advance. Simply
extend the slow-cooker cooking time to 8 hours on
low.*

*2. This is a stress-free recipe when you're
expecting guests, but you're not sure of their
arrival time. Slow Cooker Bean Soup can burble
on low heat for longer than its appointed cooking
time without being damaged.*

*3. Make a tossed salad and have the dressing
ready to go. Add dressing to salad as your guests
make their way to the table.*

Southwestern Bean Soup with Cornmeal Dumplings

Melba Eshleman
Manheim, PA

Makes 4 servings

15 1/2-oz. can red kidney beans, rinsed and
   drained
15 1/2-oz. can black beans, pinto beans, or
   Great Northern beans, rinsed and
   drained
3 cups water
14 1/2-oz. can Mexican-style stewed
   tomatoes
10-oz. pkg. frozen whole-kernel corn,
   thawed
1 cup sliced carrots
1 cup chopped onions
4-oz. can chopped green chilies
2 Tbsp. instant beef, chicken, or vegetable
   bouillon granules
1-2 tsp. chili powder
2 cloves garlic, minced

Dumplings:
1/3 cup flour
1/4 cup yellow cornmeal
1 tsp. baking powder
dash of salt
dash of pepper
1 egg white, beaten
2 Tbsp. milk
1 Tbsp. oil

1. Combine 11 soup ingredients in slow cooker.

2. Cover. Cook on low 10-12 hours or high 4-5 hours.

3. Make dumplings by mixing together flour, cornmeal, baking powder, salt, and pepper.

4. Combine egg white, milk, and oil. Add to flour mixture. Stir with fork until just combined.

5. At the end of the soup's cooking time, turn slow cooker to high. Drop dumpling mixture by rounded teaspoonfuls to make 8 mounds atop the soup.

6. Cover. Cook for 30 minutes (do not lift cover).

Garbanzo Souper

Willard E. Roth
Elkhart, IN

Makes 6 servings

1 lb. dry garbanzo beans
4 ozs. raw baby carrots, cut in halves
1 large onion, diced
3 ribs celery, cut in 1″ pieces
1 large green pepper, diced
½ tsp. dried basil
½ tsp. dried oregano
½ tsp. dried rosemary
½ tsp. dried thyme
2 28-oz. cans vegetable broth
1 broth can of water
8-oz. can tomato sauce
8 ozs. prepared hummus
½ tsp. sea salt

1. Soak beans overnight. Drain. Place in bottom of slow cooker.

2. Add carrots, onion, celery, and green pepper.

3. Sprinkle with basil, oregano, rosemary, and thyme.

4. Cover with broth and water.

5. Cover. Cook on high 6 hours.

6. Half an hour before serving, stir in tomato sauce, hummus, and salt. Cook until hot.

7. Serve with Irish soda bread and lemon curd.

A fine meal for vegetarians on St. Patrick's Day!

Hearty Bean and Vegetable Soup

Jewel Showalter
Landisville, PA

Makes 6-8 servings

2 medium onions, sliced
2 garlic cloves, minced
2 Tbsp. olive oil
8 cups chicken or vegetable broth
1 small head cabbage, chopped
2 large red potatoes, chopped
2 cups chopped celery
2 cups chopped carrots
4 cups corn
2 tsp. dried basil
1 tsp. dried marjoram
1/4 tsp. dried oregano
1 tsp. salt
1/2 tsp. pepper
2 15-oz. cans navy beans

1. Saute onions and garlic in oil. Transfer to large slow cooker.
2. Add remaining ingredients, mixing together well.
3. Cover. Cook on low 6-8 hours.

Variation: Add 2-3 cups cooked and cut-up chicken 30 minutes before serving if you wish.

I discovered this recipe after my husband's heart attack. It's a great nutritious soup using only a little fat.

Menu Idea

Hearty Bean and Vegetable Soup
Homemade Bread
Cheese Cubes and Crackers
Fruit
Cookies

Meatless

Blessing Soup

Alix Nancy Botsford
Seminole, OK

Makes 8-10 servings

2 cups mixed dried beans (10-18 different kinds)
2-2 1/2 qts. water
1 cup diced ham
1 large onion, chopped
1 garlic clove, minced
juice of 1 lemon
14.5-oz. can Italian tomatoes, chopped
1/2 cup chopped sweet red pepper
1/2 cup chopped celery
2 carrots, thinly sliced
1 tsp. salt
1 tsp. pepper

1. Sort and wash beans. Cover with water and soak several hours or overnight. Drain.
2. Place beans in cooker and add 2-2 1/2 quarts water. Cook on high for 2 hours.
3. Combine all ingredients with beans in slow cooker.
4. Add more water so that everything is just covered.
5. Cover. Cook on high 4-6 hours or low 8-12 hours.

One January that was especially dismal, I invited many friends, most of whom didn't know each other, to my home. I put on a video about rose gardens around the world. Then I made this soup and a fresh bread crouton that could be eaten on top of the soup and tossed a large salad.

Mexican Rice and Bean Soup

Esther J. Mast
East Petersburg, PA

Makes 6 servings

1/2 cup chopped onions
1/3 cup chopped green peppers
1 garlic clove, minced
1 Tbsp. oil
4-oz. pkg. sliced or chipped dried beef
18-oz. can tomato juice
15 1/2-oz. can red kidney beans, undrained
1 1/2 cups water
1/2 cup long-grain rice, uncooked
1 tsp. paprika
1/2-1 tsp. chili powder
1/2 tsp. salt
dash of pepper

1. Cook onions, green peppers, and garlic in oil in skillet until vegetables are tender but not brown. Transfer to slow cooker.
2. Tear beef into small pieces and add to slow cooker.
3. Add remaining ingredients. Mix well.
4. Cover. Cook on low 6 hours. Stir before serving.
5. Serve with relish tray and cornbread, home-canned fruit, and cookies.

This is a recipe I fixed often when our sons were growing up. We have all enjoyed it in any season of the year.

Polish Sausage Bean Soup

Janie Steele
Moore, OK

Makes 10 servings

1-lb. pkg. dried Great Northern beans
28-oz. can whole tomatoes
2 8-oz. cans tomato sauce
2 large onions, chopped
3 cloves garlic, minced
1 tsp. salt
1/4-1/2 tsp. pepper, according to your taste preference
3 celery ribs, sliced
bell pepper, sliced
large ham bone or ham hock
1-2 lbs. smoked sausage links, sliced

1. Cover beans with water and soak for 8 hours. Rinse and drain.
2. Place beans in 6-qt. cooker and cover with water.
2. Combine all other ingredients, except sausage, in large bowl. Stir into beans in slow cooker.
3. Cover. Cook on high 1-1 1/2 hours. Reduce to low. Cook 7 hours.
4. Remove ham bone or hock and debone. Stir ham pieces back into soup.
5. Add sausage links.
6. Cover. Cook on low 1 hour.

Note: For enhanced flavor, brown sausage before adding to soup.

Black Bean Soup

Janie Steele
Moore, OK

Makes 5-6 quarts, or about 18 servings

4 cups dry black beans
5 qts. water
ham bone, ham pieces, or ham hocks
3 bunches of green onions, sliced thin
4 bay leaves
1 Tbsp. salt
1/4-1/2 tsp. pepper
3 cloves minced garlic
4 celery ribs, chopped
3 large onions, chopped
10 1/2-oz. can consomme
1/2 cup butter
2 1/2 Tbsp. flour
1/2 cup minced parsley
1 cup Madeira wine, optional
chopped parsley

1. In 6-qt. slow cooker, soak beans in 5 qts. water for 8 hours. Rinse. Drain. Pour beans back into slow cooker, or divide between 2 4- or 5-qt. cookers.
2. Add ham, green onions, bay, salt, pepper, garlic, celery, and onions. Pour in consomme. Add water to cover vegetables and meat.
3. Cover. Cook on high 1 1/2-2 hours. Reduce heat to low and cook for 6-8 hours.
4. Remove ham bones and bay leaves. Cut ham off bones and set meat aside
5. Force vegetable mixture through sieve, if you wish.
6. Taste and adjust seasonings, adding more salt and pepper if needed. Return cooked ingredients and cut-up ham to cooker.
7. In saucepan, melt 1/2 cup butter. Stir in flour until smooth. Stir into soup to thicken and enrich.
8. Prior to serving, add wine to heated soup mixture. Garnish with chopped parsley.

Party Bean Soup

Jo Haberkamp
Fairbank, IA

Makes 9 servings

1 cup dry navy beans
1 qt. water
1 lb. smoked or plain ham hocks
1 cup chopped onions
1/2 cup chopped celery
1 garlic clove, minced
8-oz. can tomatoes, cut up
2 14 1/2-oz. cans chicken broth
1/8 tsp. salt
1/8 tsp. pepper
1 cup (4 ozs.) shredded cheddar cheese
1 Tbsp. dried parsley flakes

1. Place beans and water in slow cooker.
2. Cover. Cook on low for 12 hours.
3. Add ham hocks, onions, celery, garlic, tomatoes, chicken broth, salt, and pepper.
4. Cover. Cook on low 8-10 hours.
5. Add cheese and parsley. Stir until cheese is melted.

Hostess Idea

Buy 10-18 different kinds of dried beans. Mix them together in a large bag or jar. Scoop them into small bags (8-oz. is a good size). Top each with a dried bay leaf to discourage bugs, tie them shut, and present them to the friends who have just eaten from your buffet table.

A bag full of these dried beans is also a welcome and interesting addition to a gift basket.

—Alix Nancy Botsford

Navy Bean Soup

Lucille Amos
Greensboro, NC

Makes 8 servings

2 cups navy beans
1 cup chopped onions
1 bay leaf
1 tsp. salt
1 tsp. pepper
½ lb. ham, chopped

1. Soak beans in water overnight. Drain.
2. Combine ingredients in slow cooker. Add water to cover.
3. Cover. Cook on low 10-12 hours or on high 5-6 hours.
4. Remove bay leaf and serve.

Navy Bean and Bacon Chowder

Ruth A. Feister
Narvon, PA

Makes 6 servings

1½ cups dried navy beans
2 cups cold water
8 slices bacon, cooked and crumbled
2 medium carrots, sliced
1 rib celery, sliced
1 medium onion, chopped
1 tsp. dried Italian seasoning
⅛ tsp. pepper
46-oz. can chicken broth
1 cup milk

1. Soak beans in 2 cups cold water for 8 hours.
2. After beans have soaked, drain, if necessary, and place in slow cooker.
2. Add all remaining ingredients, except milk, to slow cooker.
3. Cover. Cook on low 7-9 hours, or until beans are crisp-tender.
4. Place 2 cups cooked bean mixture into blender. Process until smooth. Return to slow cooker.
5. Add milk. Cover and heat on high 10 minutes.
6. Serve with crusty French bread and additional herbs and seasonings for diners to add as they wish.

Cassoulet Chowder

Miriam Friesen
Staunton, VA

Makes 8-10 servings

1¼ cups dry pinto beans
4 cups water
12-oz. pkg. brown-and-serve sausage links,
   cooked and drained
2 cups cubed cooked chicken
2 cups cubed cooked ham
1½ cups sliced carrots
8-oz. can tomato sauce
¾ cup dry red wine
½ cup chopped onions
½ tsp. garlic powder
1 bay leaf

1. Combine beans and water in large saucepan. Bring to boil. Reduce heat and simmer 1½ hours. Refrigerate beans and liquid 4-8 hours.
2. Combine all ingredients in slow cooker.
3. Cover. Cook on low 8-10 hours or on high 4 hours. If the chowder seems too thin, remove lid during last 30 minutes of cooking time to allow it to thicken.
4. Remove bay leaf before serving.

Grandma's Barley Soup

Andrea O'Neil
Fairfield, CT

Makes 10-12 servings

2 smoked ham hocks
4 carrots, sliced
4 potatoes, cubed
1 cup dried lima beans
1 cup tomato paste
1½-2 cups cooked barley
salt, if needed

1. Combine all ingredients in slow cooker, except salt.
2. Cover with water.
3. Cover. Simmer on low 6-8 hours.
4. Debone ham hocks and return cut-up meat to soup.
5. Taste before serving. Add salt if needed.

Note: If you want to reduce the amount of meat you eat, this dish is flavorful using only 1 ham hock.

Green Bean Soup

Loretta Krahn
Mountain Lake, MN

Makes 6 servings

1 meaty ham bone, or 2 cups cubed ham
1½ qts. water
1 large onion, chopped
2-3 cups cut-up green beans
3 large carrots, sliced
2 large potatoes, peeled and cubed
1 Tbsp. parsley
1 Tbsp. summer savory
½ tsp. salt
¼ tsp. pepper
1 cup cream or milk

1. Combine all ingredients except cream in slow cooker.
2. Cover. Cook on high 4-6 hours.
3. Remove ham bone. Cut off meat and return to slow cooker.
4. Turn to low. Stir in cream or milk. Heat through and serve.

Green Bean Soup

Bernita Boyts
Shawnee Mission, KS

Makes 5-6 servings

1 medium onion, chopped
2 carrots, sliced
2 ribs celery, sliced
1 Tbsp. olive oil
5 medium potatoes, cubed
10-oz. pkg. frozen green beans
2 14½-oz. cans chicken broth
2 broth cans water
⅓ lb. link sausage, sliced, or bulk sausage, browned
2 Tbsp. chopped fresh parsley
   (2 tsp. dried)
1-2 Tbsp. chopped fresh oregano
   (1-2 tbsp. dried)
1 tsp. Italian spice
salt to taste
pepper to taste

1. Saute onion, carrots, and celery in oil in skillet until tender.
2. Combine all ingredients in slow cooker.
3. Cover. Cook on high 1-2 hours and then on low 6-8 hours.
4. Serve with freshly baked bread or cornbread.

Variation: If you like it hot, add ground red pepper or hot sauce just before serving.

Hostess Idea

It's fun to type up questions from the "Ungame" onto small pieces of paper, roll them up, and tie each with a colorful ribbon. Place one by each place-setting, or put them in a small basket on the table. As an after-dinner activity and as a way to learn to know each other, take turns opening the "scrolls" and answering the questions.
—Esther J. Mast

Broccoli, Potato, and Cheese Soup

Ruth Shank
Gridley, IL

Makes 6 servings

2 cups cubed or diced potatoes
3 Tbsp. chopped onion
10-oz. pkg. frozen broccoli cuts, thawed
2 Tbsp. butter or margarine, melted
1 Tbsp. flour
2 cups cubed Velveeta cheese
1/2 tsp. salt
51/2 cups milk

1. Cook potatoes and onion in boiling water in saucepan until potatoes are crisp-tender. Drain. Place in slow cooker.
2. Add remaining ingredients. Stir together.
3. Cover. Cook on low 4 hours.

Cheesy Broccoli Soup

Dede Peterson
Rapid City, SD

Makes 4 servings

1 lb. frozen chopped broccoli, thawed
1 lb. Velveeta cheese, cubed
10 3/4-oz. can cream of celery soup
14 1/2-oz. can chicken or vegetable broth
dash of pepper
dash of salt

1. Combine ingredients in slow cooker.
2. Cover. Cook on low 5-6 hours.

Curried Carrot Soup

Ann Bender
Ft. Defiance, VA

Makes 6-8 servings

1 garlic clove, minced
1 large onion, chopped
2 Tbsp. oil
1 Tbsp. butter
1 tsp. curry powder
1 Tbsp. flour
4 cups chicken or vegetable broth
6 large carrots, sliced
1/4 tsp. salt
1/4 tsp. ground red pepper, optional
1 1/2 cups plain yogurt, or light sour cream

1. In skillet cook minced garlic and onion in oil and butter until limp but not brown.
2. Add curry and flour. Cook 30 seconds. Pour into slow cooker.
3. Add chicken broth and carrots.
4. Cover. Cook on high for about 2 hours, or until carrots are soft.
5. Puree mixture in blender. Season with salt and pepper. Return to slow cooker and keep warm until ready to serve.
6. Add a dollop of yogurt or sour cream to each serving.

Corn Chowder

Mary Rogers
Waseca, MN

Makes 12 servings

1 lb. bacon
4 cups diced potatoes
2 cups chopped onions
2 cups sour cream
2½ cups milk
2 10¾-oz. cans cream of chicken soup
2 15¼-oz. cans corn, undrained

1. Cut bacon into 1" pieces. Cook for 5 minutes in large skillet.
2. Add potatoes and onions and a bit of water. Cook 15-20 minutes, until tender, stirring occasionally. Drain. Transfer to slow cooker.
3. Combine sour cream, milk, chicken soup, and corn. Place in slow cooker.
4. Cover. Cook on low for 2 hours.
5. Serve with homemade biscuits or a pan of steaming cornbread fresh from the oven.

Green Chile Corn Chowder

Kelly Evenson
Pittsboro, NC

Makes 8 servings

16-oz. can cream-style corn
3 potatoes, peeled and diced
2 Tbsp. chopped fresh chives
4-oz. can diced green chilies, drained
2-oz. jar chopped pimentos, drained
½-¾ cup chopped cooked ham
2 10½-oz. cans chicken broth
salt to taste
pepper to taste
Tabasco sauce to taste
1 cup milk
shredded Monterey Jack cheese

1. Combine all ingredients except milk and cheese in slow cooker.
2. Cover. Cook on low 7-8 hours or until potatoes are tender.
3. Stir in milk. Heat until hot.
4. Top individual servings with cheese. Serve with homemade bread.

Corn and Shrimp Chowder

Naomi E. Fast
Hesston, KS

Makes 6 servings

4 slices bacon, diced
1 cup chopped onions
2 cups diced, unpeeled red potatoes
2 10-oz. pkgs. frozen corn
1 tsp. Worcestershire sauce
1/2 tsp. paprika
1/2 tsp. salt
1/8 tsp. pepper
2 6-oz. cans shrimp
2 cups water
2 Tbsp. butter or margarine
12-oz. can evaporated milk
chopped chives

1. Fry bacon in skillet until lightly crisp. Add onions to drippings and saute until transparent. Using slotted spoon, transfer bacon and onions to slow cooker.
2. Add remaining ingredients to cooker except milk and chives.
3. Cover. Cook on low 3-4 hours, adding milk and chives 30 minutes before end of cooking time.
4. Serve with broccoli salad.

I learned to make this recipe in a 7th grade home economics class. It made an impression on my father who liked seafood very much. The recipe calls only for canned shrimp, but I often increase the taste appeal with extra cooked shrimp.

I frequently use frozen hash brown potatoes for speedy preparation. There is no difference in the taste.

Elijah's Cucumber Soup

Shirley Unternahrer Hinh
Wayland, IA

Makes 8 servings

1 lb. ground pork
2 Tbsp. fish sauce
1/4 tsp. black pepper
4 large cucumbers, peeled
2 qts. boiling water
2 green onions, chopped
1/8 tsp. black pepper
4 Tbsp. fish sauce
salt to taste

1. Combine pork, 2 Tbsp. fish sauce, and 1/4 tsp. black pepper in mixing bowl.
2. Cut peeled cucumbers in half and scoop out seeds, creating a channel in each cuke. Stuff pork mixture into cucumbers.
3. Form remaining meat into 1" balls. Drop balls into stockpot with 2 qts. boiling water. Boil until a layer of foam develops on the water. Skim off foam and discard.
4. Drop stuffed cucumbers into boiling water. Simmer for 15 minutes. Transfer cucumbers and pork balls into slow cooker. Add hot liquid from stockpot.
5. Add green onions, 1/8 tsp. black pepper, and 4 Tbsp. fish sauce.
6. Cover. Cook on high 1 1/2-2 hours.
7. Serve over rice in bowl, along with lemon juice and chili sauce.

This dish was brought into our family's recipe collection by my husband, Hai. Hai came to the United States, from Vietnam, 23 years ago.

We eat this soup quite often at our house. Many of our friends and family have enjoyed it over the years and we've had many requests for it.

Oriental Pork Soup

Judi Manos
West Islip, NY

Makes 6 servings

1 lb. ground pork, chicken, or turkey
1 garlic clove, minced
2 medium carrots, cut into julienne strips
4 medium green onions, cut into 1" pieces
1 garlic clove, minced
1/4 cup soy sauce
1/2 tsp. gingerroot, chopped
1/8 tsp. pepper
491/2-oz. can chicken broth
1 cup sliced mushrooms
1 cup bean sprouts

1. Cook meat with garlic in skillet until brown. Drain.
2. Combine all ingredients except mushrooms and sprouts in slow cooker.
3. Cover. Cook on low 7-9 hours or high 3-4 hours.
4. Stir in mushrooms and bean sprouts.
5. Cover. Cook on low 1 hour.

Variation: For added flavor to the meat, add 1/8 tsp. five-spice blend to Step 1.

Lentil Soup with Ham Bone

Rhoda Atzeff
Harrisburg, PA

Makes 6-8 servings

1 lb. lentils, washed and drained
1 celery rib, chopped
1 large carrot, grated
1/2 cup chopped onions
1 bay leaf
1/4 tsp. dried thyme
7-8 cups water
1 ham bone, thinly sliced kielbasa, or hot smoked sausage
1/4-1/2 tsp. crushed red hot pepper flakes
pepper to taste
salt to taste

1. Combine all ingredients except pepper and salt in slow cooker.
2. Cover. Cook on low 8-9 hours. Remove bay leaf and ham bone. Dice meat from bone and return to cooker.
3. Season to taste with pepper and salt.
4. Serve alone, or over rice with grated cheese on top.

Russian Red-Lentil Soup

Naomi E. Fast
Hesston, KS

Makes 8 servings

1 Tbsp. oil
1 large onion, chopped
3 cloves garlic, minced
1/2 cup diced, dried apricots
1 1/2 cups dried red lentils
1/2 tsp. cumin
1/2 tsp. dried thyme
3 cups water
2 14 1/2-oz. cans chicken or vegetable broth
14 1/2-oz. can diced tomatoes
1 Tbsp. honey
3/4 tsp. salt
1/2 tsp. coarsely ground black pepper
2 Tbsp. chopped fresh mint
1 1/2 cups plain yogurt

1. Combine all ingredients except mint and yogurt in slow cooker.
2. Cover. Heat on high until soup starts to simmer, then turn to low and cook 3-4 hours.
3. Add mint and dollop of yogurt to each bowl of soup.

Menu Idea

Russian Red Lentil Soup
Pita Bread Triangles
Waldorf Salad
Platter of Fresh Veggies—radishes, celery, cauliflower, carrots, and pickles

---

Onion Soup

Rosemarie Fitzgerald
Gibsonia, PA

Makes 6-8 servings

3 medium onions, thinly sliced
1/4 cup butter
1 tsp. salt
1 Tbsp. sugar
2 Tbsp. flour
1 qt. beef or vegetable broth
1/2 cup dry white wine
slices of French bread
Swiss or Parmesan cheese, grated

1. Saute onions in butter in covered skillet until soft. Uncover. Add salt and sugar. Cook 15 minutes. Stir in flour. Cook 3 more minutes.
2. Combine onions, broth, and wine in slow cooker.
3. Cover. Cook on low 6-8 hours.
4. Toast bread. Sprinkle with grated cheese and then broil.
5. Dish soup into individual bowls; then float a slice of broiled bread on top of each serving of soup.

Lentil Soup

Tina Snyder
Manheim, PA

Makes 10 servings

4 cups hot water
14 1/2-oz. can tomatoes
1/4 cup tomato juice
3 medium potatoes, peeled and diced
3 carrots, thinly sliced
1 onion, chopped

1 rib celery, sliced
1 cup dry lentils
2 garlic cloves, minced
2 bay leaves
4 tsp. curry powder
1½ tsp. salt
sour cream

1. Combine all ingredients except sour cream in slow cooker.
2. Cover. Cook on low 8 hours.
3. Serve with sour cream on top of individual servings and crusty bread as a go-along.

Potato Soup

Deborah Santiago
Lancaster, PA

Makes 6 servings

6 potatoes, peeled and cubed
2 onions, chopped
1 carrot, sliced
1 rib celery, sliced
4 chicken or vegetable bouillon cubes
1 Tbsp. parsley flakes
5 cups water
¼ tsp. pepper
1 Tbsp. salt
⅓ cup butter, melted
13-oz. can evaporated milk

1. Combine all ingredients except evaporated milk in slow cooker.
2. Cover. Cook on high 3-4 hours or low 10-12 hours.
3. Stir in evaporated milk during last hour of cooking time.
4. Serve with sandwiches, crackers, and beverage.

Potato Soup

Zona Mae Bontrager
Kokomo, IN

Makes 4 servings

½ cup chopped onions
1 tsp. butter
14½-oz. can beef, chicken, or vegetable broth
1 potato, chopped
1 carrot, shredded
1 rib celery, chopped
½-¾ tsp. salt
⅛-¼ tsp. pepper
2 cups mashed potatoes
½ cup shredded mild cheese, optional

1. Saute onions in butter in skillet.
2. Stir in broth, 1 potato, carrot, celery, and seasonings. Cook until vegetables are tender. Pour into hot slow cooker.
3. Add mashed potatoes and cheese. Stir well.
4. Cover. Heat on low until ready to serve.

Hostess Idea

Present any new recipe without apologies. Offer new foods and tastes as a wonderful experience.
—Naomi E. Fast

163

Potato Cheddar-Cheese Soup

Marla Folkerts
Holland, OH

Makes 4 servings

6-10 potatoes, peeled and cubed
½ cup vegetable broth
1 cup water
1 large onion, finely chopped
½ tsp. garlic powder
⅛ tsp. white pepper
2 cups milk, heated
1 cup shredded sharp, or extra sharp,
   cheddar cheese
paprika

1. Place potatoes, broth, water, onions, and garlic powder in slow cooker.
2. Cover. Cook on low 7-9 hours, or on high 4-6 hours.
3. Mash potatoes, leaving them a bit lumpy. Stir in pepper and milk a little at a time. Add cheese. Cook until cheese has melted, about 5 minutes. Add more milk if you'd like a thinner or creamier soup.
4. Garnish each serving with paprika.
5. Serve with homemade bread, salad, and fruit.

Ham and Potato Chowder

Penny Blosser
Beavercreek, OH

Makes 5 servings

5-oz. pkg. scalloped potatoes
sauce mix from potato pkg.
1 cup cooked ham, cut into narrow strips
4 cups chicken broth
1 cup chopped celery
⅓ cup chopped onions
salt to taste
pepper to taste
2 cups half-and-half
⅓ cup flour

1. Combine potatoes, sauce mix, ham, broth, celery, onions, salt, and pepper in slow cooker.
2. Cover. Cook on low 7 hours.
3. Combine half-and-half and flour. Gradually add to slow cooker, blending well.
4. Cover. Cook on low up to 1 hour, stirring occasionally until thickened.

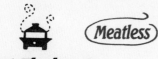

Aunt Thelma's Homemade Soup

Janice Muller
Derwood, MD

Makes 10-12 servings

7 cups water
4 chicken or vegetable bouillon cubes
1 cup thinly sliced carrots
1-lb. pkg. frozen peas
1-lb. pkg. frozen corn
1-lb. pkg. frozen lima beans
1 bay leaf
1/4 tsp. dill seed
28-oz. can whole tomatoes
1 cup diced raw potatoes
1 cup chopped onions
2-3 tsp. salt
1/2 tsp. dried basil
1/4 tsp. pepper
2 Tbsp. cornstarch
1/4 cup cold water

1. Combine all ingredients except cornstarch and 1/4 cup water in slow cooker.
2. Cover. Simmer on high 4 hours, or until vegetables are tender.
3. Thirty minutes before end of cooking time, mix cornstarch and cold water together until smooth. Remove 1 cup broth from cooker and mix with cornstarch-water. When smooth, stir into soup. Cover and continue cooking another half hour.
4. A loaf of fresh Italian bread goes well with a hot bowl of this soup.

My aunt always makes this in the winter and freezes an extra batch for unexpected guests.
I converted the recipe to crockpot-use a few years ago, but I think of her whenever I make it.

Diet Soup Unlimited

Eileen Lehman
Kidron, OH

Makes 6 servings

4 cups water
2 cups tomato juice
2 beef or vegetable bouillon cubes
1 Tbsp. soy sauce, optional
1 tsp. sweetener, optional
1 cup sliced cabbage
2 carrots, sliced
1 celery rib, sliced
1 onion, sliced
2 cups frozen green beans
1 tsp. salt
pepper to taste

1. Combine all ingredients in slow cooker.
2. Cover. Cook on low 4-8 hours.

Variation: Add mushrooms, if you like, after the first 2 hours of cooking.

After the holidays this tasty, low-calorie soup is a welcome meal. It improves in flavor the longer it cooks.

Minestrone

Bernita Boyts
Shawnee Mission, KS

Makes 8-10 servings

1 large onion, chopped
4 carrots, sliced
3 ribs celery, sliced
2 garlic cloves, minced
1 Tbsp. olive oil
6-oz. can tomato paste
14½-oz. can chicken, beef, or vegetable
  broth
24-oz. can pinto beans, undrained
10-oz. pkg. frozen green beans
2-3 cups chopped cabbage
1 medium zucchini, sliced
8 cups water
2 Tbsp. parsley
2 Tbsp. Italian spice
1 tsp. salt, or more
½ tsp. pepper
¾ cup dry acini di pepe
  (small round pasta)
grated Parmesan or Asiago cheese

1. Saute onion, carrots, celery, and garlic in oil until tender.
2. Combine all ingredients except pasta and cheese in slow cooker.
3. Cover. Cook 4-5 hours on high or 8-9 hours on low, adding pasta 1 hour before cooking is complete.
4. Top individual servings with cheese.

The Soup

Joanne Kennedy
Plattsburgh, NY

Makes 8 servings

2 14½-oz. cans vegetable broth
2 vegetable boullion cubes
4 cups water
1 qt. canned tomatoes
3-4 garlic cloves, minced
1 large onion, chopped
1 cup chopped celery
2 cups chopped carrots
1 small zucchini, cubed
1 small yellow squash, cubed
2 tsp. fresh basil
1 tsp. fresh parsley
pepper to taste
3 dashes Tabasco sauce

1. Combine ingredients in slow cooker.
2. Cover. Cook on low 9 hours.

Variation: Add cooked pasta after soup is done.

Homemade Vegetable Soup

Audrey Romonosky
Austin, TX

Makes 10-12 servings

1 lb. stewing meat, cut into pieces
1 bay leaf
1 small onion, diced
3 carrots, sliced
2 ribs celery, sliced
2-3 potatoes, diced
14½-oz. can stewed tomatoes, cut up
8-oz. can tomato sauce

¼ cup frozen corn
½ cup frozen green beans
¼ cup frozen peas
¼ cup chopped cabbage
salt to taste
pepper to taste

1. Combine all ingredients in slow cooker. Add water to fill pot.
2. Cover. Cook on low 6-8 hours.

Beef Dumpling Soup

Barbara Walker
Sturgis, SD

Makes 5-6 servings

1 lb. beef stewing meat, cubed
1 envelope dry onion soup mix
6 cups hot water
2 carrots, peeled and shredded
1 celery rib, finely chopped
1 tomato, peeled and chopped
1 cup buttermilk biscuit mix
1 Tbsp. finely chopped parsley
6 Tbsp. milk

1. Place meat in slow cooker. Sprinkle with onion soup mix. Pour water over meat.
2. Add carrots, celery, and tomato.
3. Cover. Cook on low 4-6 hours, or until meat is tender.
4. Combine biscuit mix and parsley. Stir in milk with fork until moistened. Drop dumplings by teaspoonfuls into pot.
5. Cover. Cook on high 30 minutes.

Variation: Increase the flavor of the broth by adding 2 cloves garlic, ½ tsp. dried basil, and ¼ tsp. dill weed to Step 2.

Easy Vegetable Soup

Winifred Paul
Scottdale, PA

Makes 8-10 servings

1 lb. ground beef, browned
1 cup chopped onions
15-oz. can kidney beans or butter beans, undrained
1 cup sliced carrots
¼ cup rice, uncooked
1 qt. stewed tomatoes
3½ cups water
5 beef bouillon cubes
1 Tbsp. parsley flakes
1 tsp. salt
⅛ tsp. pepper
¼ tsp. dried basil
1 bay leaf

1. Combine all ingredients in slow cooker.
2. Cover. Cook on low 8-10 hours.

Note: Add more herbs and additional seasonings for zestier flavor.

Easy Veggie-Beef Soup

Rebecca Plank Leichty
Harrisonburg, VA

Makes 6-8 servings

1 lb. browned ground beef, or 2 cups
   stewing beef
2 cups sliced carrots
1 lb. frozen green beans, thawed
14½-oz. can corn, drained,
   or 16-oz. bag frozen corn, thawed
28-oz. can diced tomatoes
3 cups beef or veggie broth
3 tsp. instant beef bouillon
2 tsp. Worcestershire sauce
1 Tbsp. sugar
1 Tbsp. minced onion
10¾-oz. can cream of celery soup

   1. Place meat in bottom of slow cooker.
   2. Add remaining ingredients except celery soup. Mix well.
   3. Stir in soup.
   4. Cover. Cook on low 7-8 hours or high 4 hours.
   5. If using stewing meat, shred and mix through soup just before serving.
   6. Serve with freshly baked bread and homemade jam.

Two modern-day conveniences—the slow cooker and bread machine—allow me to prepare tasty meals without too much last-minute dashing around. Utilizing both gives me time to plan table settings and decorations, too.

Hamburger Soup

Naomi Ressler
Harrisonburg, VA
Kay Magruder
Seminole, OK

Makes 8 servings

1½ lbs. ground beef, browned
1 medium onion, chopped
1 cup sliced carrots
1 cup sliced celery
1 cup sliced cabbage
6-oz. can tomato paste
2 tsp. Worcestershire sauce
2-3 cups beef broth, depending upon how
   thick or thin you like your soup

   1. Combine beef, onions, carrots, celery, and cabbage in slow cooker.
   2. Combine tomato paste, Worcestershire sauce, and broth. Pour into slow cooker. Mix to blend.
   3. Cover. Cook on low 8-10 hours or on high 3-4 hours.

Variation: Stir in ¼ tsp. black or cayenne pepper and 2 bay leaves in Step 2 for added flavor.

Ground Beef Soup

Nadine L. Martinitz
Salina, KS

Makes 6-8 servings

1 lb. ground beef
1 medium onion, chopped
1 Tbsp. oil
15.8-oz. can Great Northern Beans,
   undrained
15-oz. can tomato sauce
1 1/2-2 tomato-sauce cans water
2 large potatoes, cubed
14.5-oz. can tomatoes
1 tsp. salt

1. Brown ground beef and onions in oil in skillet. Drain. Place in slow cooker.
2. Add remaining ingredients.
3. Cook on high 1 hour, then low 6-8 hours.
4. Serve with grilled cheese sandwiches.

Hamburger Vegetable Soup

Joyce Shackelford
Green Bay, WI

Makes 8-10 servings

1 lb. ground chuck
1 onion, chopped
2 garlic cloves, minced
4 cups V8 juice
14 1/2-oz. can stewed tomatoes
2 cups cole slaw mix
2 cups frozen green beans
2 cups frozen corn
2 Tbsp. Worcestershire sauce

1 tsp. dried basil
1/2 tsp. salt
1/4 tsp. pepper

1. Brown beef, onion, and garlic in skillet. Drain and transfer to slow cooker.
2. Add remaining ingredients to slow cooker and combine.
3. Cover. Cook on low 8-9 hours.

Taco Soup

Suzanne Slagel
Midway, OH

Makes 6-8 servings

1 lb. ground beef
1 large onion, chopped
16-oz. can Mexican-style tomatoes
16-oz. can ranch-style beans
16-oz. can whole-kernel corn, undrained
16-oz. can kidney beans, undrained
16-oz. can black beans, undrained
16-oz. jar picante sauce
corn or tortilla chips
sour cream
shredded cheddar cheese

1. Brown meat and onions in skillet. Drain.
2. Combine with all other vegetables and picante sauce in slow cooker.
3. Cover. Cook on low 4-6 hours.
4. Serve with corn or tortilla chips, sour cream, and shredded cheese as toppings.

Taco Soup

Sue Tjon
Austin, TX

Makes 8 servings

1 lb. ground beef
1 envelope dry ranch dressing mix
1 envelope dry taco seasoning mix
3 12-oz. cans rotel tomatoes, undrained
2 24-oz. cans pinto beans, undrained
24-oz. can hominy, undrained
14.5-oz. can stewed tomatoes, undrained
1 onion, chopped
2 cups water

1. Brown meat in skillet. Pour into slow cooker.
2. Add remaining ingredients. Mix well.
3. Cover. Cook on low 4 hours.

Notes:
1. Increase or decrease the amount of water you add to make the dish either stew-like or soup-like.

2. A serving suggestion is to line each individual soup bowl with tortilla chips, ladle taco soup on top, and sprinkle with grated cheese.

Ruth's Ground Beef Vegetable Soup

Ruth Ann Penner
Hillsboro, KS

Makes 6 servings

1 lb. ground beef
1 1/2 qts. water
3/4 cup chopped celery
1 cup chopped carrots
1 large onion, chopped
2 cups cubed potatoes
1 1/2 tsp. salt
1/2 cup uncooked rice
1/4 tsp. pepper
10 3/4-oz. can tomato soup

1. Crumble ground beef in slow cooker. Add water.
2. Add remaining ingredients except soup. Mix together well.
3. Cover. Cook on low 8-10 hours.
4. Add soup 30 minutes before serving and stir through.

Menu Idea

Ruth's Ground Beef Vegetable Soup
Fresh Bread or Biscuits
Pie

Beef Barley Soup

Michelle Showalter
Bridgewater, VA

Makes 10-12 servings

1 lb. ground beef, browned
1½ qts. water
1 qt. canned tomatoes, stewed, crushed, or
  whole
3 cups sliced carrots
1 cup diced celery
1 cup diced potatoes
1 cup diced onions
¾ cup quick-cooking barley
3 tsp. beef bouillon granules, or 3 beef
  bouillon cubes
2-3 tsp. salt
¼ tsp. pepper

   1. Combine ingredients in slow cooker.
   2. Cover. Cook on low 8-10 hours or high
4-5 hours.
   3. Serve with fresh bread and cheese cubes.

*Variation: You may use pearl barley instead of
quick-cooking barley. Cook it according to
package directions and add halfway through
cooking time of soup.*

Easy Vegetable Soup

Dawn Day
Westminster, CA

Makes 6-8 servings

4 cups vegetable, beef, or chicken stock
4 cups vegetables (use any or all of corn,
  peas, carrots, broccoli, green beans,
  cauliflower, mushrooms), either fresh or
  frozen
leftover meat, cut in small pieces, or 1 lb.
  cubed beef, browned in oil in skillet
15-oz. can chopped tomatoes
1 bay leaf
¼ cup uncooked rice or barley,
  or ½ cup cooked orzo or small shells

   1. Combine all ingredients in slow cooker
except pasta.
   2. Cover. Cook on low 6 hours, adding pasta
½ hour before serving.
   3. Serve with rolls and a salad for a great
comfort meal.

Everyone's Hungry Soup

Janie Steele
Moore, OK

Makes 20-25 servings

6 thick slices bacon
3 lbs. boneless beef stewing meat, cubed
1 lb. boneless pork, cubed
3 14.5-oz. cans tomatoes
10-oz. can rotel tomatoes and chilies
3 celery ribs, chopped
3 large onions, chopped
garlic to taste
salt to taste
pepper to taste
1/2 cup Worcestershire sauce
2 Tbsp. chili powder
2 cups water
6-8 medium potatoes, peeled and cubed
1 lb. carrots, sliced
15-oz. can English peas, undrained
14 1/2-oz. can green beans, undrained
15.25-oz. can corn, undrained
1 lb. cut-up okra, optional

1. Fry bacon in skillet until crisp. Remove bacon, but reserve drippings. Crumble bacon and divide between 2 large (6 qt. or larger) slow cookers.
2. Brown stewing beef and pork in skillet in bacon drippings.
3. Combine all ingredients and divide between slow cookers.
4. Cover. Cook on low 8-10 hours.
5. Serve with loaves of homemade bread or pans of cornbread.

Hamburger Sausage Soup

Esther Becker
Gordonville, PA

Makes 4-6 servings

1 lb. ground beef
1 lb. Polish sausage, sliced
1/2 tsp. seasoning salt
1/4 tsp. dried oregano
1/4 tsp. dried basil
1 pkg. dry onion soup mix
6 cups boiling water
16-oz. can diced tomatoes
1 Tbsp. soy sauce
1/2 cup sliced celery
1/4 cup chopped celery leaves
1 cup pared, sliced carrots
1 cup uncooked macaroni

1. Brown ground beef and sausage in skillet. Drain. Place in slow cooker.
2. Add seasoning salt, oregano, basil, and onion soup mix to cooker.
3. Stir in boiling water, tomatoes, and soy sauce.
4. Add celery, celery leaves, and carrots. Stir well.
5. Cover. Cook on low 8-10 hours.
6. One hour before end of cooking time, stir in dry macaroni.
7. Serve with cornbread or corn muffins.

Hosting Idea

A simple meal of a tasty soup and a few other make-ahead items sets an atmosphere for relaxed hosting. Setting the table with my best china, in spite of the simplicity of the meal, helps to make the event special.
—Esther Becker

Delicious Sausage Soup

Karen Waggoner
Joplin, MO

Makes 4 servings

5½ cups chicken broth
½ cup heavy cream
3 carrots, grated
4 potatoes, sliced or cubed
4 cups kale, chopped
1 lb. spicy Italian sausage, browned
½ tsp. salt
½ tsp. crushed red pepper flakes

1. Combine broth and cream in slow cooker. Turn on high.
2. Add carrots, potatoes, kale, and sausage.
3. Sprinkle spices over top.
4. Cover. Cook on high 4-5 hours, stirring occasionally.

Spicy Sausage Soup

Janie Steele
Moore, OK

Makes 8-10 servings

1 lb. ground beef
1 lb. bulk spicy sausage (casings removed)
half a large onion, chopped
2 cups chopped carrots
2 cups chopped celery
1 green or red bell pepper, chopped, optional
2 tsp. salt, or to taste
¼ tsp. pepper, or to taste
1 tsp. dried oregano, or to taste
2 or 3 garlic cloves, minced
14½-oz. can stewed tomatoes with chilies
14½-oz. can green beans
¼ tsp. chili powder
1 cup instant rice, uncooked

1. Combine beef, sausage, and onions. Form into balls. Place in slow cooker.
2. Add all remaining ingredients, except rice. Stir gently so as not to break up the meatballs.
3. Cover. Cook on low 6-8 hours. Stir in rice 20 minutes before serving.
4. Serve with rolls or cornbread.

Sauerkraut-Sausage Bean Soup

Bonnie Goering
Bridgewater, VA

Makes 8-10 servings

3 15-oz. cans white beans, undrained
16-oz. can sauerkraut, drained and rinsed
1 lb. link sausage, sliced
1/4 cup brown sugar
1/2 cup ketchup

1. Combine all ingredients in slow cooker.
2. Cover. Cook on high 2-3 hours.
3. Serve with cornbread, applesauce, or coleslaw.

Note: You may add tomato juice or water if you prefer a thinner soup.

Pixie's Chicken Stew

Janice Muller
Derwood, MD

Makes 8-10 servings

2-3-lb. chicken
2 qts. water
1 pkg. dry chicken noodle soup
2 chicken bouillon cubes
15-oz. can whole-kernel corn, undrained
1 Tbsp. onion flakes
1/2 tsp. dried thyme, or according to your taste preference

1. Place chicken in slow cooker. Add water.
2. Cover. Cook on high 3-4 hours. Cool.
3. Strain liquid into container and save. Debone chicken. Return cut-up meat and strained broth to slow cooker.
4. Stir in remaining ingredients.
5. Cover. Cook on high 2 hours.

Note: I make this a day ahead so that it can sit overnight in the refrigerator making it easier to skim fat off the top.

Pixie would invite friends in for soup after long walks in the snow. She always served this with fresh bread in front of a roaring fire. Pixie finished these meals by offering us a plate of chocolate fudge. Life couldn't get any better.

Chicken Noodle Soup

Jennifer J. Gehman
Harrisburg, PA

Makes 6-8 servings

2 cups cubed chicken
15 1/4-oz. can corn, or 2 cups frozen corn
1 cup frozen peas or green beans
10 cups water
10-12 chicken bouillon cubes
3 Tbsp. bacon drippings
1/2 pkg. dry Kluski (or other very sturdy) noodles

1. Combine all ingredients except noodles in slow cooker.
2. Cover. Cook on high 4-6 hours or low 6-8 hours. Add noodles during last 2 hours.
3. Serve with potato rolls and butter or grilled cheese sandwiches.

Santa Fe Chicken Soup

Sherry Conyers
McPherson, KS

Makes 6-8 servings

4 whole chicken breasts, cooked and
   shredded
1 small onion, diced
15¼-oz. can whole-kernel corn, undrained
24-oz. can pinto beans, undrained
14½-oz. can diced tomatoes, undrained
10-oz. can rotel tomatoes, undrained
½ lb. mild Velveeta cheese, cubed
½ lb. regular Velveeta cheese, cubed
¼ cup milk

  1. Place chicken and onions in slow cooker.
  2. Add corn, beans, tomatoes, cubed cheese,
and milk.
  3. Cover. Cook on low 3-4 hours, or until
cheese is melted. Try not to let soup boil.

Matzoh Ball Soup

Audrey Romonosky
Austin, TX

Makes 6 servings

2 eggs
2 Tbsp. oil
2 Tbsp. water
½ cup matzoh meal*
1 tsp. salt, optional
1½ qts. water
32-oz. can chicken broth

  1. Lightly beat eggs, oil, and 2 Tbsp. water
together.
  2. Add matzoh meal and salt. Mix well.
  3. Cover and refrigerate for 20 minutes.
  4. Bring 1½ qts. water to boil in saucepan.
  5. Wet hands. Roll matzoh mixture into
1" balls. Drop into boiling water and cook for
20 minutes. Remove from water. (Cooked balls
can be stored in refrigerator for up to 2 days.)
  6. Pour chicken broth into slow cooker. Add
matzoh balls.
  7. Cover. Cook on high 2-3 hours or on low
5-6 hours.

* Finely crushed matzoh may be substituted.

*I made this soup for an ethnic luncheon at
work. Everyone enjoyed it. Matzoh ball soup is
traditionally served on the Jewish holiday of
Passover. It is also known as "Jewish penicillin,"
and I make it all year-round.*

Lidia's Egg Drop Soup

Shirley Unternahrer Hinh
Wayland, IA

Makes 8 servings

2 14 1/2-oz. cans chicken broth
1 qt. water
2 Tbsp. fish sauce
1/4 tsp. salt
4 Tbsp. cornstarch
1 cup cold water
2 eggs, beaten
1 chopped green onion
pepper to taste

1. Combine broth and water in large saucepan.
2. Add fish sauce and salt. Bring to boil.
3. Mix cornstarch into cold water until smooth. Add to soup. Bring to boil while stirring. Remove from heat.
4. Pour beaten eggs into thickened broth, but do not stir. Instead, pull fork through soup with 2 strokes.
5. Transfer to slow cooker. Add green onions and pepper.
6. Cover. Cook on low 1 hour. Keep warm in cooker.
7. Eat plain or with rice.

One day when the kids were sledding I surprised them with something other than hot cocoa when they came in. "Mmmmm," was all I heard, and, "This tastes great!" "You're the best, Mom!" They finished all the egg drop soup and wondered if I'd make more.

Buffalo Chicken Wing Soup

Anna Stoltzfus
Honey Brook, PA

Makes 8 servings

6 cups milk
3 10 3/4-oz. cans cream of chicken soup
3 cups shredded cooked chicken
1 cup sour cream
1/4-1/2 cup hot pepper sauce (or if you're timid, use 2 Tbsp.)

1. Combine ingredients in slow cooker.
2. Cover. Cook on low 4-5 hours.

White Chicken Chili

Jewel Showalter
Landisville, PA

Makes 6-8 servings

2 whole skinless chicken breasts
6 cups water
2 chopped onions
2 garlic cloves, minced
1 Tbsp. oil
2-4 4-oz. cans chopped green chilies
1-2 diced jalapeno peppers
2 tsp. ground cumin
1 1/2 tsp. dried oregano
1/4 tsp. cayenne pepper
1/2 tsp. salt
3-lb. can navy beans, undrained
1-2 cups shredded cheese
sour cream
salsa

1. Place chicken in slow cooker. Add 6 cups water.

2. Cover. Cook on low 3-4 hours, or until tender.

3. Remove chicken from slow cooker. Cube and set aside.

4. Saute onions and garlic in oil in skillet. Add chilies, jalapeno peppers, cumin, oregano, pepper, and salt. Saute 2 minutes. Transfer to broth in slow cooker.

5. Add navy beans.

6. Cover. Cook on low 30-60 minutes.

7. Right before serving add chicken and cheese.

8. Serve topped with sour cream and salsa. Cornbread or corn chips are good go-alongs with this chili.

Variation: If you want to use dried beans, use 3 cups navy beans and cover with water in saucepan, soaking overnight. In the morning, drain and cover with fresh water. Cook in saucepan on low 7-8 hours, or until tender. Drain of excess moisture and stir into chicken and broth.

White Chili

Rebecca Plank Leichty
Harrisonburg, VA

Makes 6-8 servings

15-oz. can chickpeas or garbanzo beans, undrained
15-oz. can small Northern beans, undrained
15-oz. can pinto beans, undrained
1 qt. frozen corn, or 2 1-lb. bags frozen corn
1½ cups shredded cooked chicken
2 Tbsp. minced onion
1 red bell pepper, diced
3 tsp. minced garlic
3 tsp. ground cumin
½ tsp. salt
½ tsp. dried oregano
2 15-oz. cans chicken broth

1. Combine all ingredients in slow cooker.

2. Cover. Cook on low 8-10 hours, or high 4-5 hours.

3. Serve with warmed tortilla chips topped with melted cheddar cheese

Variations: For more zip, add 2 tsp. chili powder, or one or more chopped jalapeno peppers, to Step 1.

Pumpkin Black-Bean Turkey Chili

Rhoda Atzeff
Harrisburg, PA

Makes 10-12 servings

1 cup chopped onions
1 cup chopped yellow bell pepper
3 garlic cloves, minced
2 Tbsp. oil
1½ tsp. dried oregano
1½-2 tsp. ground cumin
2 tsp. chili powder
2 15-oz. cans black beans, rinsed and drained
2½ cups chopped cooked turkey
16-oz. can pumpkin
14½-oz. can diced tomatoes
3 cups chicken broth

1. Saute onions, yellow pepper, and garlic in oil for 8 minutes, or until soft.

2. Stir in oregano, cumin, and chili powder. Cook 1 minute. Transfer to slow cooker.

3. Add remaining ingredients.

4. Cover. Cook on low 7-8 hours.

Turkey Chili

Reita F. Yoder
Carlsbad, NM

Makes 6-8 servings

2 lbs. ground turkey
16-oz. can pinto, or kidney, beans
2 cups fresh or canned tomatoes, chopped
2 cups tomato sauce
1 garlic clove, minced
1 small onion, chopped
16-oz. can rotel tomatoes
1-oz. pkg. Williams chili seasoning

1. Crumble ground turkey in bottom of slow cooker.
2. Add remaining ingredients. Mix well.
3. Cover. Cook on low 6-8 hours.

Chilly-Chili

Alix Nancy Botsford
Seminole, OK

Makes 6-8 servings

2 cups dried beans
1 tsp. salt
2 Tbsp. olive oil
1 large onion, chopped
1 lb. ground turkey
2 tsp. minced garlic
oil
1 tsp. salt
2 celery ribs, chopped
1 green pepper, diced
10-oz. can tomatoes and green chilies

1. Sort, wash, and cover beans with water. Soak 6-8 hours. Drain.

2. Place beans in slow cooker. Cover with fresh water. Add 1 tsp. salt.
3. Cover. Cook on high 2-3 hours, or until a bean can be crushed with a fork. Drain off all but 1-2 cups liquid.
4. Brown onion, turkey, and garlic in oil in skillet. Add 1 tsp. salt, celery, and green pepper. Cook until vegetables have started to soften. Add tomatoes. Place in slow cooker.
5. Cover. Cook on low 1-8 hours.
6. Serve with slices of cheese and crackers.

This is a good meal for guests—or when we're all working outdoors and need our meal to be ready when we come in, like early spring when we're getting the garden ready.

Three-Bean Chili

Chris Kaczynski
Schenectady, NY

Makes 8-10 servings

2 lbs. ground beef
2 medium onions, diced
16-oz. jar medium salsa
2 pkgs. dry chili seasoning
2 16-oz. cans red kidney beans, drained
2 16-oz. cans black beans, drained
2 16-oz. cans white kidney, or garbanzo, beans drained
28-oz. can crushed tomatoes
16-oz. can diced tomatoes
2 tsp. sugar

1. Brown beef and onions in skillet.
2. Combine all ingredients in 6-qt. slow cooker, or in 2 4- or 5-qt. cookers.
3. Cover. Cook on low 8-10 hours.
4. Serve with chopped raw onion and/or shredded cheddar cheese.

Note: This recipe can be cut in half without injuring the flavor, if you don't have a cooker large enough to handle the full amount.

Hearty Chili

Joylynn Keener
Lancaster, PA

Makes 8 servings

1 onion, chopped
2 ribs celery, chopped
1 lb. ground beef
2 14-oz. cans kidney beans, undrained
14-oz. can pinto beans, undrained
14-oz. can diced tomatoes
2 14-oz. cans tomato sauce
1 green pepper, chopped
1 Tbsp. sugar
1 tsp. salt
1 tsp. dried thyme
1 tsp. dried oregano
1 Tbsp. chili powder, or to taste

1. Brown onion, celery, and beef in skillet. Pour into slow cooker.
2. Add remaining ingredients. Mix well.
3. Cover. Cook on low 8 hours.

Slow-Cooker Chili

Kay Magruder
Seminole, OK

Makes 8-10 servings

3 lbs. stewing meat, browned
2 cloves garlic, minced
1/4 tsp. pepper
1/2 tsp. cumin
1/4 tsp. dry mustard
71/2-oz. can jalapeno relish
1 cup beef broth
1-11/2 onions, chopped, according to your taste preference
1/2 tsp. salt
1/2 tsp. dried oregano
1 Tbsp. chili powder
7-oz. can green chilies, chopped
141/2-oz. can stewed tomatoes, chopped
15-oz. can tomato sauce
2 15-oz. cans red kidney beans, rinsed and drained
2 15-oz. cans pinto beans, rinsed and drained

1. Combine all ingredients except kidney and pinto beans in slow cooker.
2. Cover. Cook on low 10-12 hours or on high 6-7 hours. Add beans halfway through cooking time.
3. Serve with Mexican cornbread.

So-Easy Chili

Sue Graber
Eureka, IL

Makes 4 servings

1 lb. ground beef
1 onion, chopped
15-oz. can chili, with or without beans
14.5-oz. can diced tomatoes with green chilies, or with basil, garlic, and oregano
1 cup tomato juice
chopped onion
grated cheddar cheese

1. Brown ground beef and onion in skillet. Drain and put in slow cooker.
2. Add chili, diced tomatoes, and tomato juice.
3. Cover. Cook on low 4-6 hours.
4. Serve with onion and cheese on top of each individual serving.

Note: This chili is of a good consistency for serving over rice. For a thicker chili, add 4-6 ozs. tomato paste 20 minutes before end of cooking time.

Extra Easy Chili

Jennifer Gehman
Harrisburg, PA

Makes 4-6 servings

1 lb. ground beef or turkey, uncooked
1 pkg. dry chili seasoning mix
16-oz. can chili beans in sauce
2 28-oz. cans crushed or diced tomatoes seasoned with garlic and onion

1. Crumble meat in bottom of slow cooker.
2. Add remaining ingredients. Stir.
3. Cover. Cook on high 4-6 hours or low 6-8 hours. Stir halfway through cooking time.
4. Serve over white rice, topped with shredded cheddar cheese and chopped raw onions.

I decided to make this chili recipe one year for Christmas. Our family was hosting other family members—and we had had guests for about a week prior to Christmas. Needless to say, I was tired of cooking so this seemed easy enough. It was so nice to put the ingredients in the slow cooker and let it cook all day long. Not only did the chili warm us up on a cold day, but it was a welcomed change from the traditional Christmas meal. It has been my tradition ever since!

Menu Idea

Extra Easy Chili
Baked Potatoes
Buttered Macaronis
Cornbread Muffins

Grandma's Chili

Beverly (Flatt) Getz
Warriors Mark, PA

Makes 8 servings

1 large onion, chopped
2 lbs. ground beef
28-oz. can stewed tomatoes
16-oz. can dark kidney beans, undrained
15-oz. can Hormel chili with beans
10¾-oz. can tomato soup
1 tsp. K.C. Masterpiece BBQ sauce
¼ tsp. garlic salt
¼ tsp. garlic powder
¼ tsp. onion salt
¼ tsp. chili powder
pinch of sugar

1. Brown onion and beef in skillet, leaving meat in larger chunks. Place in slow cooker.

2. Add remaining ingredients. Stir.

3. Cover. Cook on high 4 hours.

4. Serve with crackers, rolls, butter, and apple crisp with whipped topping.

When the grandchildren come to visit from five different states, they always ask for Grandma's Chili. I just made up the recipe. Now I'm afraid to change it!

Chili Soup

Fannie Miller
Hutchinson, KS

Makes 12-15 servings

4 lbs. ground beef
1 large onion, diced
2 cups cold water
2 Tbsp. brown sugar
2 Tbsp. chili powder
2 tsp. salt
2 tsp. dried oregano
1/2 tsp. garlic salt
1/4 tsp. ground coriander

1. Brown hamburger and onion in skillet. Drain and transfer to slow cooker.

2. Add remaining ingredients. Mix well.

3. Cover. Cook on low 4-6 hours.

Our Favorite Chili

Ruth Shank
Gridley, IL

Makes 10-12 servings

1 1/2 lbs. ground beef
1/4 cup chopped onions
1 rib celery, chopped
29-oz. can stewed tomatoes
2 15.5-oz. cans red kidney beans, undrained
2 16-oz. cans chili beans, undrained
1/2 cup ketchup
1 1/2 tsp. lemon juice
2 tsp. vinegar
1 1/2 tsp. brown sugar
1 1/2 tsp. salt
1 tsp. Worcestershire sauce
1/2 tsp. garlic powder
1/2 tsp. dry mustard powder
1 Tbsp. chili powder
2 6-oz. cans tomato paste

1. Brown ground beef, onions, and celery in skillet. Drain. Place in slow cooker.

2. Add remaining ingredients. Mix well.

3. Cover. Cook on low 8-10 hours or high 4-5 hours.

4. Serve with fresh warm cornbread and slices of Colby or Monterey Jack cheese.

Slow-Cooked Chili

Jean A. Shaner
York, PA

Makes 10 servings

2 lbs. ground beef, browned
2 16-oz. cans kidney beans, rinsed and
  drained
2 14½-oz. cans diced tomatoes
8-oz. can tomato sauce
2 onions, chopped
1 green pepper, chopped
2 garlic cloves, minced
2 Tbsp. chili powder
2 tsp. salt
1 tsp. pepper
shredded cheddar cheese

1. Combine all ingredients except cheese in slow cooker.
2. Cover. Cook on low 8-10 hours.
3. Ladle chili into individual bowls and top with cheese just before serving.

Chili Soup

Glenna Fay Bergey
Lebanon, OR

Makes 5 quarts

3 lbs. ground beef
¾ cup chopped onions
2 Tbsp. celery flakes
2 tsp. salt
1 Tbsp. chili powder, or more, according to
  taste
3 15-oz. cans kidney beans
1 qt. tomato juice
2 10¾-oz. cans tomato soup
1 cup ketchup
¼ cup brown sugar

1. Brown meat, onions, and seasonings in large skillet. Transfer to large bowl and stir in remaining ingredients.
2. Divide between 2 4- or 5-qt. slow cookers (this is a large recipe!).
3. Cover. Cook on high 2 hours or low 4-6 hours.
4. Serve with cornbread.

Country Auction Chili Soup

Clara Newswanger
Gordonville, PA

Makes 20 servings

1½ lbs. ground beef
¼ cup chopped onions
½ cup flour
1 Tbsp. chili powder
1 tsp. salt
6 cups water
2 cups ketchup
⅓ cup brown sugar
3 15.5-oz. cans kidney beans, undrained

1. Brown ground beef and onions in skillet. Drain. Spoon meat mixture into slow cooker.
2. Stir flour into meat and onions. Add seasonings.
3. Slowly stir in water. Add ketchup, brown sugar, and beans.
4. Cover. Cook on high 4 hours or low 8 hours.

The Chili Connection

Anne Townsend
Albuquerque, NM

Makes 6 servings

1½ lbs. ground beef
1 cup chopped onions
28-oz. can tomatoes, chopped
15-oz. can kidney beans, undrained
1 Tbsp. brown or granulated sugar
2-4 tsp. chili powder, according to your taste preference
1 tsp. salt

1. Brown ground beef and onions in skillet.
2. Combine all ingredients in slow cooker.
3. Cover. Cook on low 3-5 hours.

Variation: In order to have a thicker chili, stir in a 6-oz. can of tomato paste in Step 2.

Notes:
1. *An assortment of toppings can take the place of a salad with this chili. I usually offer chopped onions, tomatoes, grated cheddar cheese, picante sauce, and, when avocados are in season, guacamole. Cornbread or refrigerated twist rolls sprinkled with garlic salt are delicious. Either chocolate or apple cake with ice cream makes a happy ending.*

2. *This is a fun informal party dish which connects the guests as they get involved in selecting their favorite toppings.*

3. *As a frequently enjoyed dish, this recipe has stood the test of time. Our children thought it was delicious when they were young and now they enjoy preparing it for their own families.*

Hot and Good Chili

Rose Hankins
Stevensville, MD

Makes 12 servings

1 lb. ground beef
1 cup chopped onions
1 cup chopped celery
1 cup chopped green peppers
28-oz. can tomatoes
14-oz. can tomato sauce
2 14-oz. cans kidney beans, undrained
2 Tbsp. chili powder
1 Tbsp. garlic powder
1 Tbsp. hot sauce

1. Brown beef in skillet. Reserve drippings and transfer drained beef to slow cooker.
2. Saute onions, celery, and green peppers in drippings. Drain and transfer to slow cooker.
3. Stir in remaining ingredients.
4. Cover. Cook on high 4-5 hours or on low 8-10 hours.

Slowly Cooked Chili

Beatrice Martin
Goshen, IN

Makes 6-8 servings

2 lbs. ground beef or turkey, browned in skillet
15½-oz. can kidney beans, undrained
3 cups tomato juice
3 Tbsp. chili powder
1 tsp. minced garlic
1 pkg. dry onion soup mix
½-1 tsp. salt, according to taste
¼ tsp. pepper

1. Combine all ingredients in slow cooker.
2. Cover. Cook on low 10-12 hours or on high 5-6 hours.
3. Serve in soup bowls with crackers, or over rice.

Note: This chili freezes well.

Hearty Potato Chili

Janice Muller
Derwood, MD

Makes 8 servings

1 lb. ground beef
½ cup chopped onions, or 2 Tbsp. dried minced onions
½ cup chopped green peppers
1 Tbsp. poppy seeds (optional)
1 tsp. salt
½ tsp. chili powder
1 pkg. au gratin or scalloped potato mix
1 cup hot water
15-oz. can kidney beans, undrained
16-oz. can stewed tomatoes
4-oz. can mushroom pieces, undrained

1. Brown ground beef in skillet. Remove meat and place in slow cooker. Saute onions and green peppers in drippings until softened.
2. Combine all ingredients in slow cooker.
3. Cover. Cook on high 4 hours, or until liquid is absorbed and potatoes are tender.

Spicy Chili
Deborah Swartz
Grottoes, VA

Makes 4-6 servings

½ lb. sausage, either cut in thin slices or
   removed from casings
½ lb. ground beef
½ cup chopped onions
½ lb. fresh mushrooms, sliced
⅛ cup chopped celery
⅛ cup chopped green peppers
1 cup salsa
16-oz. can tomato juice
6-oz. can tomato paste
½ tsp. sugar
½ tsp. salt
½ tsp. dried oregano
½ tsp. Worcestershire sauce
¼ tsp. dried basil
¼ tsp. pepper

1. Brown sausage, ground beef, and onion
in skillet. During last 3 minutes of browning,
add mushrooms, celery, and green peppers.
Continue cooking; then drain.

2. Add remaining ingredients. Pour into
slow cooker.

3. Cover. Cook on high 2-3 hours.

Variations:
Add any or all of the following to Step 2:
   1 tsp. chili powder
   1 tsp. ground cumin
   15-oz. can black beans, undrained
   15-oz. can whole-kernel corn,
      undrained

M&T's Chili
Sherry Conyers
McPherson, KS

Makes 4 servings

1 lb. ground beef, browned
½ lb. sausage links, sliced and browned
1 pkg. Williams chili seasoning
2 10-oz. cans Mexican tomatoes
15-oz. can chili with no beans
2 10-oz. cans rotel tomatoes
1-lb. can refried beans
¼ cup diced onions

1. Combine ingredients in slow cooker.
2. Cover. Cook on low 5-6 hours.

*Variations: If you want a soupier, and less spicy,
chili, add a 1-lb. can of stewed tomatoes or 2 cups
tomato juice.*

Wintertime Vegetable Chili

Maricarol Magill
Freehold, NJ

Makes 6 servings

1 medium butternut squash, peeled and
   cubed
2 medium carrots, peeled and diced
1 medium onion, diced
3 tsp.—3 Tbsp. chili powder, depending
   upon how hot you like your chili
2 14-oz. cans diced tomatoes
4-oz. can chopped mild green chilies
1 tsp. salt, optional
1 cup vegetable broth
2 16-oz. cans black beans, drained and
   rinsed
sour cream, optional

1. In slow cooker, layer ingredients in order
given—except sour cream.
2. Cover. Cook on low 6-8 hours, or until
vegetables are tender.
3. Stir before serving.
4. Top individual servings with dollops of
sour cream.
5. Serve with crusty French bread.

Black Bean Chili Con Carne

Janie Steele
Moore, OK

Makes 18 1-cup servings

1 lb. black beans
3 lbs. ground beef
oil, if needed
2 large onions, chopped
1 green pepper, chopped
3 cloves garlic, minced
2 tsp. salt
1 tsp. pepper
6-oz. can tomato paste
3 cups tomato juice, or more
1 tsp. celery salt
1 Tbsp. Worcestershire sauce
1 tsp. dry mustard
cayenne pepper to taste
cumin to taste
3 Tbsp. chili powder

1. Soak beans 8 hours or overnight. Rinse
and drain.
2. Brown ground beef in batches in large
skillet, in oil if needed.
3. Combine all ingredients in 6-qt. or larger
slow cooker, or divide between 2 smaller
cookers.
4. Cover. Cook on low 8 hours.
5. Serve over salad greens or wrapped in
tortillas, topped with lettuce and grated cheese.

Norma's Vegetarian Chili
Kathy Hertzler
Lancaster, PA

Makes 8-10 servings

2 Tbsp. oil
2 cups minced celery
1½ cups chopped green pepper
1 cup minced onions
4 garlic cloves, minced
5½ cups stewed tomatoes
2 1-lb. cans kidney beans, undrained
1½-2 cups raisins
¼ cup wine vinegar
1 Tbsp. chopped parsley
2 tsp. salt
1½ tsp. dried oregano
1½ tsp. cumin
¼ tsp. pepper
¼ tsp. Tabasco sauce
1 bay leaf
¾ cup cashews
1 cup grated cheese, optional

1. Combine all ingredients except cashews and cheese in slow cooker.
2. Cover. Simmer on low for 8 hours. Add cashews and simmer 30 minutes.
3. Garnish individual servings with grated cheese.

Menu Idea

Norma's Vegetarian Chili
Cornbread
Plate of Crudites
Chocolate Chip Cookies

Easy Cheese Soup
Nancy Wagner Graves
Manhattan, KS

Makes 4 servings

2 10¾-oz. cans cream of mushroom or cream of chicken soup
1 cup beer or milk
1 lb. cheddar cheese, grated
1 tsp. Worcestershire sauce
¼ tsp. paprika
croutons

1. Combine all ingredients except croutons in slow cooker.
2. Cover. Cook on low 4-6 hours.
3. Stir thoroughly 1 hour before serving, to make sure cheese is well distributed and melted.
4. Serve topped with croutons or in bread bowls.

Wonderful Clam Chowder

Carlene Horne
Bedford, NH

Makes 4-6 servings

2 12-oz. cans evaporated milk
1 evaporated milk can of water
2 6-oz. cans whole clams, undrained
6-oz. can minced clams, undrained
1 small onion, chopped
2 small potatoes, diced
2 Tbsp. cornstarch
1/4 cup water

1. Combine all ingredients except cornstarch and 1/4 cup water in slow cooker.

2. Cover. Cook on low 6-7 hours.

3. One hour before end of cooking time, mix cornstarch and 1/4 cup water together. When smooth, stir into soup. Stir until soup thickens.

Clam Chowder

Ruth Shank
Gridley, IL

Makes 8-12 servings

2 10³/4-oz. cans cream of potato soup
10³/4-oz. can cream of celery soup
2 6¹/2-oz. cans minced clams, drained
3 slices bacon, diced and fried
1 soup can of water
1 small onion, minced
1 Tbsp. fresh parsley
dash of dried marjoram
1 Tbsp. Worcestershire sauce
pepper to taste
2 soup cans of milk

1. Combine all ingredients, except 2 soup cans of milk, in slow cooker.

2. Cover. Cook on low 6-8 hours.

3. Twenty minutes before end of cooking time, stir in milk. Continue cooking until heated through.

Vegetables

Easy Flavor-Filled Green Beans

Paula Showalter
Weyers Cave, VA

Makes 10 servings

2 qts. green beans, drained
1/3 cup chopped onions
4-oz. can mushrooms, drained
2 Tbsp. brown sugar
3 Tbsp. butter
pepper to taste

1. Combine beans, onions, and mushrooms in slow cooker.
2. Sprinkle with brown sugar.
3. Dot with butter.
4. Sprinkle with pepper.
5. Cover. Cook on high 3-4 hours. Stir just before serving.

Green Bean Casserole

Brenda S. Burkholder
Port Republic, VA

Makes 6-8 servings

1 qt. cooked green beans
1/2 tsp. sugar
10¾-oz. can cream of mushroom soup
¾ cup grated cheddar cheese

1. Combine ingredients in slow cooker.
2. Cover. Cook on low 3-4 hours.

If I ask my husband what to make for a company meal, he quite frequently asks for these beans.

189

Green Bean Casserole

Mary Sommerfeld
Lancaster, PA

Makes 6 servings

2 lbs. fresh green beans, cut up,
   or 4 10-oz. pkgs. frozen beans
10³/4-oz. can cream of mushroom soup
3-oz. can French-fried onion rings
1 cup grated cheddar cheese
8-oz. can water chestnuts, thinly sliced
slivered almonds, optional
salt to taste
pepper to taste
1 cup water

1. In slow cooker, layer one-third of ingredients, except water, in order given. Repeat 2 times, saving a few onion rings for top.
2. Pour water into slow cooker.
3. Cover. Cook on high 4-5 hours or on low 8-10 hours. Sprinkle reserved onion rings on top 20 minutes before serving.

Green Bean Casserole

Jane Meiser
Harrisonburg, VA

Makes 4-5 servings

14¹/2-oz. can green beans, drained
3¹/2-oz. can French fried onions
1 cup grated cheddar cheese
8-oz. can water chestnuts, drained
10³/4-oz. can cream of chicken soup
¹/4 cup white wine or water
¹/2 tsp. curry powder
¹/4 tsp. pepper

1. Alternate layers of half the beans, half the onions, half the cheese, and half the water chestnuts in slow cooker. Repeat.
2. Combine remaining ingredients. Pour over vegetables in slow cooker.
3. Cover. Cook on low 6-7 hours or high 3-4 hours.

Green Bean Casserole

Vicki Dinkel
Sharon Springs, KS

Makes 9-11 servings

3 10-oz. pkgs. frozen, cut green beans
2 10¹/2-oz. cans cheddar cheese soup
¹/2 cup water
¹/4 cup chopped green onions
4-oz. can sliced mushrooms, drained
8-oz. can water chestnuts, drained and
   sliced (optional)
¹/2 cup slivered almonds
1 tsp. salt
¹/4 tsp. pepper

1. Combine all ingredients in lightly greased slow cooker. Mix well.
2. Cover. Cook on low 8-10 hours or on high 3-4 hours.

Creamy Cheesy Bean Casserole

Martha Hershey
Ronks, PA

Makes 5 servings

16-oz. bag frozen green beans, cooked
3/4 cup milk
1 cup grated American cheese
2 slices bread, crumbled

1. Place beans in slow cooker.
2. Combine milk and cheese in saucepan. Heat, stirring continually, until cheese melts. Fold in bread cubes and pour mixture over beans.
3. Cover. Heat on high 2 hours.

Variation: Use 15-oz. container of Cheez Whiz instead of making cheese sauce. Mix crumbled bread into Cheez Whiz and pour over beans. Proceed with Step 3.

Au Gratin Green Beans

Donna Lantgen
Rapid City, SD

Makes 8 servings

2 16-oz. cans green beans, drained
1/4 cup diced onions
1/2 cup cubed Velveeta cheese
1/4 cup evaporated milk
1 tsp. flour
1/2 tsp. salt
dash of pepper

1. Combine all ingredients in slow cooker.
2. Cover. Cook on low 4 hours.
3. Garnish with sliced almonds at serving time, if you wish.

Green Bean Casserole

Darla Sathre
Baxter, MN

Makes 8 servings

4 14 1/2-oz. cans French-style green beans, drained
2 10 3/4-oz. cans cream of celery soup
6-oz. can French-fried onion rings
2 cups shredded cheddar cheese
2 tsp. dried basil
5-oz. can evaporated milk

1. In greased slow cooker, layer half of each ingredient, except milk, in order given. Repeat. Pour milk over all.
2. Cover. Cook on low 6-10 hours.

Super Creamed Corn

Ruth Ann Penner
Hillsboro, KS

Alix Nancy Botsford
Seminole, OK

Makes 8-12 servings

2-3 lbs. frozen corn
8-oz. pkg. cream cheese, cubed
1/4 cup butter or margarine, melted
2-3 Tbsp. sugar or honey
2-3 Tbsp. water, optional

1. Combine ingredients in slow cooker.
2. Cover. Cook on low 4 hours.
3. Serve with meat loaf, turkey, or hamburgers.

A great addition to a holiday that is easy and requires no last-minute preparation. It also frees the stove and oven for other food preparation.

Corn Pudding

Lizzie Weaver
Ephrata, PA

Makes 3-4 servings

2 eggs, beaten slightly
1/4 cup sugar
1 tsp. salt
1/8 tsp. pepper
2 Tbsp. melted butter
2 Tbsp. flour
1/2 cup milk
16-oz. can cream-style corn

1. Combine all ingredients except corn. Pour into slow cooker.
2. Add corn. Mix well.
3. Cover. Cook on low 4 hours.

Variation: Add 1/2 cup grated cheese to Step 2.
—Brenda S. Burkholder, Port Republic, VA

This recipe frees your oven space for other dishes. It's perfect, too, for Sunday lunch if you've been gone all morning.

Baked Corn

Velma Stauffer
Akron, PA

Makes 8 servings

1 qt. corn, frozen or fresh
2 eggs, beaten
1 tsp. salt
1 cup milk
1/8 tsp. pepper
2 tsp. oil
3 Tbsp. sugar
3 Tbsp. flour

1. Combine all ingredients well. Pour into greased slow cooker.
2. Cover. Cook on high 3 hours and then on low 45 minutes.

Note: If you use home-grown sweet corn, you could reduce the amount of sugar.

Scalloped Corn

Rebecca Plank Leichty
Harrisonburg, VA

Makes 6 servings

2 eggs
10³/4-oz. can cream of celery soup
²/3 cup unseasoned bread crumbs
2 cups whole-kernel corn, drained, or
   cream-style corn
1 tsp. minced onion
1/4-1/2 tsp. salt, according to your taste
   preference
1/8 tsp. pepper
1 Tbsp. sugar
2 Tbsp. melted butter

1. Beat eggs with fork. Add soup and bread crumbs. Mix well.
2. Add remaining ingredients and mix thoroughly. Pour into greased slow cooker.
3. Cover. Cook on high 3 hours or on low 6 hours.

Hosting Idea

Because not all guests enjoy the same vegetable, I usually prepare two or three different ones. By utilizing my slow cooker for a vegetable dish, as well as the oven and stove-top, I have alot of freedom to plan and make a desirable variety.

— Rebecca Plank Leichty

Scalloped Corn and Celery

Darla Sathre
Baxter, MN

Makes 8 servings

2 16-oz. cans whole-kernel corn, drained
2 16-oz. cans cream-style corn
2 cups chopped celery
40 saltine crackers, crushed
1/8-1/4 tsp. pepper
2 Tbsp. butter
12-oz. can evaporated milk

1. Layer in greased slow cooker, half of whole-kernel corn, cream-style corn, celery, crackers, pepper, and butter. Repeat. Pour milk over all.
2. Cover. Cook on low 8-12 hours.

Baked Corn and Noodles

Ruth Hershey
Paradise, PA

Makes 6 servings

3 cups noodles, cooked al dente
2 cups fresh or frozen corn, thawed
³/4 cup grated cheddar cheese, or cubed
   Velveeta cheese
1 egg, beaten
1/2 cup butter, melted
1/2 tsp. salt

1. Combine all ingredients in slow cooker.
2. Cover. Cook on low 6-8 hours or on high 3-4 hours.

Mexican Corn

Betty K. Drescher
Quakertown, PA

Makes 8-10 servings

2 10-oz. pkgs. frozen corn, partially
   thawed
4-oz. jar chopped pimentos
1/3 cup chopped green peppers
1/3 cup water
1 tsp. salt
1/4 tsp. pepper
1/2 tsp. paprika
1/2 tsp. chili powder

1. Combine all ingredients in slow cooker.
2. Cover. Cook on high 45 minutes, then on
low 2-4 hours. Stir occasionally.

*Variations: For more fire, add 1/3 cup salsa to the
ingredients, and increase the amounts of pepper,
paprika, and chili powder to match your taste.*

Confetti Scalloped Corn

Rhoda Atzeff
Harrisburg, PA

Makes 6-8 servings

2 eggs, beaten
1 cup sour cream
1/4 cup butter or margarine, melted
1 small onion, finely chopped, or 2 Tbsp.
   dried chopped onion
11-oz. can Mexicorn, drained
14-oz. can cream-style corn
2-3 Tbsp. green jalapeno salsa, regular
   salsa, or chopped green chilies
8 1/2-oz. pkg. cornbread mix

1. Combine all ingredients. Pour into lightly
greased slow cooker.
2. Cover. Bake on high 2-2 1/2 hours, or until
corn is fully cooked.

Cornbread Casserole

Arlene Groff
Lewistown, PA

Makes 8 servings

1 qt. whole-kernel corn
1 qt. creamed corn
1 pkg. corn muffin mix
1 egg
2 Tbsp. butter
1/4 tsp. garlic powder
2 Tbsp. sugar
1/4 cup milk
1/2 tsp. salt
1/4 tsp. pepper

1. Combine ingredients in greased slow
cooker.
2. Cover. Cook on low 3 1/2-4 hours, stirring
once halfway through.

Cheesy Hominy

Michelle Showalter
Bridgewater, VA

Makes 12-14 servings

2 cups cracked hominy
6 cups water
2 Tbsp. flour
1½ cups milk
4 cups sharp cheddar cheese, grated
1-2 tsp. salt
¼ tsp. pepper
4 Tbsp. butter

1. Combine hominy and water in 5-6 qt. slow cooker.
2. Cover. Cook on high 3-4 hours or on low 6-8 hours.
3. Stir in remaining ingredients.
4. Cover. Cook 30-60 minutes.

Cheesy Hominy is a nice change if you're tired of the same old thing. It's wonderful with ham, slices of bacon, or meatballs. Add a green vegetable and you have a lovely meal. Hominy is available at bulk-food stores.

Hosting Idea

The most important thing to remember when hosting is to relax and be yourself. This will make your company feel at home.
—Michelle Showalter

Southwest Posole

Becky Harder
Monument, CO

Makes 6 servings

2 12-oz. pkgs. dry posole
1 garlic clove, minced
2 14-oz. cans vegetable or chicken broth
2 10-oz. cans rotel Mexican diced tomatoes
4-oz. can diced green chilies, optional
salt to taste

1. Soak posole for 4-8 hours. Drain water.
2. Combine ingredients in slow cooker.
3. Cover. Cook on high 3 hours; then turn to low for 2 hours.
4. Serve with enchiladas, black beans, Spanish rice, and chopped lettuce with black olives and tomatoes.

Note: Dry posole can be found in the Mexican food department of the grocery store. If you cannot find dry posole, you can used canned hominy and skip to Step 2.

Fruited Wild Rice with Pecans

Dottie Schmidt
Kansas City, MO

Makes 4 servings

1/2 cup chopped onions
2 Tbsp. margarine
6-oz. pkg. long-grain and wild rice
seasoning packet from wild rice pkg.
1 1/2 cups hot water
2/3 cup apple juice
1 large tart apple, chopped
1/4 cup raisins
1/4 cup coarsely chopped pecans

1. Combine all ingredients except pecans in greased slow cooker.
2. Cover. Cook on high 2-2 1/2 hours.
3. Stir in pecans. Serve.

Menu Idea

Grilled Chicken Breasts
Fruited Wild Rice with Pecans
Tossed Salad

Mjeddrah

Dianna Milhizer
Brighton, MI

Makes 20-24 servings

10 cups water
4 cups dried lentils, rinsed
2 cups uncooked brown rice
1/4 cup olive oil
2 tsp. salt

1. Combine ingredients in large slow cooker
2. Cover. Cook on high 8 hours, then on low 2 hours. Add 2 more cups water, if needed, to allow rice to cook and to prevent dish from drying out.
3. This is traditionally eaten with a salad with an oil-and-vinegar dressing over the lentil-rice mixture, similar to a tostada without the tortilla.

Broccoli Casserole

Dorothy Van Deest
Memphis, TN

Makes 4-6 servings

10-oz. pkg. frozen chopped broccoli
6 eggs, beaten
24-oz. carton small-curd cottage cheese
6 Tbsp. flour
8 ozs. mild cheese of your choice, diced
1/4 cup butter, melted
2 green onions, chopped
salt to taste

1. Place frozen broccoli in colander. Run cold water over it until it thaws. Separate into pieces. Drain well.
2. Combine remaining ingredients in large bowl and mix until well blended. Stir in broccoli. Pour into greased slow cooker.
3. Cover. Cook on high 1 hour. Stir well, then resume cooking on low 2-4 hours.

Quick Broccoli Fix

Willard E. Roth
Elkhart, IN

Makes 6 servings

1 lb. fresh or frozen broccoli, cut up
10³/4-oz. can cream of mushroom soup
¹/2 cup mayonnaise
¹/2 cup plain yogurt
¹/2 lb. sliced fresh mushrooms
1 cup shredded cheddar cheese, divided
1 cup crushed saltine crackers
sliced almonds, optional

1. Microwave broccoli for 3 minutes. Place in greased slow cooker.
2. Combine soup, mayonnaise, yogurt, mushrooms, and ¹/2 cup cheese. Pour over broccoli.
3. Cover. Cook on low 5-6 hours.
4. Top with remaining cheese and crackers for last half hour of cooking time.
5. Top with sliced almonds, for a special touch, before serving.

Broccoli and Rice Casserole

Deborah Swartz
Grottoes, VA

Makes 4-6 servings

1 lb. chopped broccoli, fresh or frozen, thawed
1 medium onion, chopped
¹/4 cup butter or margarine
1 cup minute rice, or 1¹/2 cups cooked rice
10³/4-oz. can cream of chicken or mushroom soup
¹/4 cup milk
1¹/3 cups Velveeta cheese, cubed, or cheddar cheese, shredded
1 tsp. salt

1. Cook broccoli for 5 minutes in saucepan in boiling water. Drain and set aside.
2. Saute onion in butter in saucepan until tender. Add to broccoli.
3. Combine remaining ingredients. Add to broccoli mixture. Pour into greased slow cooker.
4. Cover. Cook on low 3-4 hours.

Squash Medley

Evelyn Page
Riverton, WY

Makes 8 servings

8 summer squash, each about 4″ long,
   thinly sliced
1/2 tsp. salt
2 tomatoes, peeled and chopped
1/4 cup sliced green onions
half a small sweet green pepper, chopped
1 chicken bouillon cube
1/4 cup hot water
4 slices bacon, fried and crumbled
1/4 cup fine dry bread crumbs

1. Sprinkle squash with salt.
2. In slow cooker, layer half the squash, tomatoes, onions, and pepper. Repeat layers.
3. Dissolve bouillon in hot water. Pour into slow cooker.
4. Top with bacon. Sprinkle bread crumbs over top.
5. Cover. Cook on low 4-6 hours.

Variation: For a sweeter touch, sprinkle 1 Tbsp. brown sugar over half the layered vegetables. Repeat over second half of layered vegetables.

Baked Acorn Squash

Dale Peterson
Rapid City, SD

Makes 4 servings

2 acorn squash
2/3 cup cracker crumbs
1/2 cup coarsely chopped pecans
1/3 cup butter or margarine, melted
4 Tbsp. brown sugar
1/2 tsp. salt
1/4 tsp. ground nutmeg
2 Tbsp. orange juice

1. Cut squash in half. Remove seeds.
2. Combine remaining ingredients. Spoon into squash halves. Place squash in slow cooker.
3. Cover. Cook on low 5-6 hours, or until squash is tender.

Apple Walnut Squash

Michele Ruvola
Selden, NY

Makes 4 servings

1/4 cup water
2 small acorn squash
1/4 cup packed brown sugar
1/4 cup butter, melted
3 Tbsp. apple juice
1 1/2 tsp. ground cinnamon
1/4 tsp. salt
1 cup toasted walnuts
1 apple, chopped

1. Pour water into slow cooker.
2. Cut squash crosswise in half. Remove seeds. Place in slow cooker, cut sides up.

3. Combine brown sugar, butter, apple juice, cinnamon, and salt. Spoon into squash.

4. Cover. Cook on high 3-4 hours, or until squash is tender.

5. Combine walnuts and chopped apple. Add to center of squash and mix with sauce to serve.

6. Serve with a pork dish.

Stuffed Acorn Squash

Jean Butzer
Batavia, NY

Makes 6 servings

3 small carnival or acorn squash
5 Tbsp. instant brown rice
3 Tbsp. dried cranberries
3 Tbsp. diced celery
3 Tbsp. minced onion
pinch of ground or dried sage
1 tsp. butter, divided
3 Tbsp. orange juice
1/2 cup water

1. Slice off points on the bottoms of squash so they will stand in slow cooker. Slice off tops and discard. Scoop out seeds. Place squash in slow cooker.

2. Combine rice, cranberries, celery, onion, and sage. Stuff into squash.

3. Dot with butter.

4. Pour 1 Tbsp. orange juice into each squash.

5. Pour water into bottom of slow cooker.

6. Cover. Cook on low 2½ hours.

7. Serve with cooked turkey breast.

Note: To make squash easier to slice, microwave whole squash on high for 5 minutes to soften skin.

Tzimmes

Elaine Vigoda
Rochester, NY

Makes 6-8 servings

1-2 sweet potatoes
6 carrots, sliced
1 potato, peeled and diced
1 onion, chopped
2 apples, peeled and sliced
1 butternut squash, peeled and sliced
1/4 cup dry white wine or apple juice
1/2 lb. dried apricots
1 Tbsp. ground cinnamon
1 Tbsp. apple pie spice
1 Tbsp. maple syrup or honey
1 tsp. salt
1 tsp. ground ginger

1. Combine all ingredients in large slow cooker, or mix all ingredients in large bowl and then divide between 2 4- or 5-qt. cookers.

2. Cover. Cook on low 10 hours.

This is a special dish served primarily on Jewish holidays, such as Rosh Hashana and Passover. The sweetness of the vegetables and fruit signifies wishes for a sweet year.

Stewed Tomatoes

Michelle Showalter

Bridgewater, VA

Makes 10-12 servings

2 qts. canned tomatoes
1/3 cup sugar
1 1/2 tsp. salt
dash of pepper
3 Tbsp. butter
2 cups bread cubes

1. Place tomatoes in slow cooker.
2. Sprinkle with sugar, salt, and pepper.
3. Lightly toast bread cubes in melted butter. Spread over tomatoes.
4. Cover. Cook on high 3-4 hours.

Variation: If you prefer bread that is less moist and soft, add bread cubes 15 minutes before serving and continue cooking without lid.

Stuffed Mushrooms

Melanie L. Thrower

McPherson, KS

Makes 4-6 servings

8-10 large mushrooms
1/4 tsp. minced garlic
1 Tbsp. oil
dash of salt
dash of pepper
dash of cayenne pepper
1/4 cup grated Monterey Jack cheese

1. Remove stems from mushrooms and dice.
2. Heat oil in skillet. Saute diced stems with garlic until softened. Remove skillet from heat.
3. Stir in seasonings and cheese. Stuff into mushroom shells. Place in slow cooker.
4. Cover. Heat on low 2-4 hours.

Variations:
1. Add 1 Tbsp. minced onion to Step 2.

2. Use Monterey Jack cheese with jalapenos.

Easy Olive Bake

Jean Robinson

Cinnaminson, NJ

Makes 8 servings

1 cup uncooked rice
2 medium onions, chopped
1/2 cup butter or margarine, melted
2 cups stewed tomatoes
2 cups water
1 cup black olives, quartered
1/2-3/4 tsp. salt
1/2 tsp. chili powder
1 Tbsp. Worcestershire sauce
4-oz. can mushrooms with juice
1/2 cup grated cheese

1. Wash and drain rice. Place in slow cooker.
2. Add remaining ingredients except cheese. Mix well.
3. Cover. Cook on high 1 hour, then on low 2 hours, or until rice is tender but not mushy.
4. Add cheese before serving.
5. This is a good accompaniment to baked ham.

Caponata

Katrine Rose
Woodbridge, VA

Makes 8-10 servings

1 medium eggplant, peeled and cut into
    1/2" cubes
14-oz. can diced tomatoes
1 medium onion, chopped
1 red bell pepper, cut into 1/2" pieces
3/4 cup salsa
1/4 cup olive oil
2 Tbsp. capers, drained
3 Tbsp. balsamic vinegar
3 garlic cloves, minced
1 1/4 tsp. dried oregano
1/3 cup chopped fresh basil, packed in
    measuring cup
toasted, sliced French bread

1. Combine all ingredients except basil and
bread in slow cooker.
2. Cover. Cook on low 7-8 hours, or until
vegetables are tender.
3. Stir in basil. Serve on toasted bread.

Baked Sweet Potatoes

Shari Mast
Harrisonburg, VA

Makes 6-8 servings

6-8 medium-sized sweet potatoes

1. Scrub and prick sweet potatoes with fork.
Wrap each in tin foil and arrange in slow
cooker.
2. Cover. Cook on low 6-8 hours or high
4-5 hours, or until each potato is soft.

3. Remove from foil and serve with butter
and salt.

Sweet Potato Casserole

Jean Butzer
Batavia, NY

Makes 8 servings

2 29-oz. cans sweet potatoes, drained and
    mashed
1/3 cup (5 1/3 Tbsp.) butter, melted
2 Tbsp. sugar
2 Tbsp. brown sugar
1 Tbsp. orange juice
2 eggs, beaten
1/2 cup milk
1/3 cup chopped pecans
1/3 cup brown sugar
2 Tbsp. flour
2 tsp. butter, melted

1. Combine sweet potatoes, 1/3 cup butter,
2 Tbsp. sugar, and 2 Tbsp. brown sugar.
2. Beat in orange juice, eggs, and milk.
Transfer to greased slow cooker.
3. Combine pecans, 1/3 cup brown sugar,
flour, and 2 tsp. butter. Spread over sweet
potatoes.
4. Cover. Cook on high 3-4 hours.

Meal Idea

Ham in Foil or a Bag (page 85)
Sweet Potato Casserole
Asparagus

Glazed Sweet Potatoes

Martha Hershey
Ronks, PA

Makes 8 servings

10 medium-sized sweet potatoes
½ cup butter, melted
¼ cup brown sugar
½ cup orange juice
½ tsp. salt

1. Cook sweet potatoes until just soft. Peel and cut in half.
2. Combine remaining ingredients. Pour over potatoes.
3. Cover. Cook on high 2½-3 hours, or until tender but not mushy.

Note: The sweet potatoes can be cooked and peeled ahead of time, and frozen in a single layer. Defrost before putting in slow cooker.

These are great to serve with Thanksgiving dinner.

Orange Yams

Gladys Longacre
Susquehanna, PA

Makes 6-8 servings

40-oz. can yams, drained
2 apples, cored, peeled, thinly sliced
3 Tbsp. butter, melted
2 tsp. orange zest
1 cup orange juice
2 Tbsp. cornstarch
½ cup brown sugar
1 tsp. salt
dash of ground cinnamon and/or nutmeg

1. Place yams and apples in slow cooker.
2. Add butter and orange zest.
3. Combine remaining ingredients and pour over yams.
4. Cover. Cook on high 1 hour and on low 2 hours, or until apples are tender.

Variation: Substitute 6-8 medium-sized cooked sweet potatoes, or approximately 4 cups cubed butternut squash, for yams.

Apples n' Yams

Rebecca Plank Leichty
Harrisonburg, VA

Makes 8-10 servings

1 Tbsp. lemon juice or lemonade
6 apples, peeled and sliced
6 large yams or sweet potatoes,
  peeled and thinly sliced
¼ cup apple juice
1 Tbsp. butter, melted

1. Toss sliced apples and yams in lemon juice.
2. Combine apple juice and butter. Pour over apples and sweet potatoes. Pour into greased slow cooker.
3. Cover. Cook on high 4 hours or low 6 hours.

This is a tasty vegetable dish to add to a meal when serving children. The apples smell wonderful when cooking and truly moisten the potatoes when served together. It is a well-rounded and easy way to serve sweet potatoes.

Sweet Potatoes and Apples

Bernita Boyts
Shawnee Mission, KS

Makes 8-10 servings

3 large sweet potatoes, peeled and cubed
3 large tart and firm apples, peeled and
   sliced
1/2-3/4 tsp. salt
1/8-1/4 tsp. pepper
1 tsp. sage
1 tsp. ground cinnamon
4 Tbsp. (1/2 stick) butter, melted
1/4 cup maple syrup
toasted sliced almonds or chopped pecans,
   optional

1. Place half the sweet potatoes in slow cooker. Layer in half the apple slices.
2. Mix together seasonings. Sprinkle half over apples.
3. Mix together butter and maple syrup. Spoon half over seasonings.
4. Repeat layers.
5. Cover. Cook on low 6-8 hours or until potatoes are soft, stirring occasionally.
6. To add a bit of crunch, sprinkle with toasted almonds or pecans when serving.
7. Serve with pork or poultry.

Sweet Potatoes with Applesauce

Judi Manos
West Islip, NY

Makes 6-8 servings

6 medium-sized sweet potatoes or yams
1 1/2 cups applesauce
2/3 cup packed brown sugar
3 Tbsp. butter, melted
1 tsp. ground cinnamon
1/2 cup chopped toasted nuts

1. Peel sweet potatoes and cut into 1/2" cubes. Place in slow cooker.
2. Combine remaining ingredients, except nuts. Spoon over potatoes.
3. Cover. Cook on low 6-7 hours or until potatoes are very tender.
4. Sprinkle with nuts.

Variation: If you prefer a less sweet dish, cut the sugar back to 1/3 cup.

Meal Idea

Turkey Breast (pages 125-127)
Sweet Potatoes with Applesauce
Green Salad

Barbecued Black Beans with Sweet Potatoes

Barbara Jean Fabel
Wausau, WI

Makes 4-6 servings

4 large sweet potatoes, peeled and cut into
    8 chunks each
15-oz. can black beans, rinsed and drained
1 medium onion, diced
2 ribs celery, sliced
9 ozs. Sweet Baby Ray's Barbecue Sauce

1. Place sweet potatoes in slow cooker.
2. Combine remaining ingredients. Pour over sweet potatoes.
3. Cover. Cook on high 2-3 hours, or on low 4 hours.

Mashed Potatoes

Mrs. Audrey L. Kneer
Williamsfield, IL

1-2 medium-sized potatoes per person
3 Tbsp. milk per potato
1/2 Tbsp. butter per potato, melted
1/8 tsp. salt per potato

1. Peel and boil potatoes until soft. Mash.
2. While mashing potatoes, heat milk to scalding. Then add hot milk, butter, and salt to mashed potatoes, stirring in well.
3. Put in slow cooker a couple of hours before serving. Set cooker on low. Stir once in a while. These will be the same as fresh mashed potatoes.

Note: This saves needing to mash potatoes at the last minute.

Garlic Mashed Potatoes

Katrine Rose
Woodbridge, VA

Makes 6 servings

2 lbs. baking potatoes, unpeeled
    and cut into 1/2" cubes
1/4 cup water
3 Tbsp. butter, sliced
1 tsp. salt
3/4 tsp. garlic powder
1/4 tsp. black pepper
1 cup milk

1. Combine all ingredients, except milk, in slow cooker. Toss to combine.
2. Cover. Cook on low 7 hours, or on high 4 hours.
3. Add milk to potatoes during last 30 minutes of cooking time.
4. Mash potatoes with potato masher or electric mixer until fairly smooth.

Company Mashed Potatoes

Eileen Eash
Carlsbad, NM

Makes 12 servings

15 medium-sized potatoes
1 cup sour cream
1 small onion, diced fine
1 tsp. salt
1/8-1/4 tsp. pepper, according to your taste
  preference
1-2 cups buttermilk
1 cup fresh, chopped spinach, optional
1 cup grated Colby or cheddar cheese,
  optional

1. Peel and quarter potatoes. Place in slow cooker. Barely cover with water.
2. Cover. Cook on low 8-10 hours. Drain water.
3. Mash potatoes. Add remaining ingredients except cheese.
4. Cover. Heat on low 4-6 hours.
5. Sprinkle with cheese 5 minutes before serving.

Buttermilk gives mashed potatoes a unique flavor that most people enjoy. I often serve variations of this recipe for guests and they always ask what I put in the potatoes.

Notes:
1. I save the water drained from cooking the potatoes and use it to make gravy or a soup base.

2. Small amounts of leftovers from this recipe add a special flavor to vegetable or noodle soup for another meal.

Refrigerator Mashed Potatoes

Deborah Swartz
Grottoes, VA

Makes 8-10 servings

5 lbs. potatoes
8-oz. pkg. cream cheese, softened
1 cup sour cream
1 tsp. salt
1/4 tsp. pepper
1/4 cup crisp bacon, crumbled
2 Tbsp. butter

1. Cook and mash potatoes.
2. Add remaining ingredients except butter. Put in slow cooker. Dot with butter.
3. Cover. Cook on low 2 hours.

Variations:
1. These potatoes can be made several days ahead and refrigerated. Cook refrigerated potatoes on low for 5 hours.

2. If you wish, sprinkle 1 cup cheddar cheese over the top of the potatoes during their last half hour in slow cooker.

3. Substitute chopped ham for the bacon.

4. Add 2 Tbsp. chopped fresh chives to Step 2.

Hosting Idea

My mom always prepared mashed potatoes for any get-togethers at my grandmother's house. She made them ahead of time, put them in her slow cooker, and transported them, turning on the cooker when we arrived. The potatoes were always hot, steamy, and wonderful whenever we got around to eating.

— Lucille Amos

Creamy Mashed Potatoes

Brenda S. Burkholder
Port Republic, VA

Makes 10-12 servings

2 tsp. salt
6 Tbsp. (3/4 stick) butter, melted
2¼ cups milk
6⅞ cups potato flakes
6 cups water
1 cup sour cream
4-5 ozs. (approximately half of a large
    pkg.) cream cheese, softened

1. Combine first five ingredients as directed
on potato box.
2. Whip cream cheese with electric mixer
until creamy. Blend in sour cream.
3. Fold potatoes into cheese and sour
cream. Beat well. Place in slow cooker.
4. Cover. Cook on low 3-5 hours.

Sunday Dinner Potatoes

Ruth Ann Penner
Hillsboro, KS

Makes 8 servings

4 cups cooked, sliced potatoes
⅓ cup margarine
¼ cup flour
2 cups milk
1 tsp. salt
pepper to taste
1 tsp. onion powder

1. Place potatoes in slow cooker.
2. Melt butter in small skillet. Add flour and
stir. Slowly add milk, stirring constantly.

3. Add salt, pepper, and onion powder.
When smooth and thickened, pour over
potatoes.
4. Cover. Cook on high 2-3 hours or low
4-5 hours.

Swiss-Irish Hot Sauce

Jo Haberkamp
Fairbank, IA

Makes 6-8 servings

2 medium onions, diced
5 garlic cloves, minced
¼ cup oil
1-lb. can tomatoes, pureed
15-oz. can tomato sauce
12-oz. can tomato paste
2 Tbsp. parsley, fresh or dried
½ tsp. red pepper
½ tsp. black pepper
1 tsp. chili powder
1 tsp. dried basil
2 tsp. Worcestershire sauce
2 tsp. Tabasco sauce
¼ cup red wine

1. Saute onions and garlic in oil in skillet.
2. Combine all ingredients in slow cooker.
3. Cover. Cook on low 4 hours.
4. This is a flavorful sauce for eating over
pasta or baked potatoes. Serve with French
bread and a tossed salad.

Herbed Potatoes

Jo Haberkamp
Fairbank, IA

Makes 6 servings

1½ lbs. small new potatoes
¼ cup water
¼ cup butter or margarine, melted
3 Tbsp. chopped fresh parsley
1 Tbsp. lemon juice
1 Tbsp. chopped fresh chives
1 Tbsp. dill weed
¼-½ tsp. salt, according to your taste
 preference
⅛-¼ tsp. pepper, according to your taste
 preference

1. Wash potatoes. Peel a strip around the center of each potato. Place in slow cooker.
2. Add water.
3. Cover. Cook on high 2½-3 hours. Drain well.
4. In saucepan, heat butter, parsley, lemon juice, chives, dill, salt, and pepper. Pour over potatoes.
5. Serve with ham or any meat dish that does not make gravy.

Onion Potatoes

Donna Lantgen
Rapid City, SD

Makes 6 servings

6 medium potatoes, diced
⅓ cup olive oil
1 pkg. dry onion soup mix

1. Combine potatoes and olive oil in plastic bag. Shake well.
2. Add onion soup mix. Shake well.
3. Pour into slow cooker.
4. Cover. Cook on low 6 hours or high 3 hours.

Variations: Add more zest to the potatoes by stirring in 1 small onion, chopped; 1 bell pepper, chopped; ½ tsp. salt; and ¼ tsp. black pepper, after pouring the potatoes into the slow cooker. Continue with Step 4.

Potatoes Perfect

Naomi Ressler
Harrisonburg, VA

Makes 4-6 servings

¼ lb. bacon, diced and browned until
 crisp
2 medium-sized onions, thinly sliced
6-8 medium-sized potatoes, thinly sliced
½ lb. cheddar cheese, thinly sliced
salt to taste
pepper to taste
2-4 Tbsp. butter or margarine

1. Layer half of bacon, onions, potatoes, and cheese in greased slow cooker. Season to taste.
2. Dot with butter. Repeat layers.
3. Cover. Cook on low 8-10 hours or on high 3-4 hours, or until potatoes are soft.

Pete's Scalloped Potatoes

Dede Peterson
Rapid City, SD

Makes 8-10 servings

5 lbs. red potatoes, peeled and sliced
2 cups water
1 tsp. cream of tartar
1/4 lb. bacon, cut in 1" squares, browned
    until crisp, and drained
dash of salt
1/2 pt. whipping cream
1 pt. half-and-half

1. Toss potatoes in water and cream of tartar. Drain.
2. Layer potatoes and bacon in large slow cooker. Sprinkle with salt.
3. Mix whipping cream and half-and-half. Pour over.
4. Cover. Cook on low 6-7 hours.

Variations: For added flavor, cut one large onion into thin rings. Saute in bacon drippings; then layer onion along with potatoes and bacon. Sprinkle each layer of potatoes with salt and pepper. Continue with Step 3.

Scalloped Potatoes

Zona Mae Bontrager
Kokomo, IN

Makes 10 servings

5-oz. box scalloped potatoes
5.25-oz. box au gratin potatoes
6 hot dogs, sliced, or 1 cup cubed pre-
    cooked ham
1/4 tsp. pepper, optional

1. Mix both potatoes per package instructions. Combine in slow cooker.
2. Cover. Cook on high 30 minutes.
3. Add meat. Reduce heat to low and cook on low for 4-5 hours.

I often fix this for church dinners, and I always bring home an empty slow cooker. The children love it with hot dogs. A quick dish to prepare and forget.

Lotsa Scalloped Potatoes

Fannie Miller
Hutchinson, KS

Makes 20-25 servings

5 lbs. potatoes, cooked and sliced
2 lbs. cooked ham, cubed
1/4 lb. butter
1/2 cup flour
2 cups cream or milk
1/4 lb. mild cheese (your favorite), shredded
1 1/2 tsp. salt
1/4-1/2 tsp. pepper

1. Place layers of sliced potatoes and ham in very large (or two smaller) slow cooker(s).

2. Melt butter in saucepan on stove. Stir in flour. Gradually add milk to make a white sauce, stirring constantly until smooth and thickened.

3. Stir in cheese, salt, and pepper. Stir until cheese is melted. Pour over potatoes and ham.

4. Cover. Cook on low 2-3 hours.

Note: A great way to free up oven space.

Cheese Potatoes

Joyce Shackelford
Green Bay, WI

Makes 10 servings

6 potatoes, peeled and cut into 1/4" strips
2 cups sharp cheddar cheese, shredded
10 3/4-oz. can cream of chicken soup
1 small onion, chopped
4 Tbsp. butter or margarine, melted
1 tsp. salt
1 tsp. pepper
1 cup sour cream
2 cups seasoned stuffing cubes
3 Tbsp. butter or margarine, melted

1. Toss together potatoes and cheese. Place in slow cooker.

2. Combine soup, onion, 4 Tbsp. butter, salt, and pepper. Pour over potatoes.

3. Cover. Cook on low 8 hours.

4. Stir in sour cream. Cover and heat for 10 more minutes.

5. Meanwhile, toss together stuffing cubes and 3 Tbsp. butter. Sprinkle over potatoes just before serving.

Company Potatoes

Deborah Swartz
Grottoes, VA
Julia A. Fisher
New Carlisle, OH

Makes 6-8 servings

6 medium-sized potatoes, cooked, cooled,
  and shredded
2 cups shredded cheddar cheese
1/3 cup finely chopped onions
1/4 cup butter or margarine, melted
1 tsp. salt
1/4 tsp. pepper
1 1/2-2 cups sour cream
butter

1. Combine potatoes, cheese, onions, melted butter, salt, pepper, and sour cream in slow cooker. Dot with butter.

2. Cover. Cook on low 4 hours.

Variations:
1. Use garlic salt instead of regular salt.

2. Add 1/2 tsp. chopped parsley to Step 1.

3. Use 1 cup milk and 1 cup sour cream instead of 2 cups sour cream.
  —Kim Stoltzfus, New Holland, PA

Creamy Scalloped Potatoes

Sara Kinsinger
Stuarts Draft, VA

Makes 6 servings

6 large potatoes, peeled and thinly sliced
1 small onion, thinly sliced
1/4 cup flour
1 tsp. salt
1/4 tsp. pepper
2 Tbsp. butter, melted
1/4 cup milk
10³/4-oz. can cream of mushroom soup
4 slices American cheese, or 1 cup grated
  cheddar cheese

1. Place half of potatoes in slow cooker. Top with half of onion, flour, salt, and pepper. Repeat layers.
2. Mix together butter, milk, and soup. Pour over potato layers.
3. Cover. Cook on low 6-9 hours, on high 3-4 hours, or until potatoes are soft.
4. Add cheese 30 minutes before serving.

Variation:
Eliminate 1/4 cup milk. Simply top seasoned and layered vegetables with chunks of butter and then pour soup over top.

I make this recipe often when I'm having company for lunch after church. (For that, I cook the dish on high.) Using a slow cooker for the potatoes allows you to have more room in your oven for other dishes on the menu.
  —Ruth Hershey, Paradise, PA

Cheese Scalloped Potatoes

Mary Jane Musser
Manheim, PA
Miriam Nolt
New Holland, PA

Makes 6-10 servings

6-8 good-sized potatoes
3 Tbsp. butter
2 Tbsp. flour
3 cups milk
2 Tbsp. chopped onion
1 tsp. salt
1/8 tsp. pepper
1 tsp. parsley
1 1/2 cups diced mild cheese

1. Cook potatoes in saucepan until tender. Peel and refrigerate. When thoroughly cooled, shred.
2. Melt butter in saucepan. Stir in flour. Gradually add milk, stirring constantly until smooth and thickened.
3. Stir in onions, seasonings, and cheese, a half cup at a time. Continue stirring over heat until cheese melts.
4. Combine potatoes and sauce in slow cooker.
5. Cover. Cook on low 4 hours.

Note: Cook and shred the potatoes the day before serving them. That will relieve the pressure on the day you're having guests.

Hash Brown Potato Casserole

Michelle Strite
Goshen, IN

Makes 8-10 servings

26-oz. pkg. frozen shredded hash browns
3 Tbsp. oil
2 cups chopped ham, optional
2 10¾-oz. cans cream of potato soup
½ cup grated Parmesan cheese
16-oz. container sour cream
8 ozs. shredded cheddar cheese

1. Brown hash browns in oil in skillet. Transfer to slow cooker.
2. Add remaining ingredients and stir well.
3. Cover. Cook on low 3 hours.

Meal Idea

Ham Balls (page 94)
Hash Brown Potato Casserole
Apple Crisp or Baked Apples
(pages 221-225)

Shredded Potatoes with Canadian Bacon

Carol Eberly
Harrisonburg, VA

Makes 8 serving

32-oz. bag frozen hash browns
6-8 thin slices of Canadian bacon,
  or fully cooked ham
1 cup shredded sharp cheese
2 cups shredded mild cheddar cheese
¾ cup chopped onions
salt to taste

pepper to taste
10¾-oz. can cream of mushroom soup
10¾-oz. can cream of chicken soup

1. Layer half of potatoes, meat, cheeses, and onions in slow cooker. Season with salt and pepper. Repeat layers.
2. Combine soups. Pour over top.
3. Cover. Cook on low 5 hours.

We used this recipe, minus the meat, for our daughter's wedding reception meal. We made 12 slow-cookers-full. We put the recipe together the night before, put the mixture in the refrigerator overnight, and got up at 4 a.m. to plug in the cookers. They were ready for lunch.

Hot German Potato Salad

Judi Manos
West Islip, NY

Makes 6 servings

5 medium-sized potatoes, cut ¼" thick
1 large onion, chopped
⅓ cup water
⅓ cup vinegar
2 Tbsp. flour
2 Tbsp. sugar
1 tsp. salt
½ tsp. celery seed
¼ tsp. pepper
4 slices bacon, cooked crisp and crumbled
chopped fresh parsley

1. Combine potatoes and onions in slow cooker.
2. Combine remaining ingredients, except bacon and parsley. Pour over potatoes.
3. Cover. Cook on low 8-10 hours.
4. Stir in bacon and parsley.
5. Serve warm or at room temperature with grilled bratwurst or Polish sausage, dilled pickles, pickled beets, and apples.

Mushroom Stuffing

Laverne Stoner
Scottdale, PA

Makes 7-8 cups stuffing

1/2 cup butter or margarine
1 cup finely chopped onions
1 cup finely chopped celery
8-oz. can sliced mushrooms, drained
1/4 cup chopped parsley
11/2-2 tsp. poultry seasoning
1/2 tsp. salt
1/8 tsp. pepper
12 cups toasted bread cubes*
2 eggs, well beaten
11/2 cups chicken broth

1. Saute onion and celery in butter in skillet until cooked. Stir in mushrooms and parsley.
2. Combine seasonings and sprinkle over bread cubes.
3. Gently add remaining ingredients. Spoon lightly into slow cooker.
4. Cover. Cook on high 1 hour, then reduce to low and cook 1-2 hours.

Toast 18-22 slices of bread for 15 minutes at 300°.

Note: *This is not as much a time-saver as it is a space-saver. If your oven is full, make your stuffing in your slow cooker.*

Slow Cooker Stuffing

Allison Ingels
Maynard, IA

Makes 10-12 servings

12-13 cups dry bread cubes
   (equal to a 20-oz. loaf of bread)
1/4 cup dried parsley
2 eggs, beaten
giblets, cooked and chopped (reserve
   broth)
1 tsp. salt
1/4 tsp. pepper
1/2 tsp. sage
11/2 tsp. poultry seasoning
31/2-41/2 cups turkey broth (from cooking
   giblets)
2 chicken bouillon cubes
2 cups finely chopped celery
1 cup finely chopped onion
1 cup butter or margarine

1. Combine bread cubes and parsley in slow cooker.
2. Add eggs, giblets, and seasonings.
3. Dissolve bouillon in turkey broth. Add to slow cooker.
4. Saute celery and onion in butter in skillet. Stir into bread mixture.
5. Cover. Cook on high 1 hour and then on low 2 hours, stirring occasionally.

Note: *A convenient way to free up oven space— or keep your kitchen cool.*

Poultry Stuffing

Evelyn L. Ward
Greeley, CO

Makes 8 servings

1 cup butter, melted
2 cups chopped celery
1/2 cup chopped onions
1 tsp. poultry seasoning
1/2 tsp. sage
1 tsp. salt
2 eggs, beaten
4 cups chicken broth
12 cups fresh bread crumbs, slightly dried

1. Combine everything but crumbs. Mix well. Add crumbs. Stir to blend.
2. Place in 5- or 6-qt. lightly greased slow cooker.
3. Cover. Cook on high 45 minutes, then on low 4-6 hours.

Slow Cooker Dressing

Marie Shank
Harrisonburg, VA

Makes 16 servings

2 boxes Jiffy Cornbread mix
8 slices day-old bread
4 eggs
1 onion, chopped
1/2 cup chopped celery
2 10³/4-oz. cans cream of chicken soup
2 cups chicken broth
1 tsp. salt
1/2 tsp. pepper
1¹/2 Tbsp. sage or poultry seasoning
1/2-³/4 cup butter or margarine

1. Prepare cornbread according to package instructions.
2. Crumble cornbread and bread together.
3. In large bowl combine all ingredients except butter and spoon into 6-qt. greased slow cooker, or 2 smaller cookers. Dot top with butter.
4. Cover. Cook on high 2-4 hours or on low 3-8 hours

Variations:
1. Prepare your favorite cornbread recipe in an 8"-square baking pan instead of using the cornbread mix.

2. For a more moist dressing, use 2 14¹/2-oz. cans chicken broth instead of 2 cups chicken broth.

3. You may reduce the butter to 2 Tbsp.

Serve with roast chicken or turkey drumsticks.
—**Helen Kenagy, Carlsbad, NM**

Mashed Potato Filling
Betty K. Drescher
Quakertown, PA

Makes 8-10 servings

1/2 cup diced onions
1 cup diced celery
1/2 cup butter
2 1/2 cups milk
4 large eggs, beaten
8 ozs. bread cubes
4 cups mashed potatoes
1 1/2 tsp. salt
1/4 tsp. pepper

1. Saute onions and celery in butter in skillet for 5-10 minutes, or until vegetables are tender.
2. Combine onions and celery, milk, and eggs. Pour over bread cubes. Mix lightly to absorb liquid.
3. Stir in potatoes and seasonings. Pour into greased slow cooker.
4. Cover. Cook on low 4 hours.

Variation: For more flavor, add the packet of seasoning from the bread cube package in Step 3.

Sweet Potato Stuffing
Tina Snyder
Manheim, PA

Makes 8 servings

1/2 cup chopped celery
1/2 cup chopped onions
1/4 cup butter
6 cups dry bread cubes
1 large sweet potato, cooked, peeled, and cubed
1/2 cup chicken broth
1/4 cup chopped pecans
1/2 tsp. poultry seasoning
1/2 tsp. rubbed sage
1/2 tsp. salt
1/4 tsp. pepper

1. Saute celery and onion in skillet in butter until tender. Pour into greased slow cooker.
2. Add remaining ingredients. Toss gently.
3. Cover. Cook on low 4 hours.

Sweets

Boston Brown Bread

Jean Butzer
Batavia, NY

Makes 3 loaves

3 16-oz. vegetable cans, cleaned and emptied
1/2 cup rye flour
1/2 cup yellow cornmeal
1/2 cup whole wheat flour
3 Tbsp. sugar
1 tsp. baking soda
3/4 tsp. salt
1/2 cup chopped walnuts
1/2 cup raisins
1 cup buttermilk*
1/3 cup molasses

1. Spray insides of vegetable cans, and one side of 3 6"-square pieces of foil, with nonstick cooking spray. Set aside.

2. Combine rye flour, cornmeal, whole wheat flour, sugar, baking soda, and salt in a large bowl.

3. Stir in walnuts and raisins.

4. Whisk together buttermilk and molasses. Add to dry ingredients. Stir until well mixed. Spoon into prepared cans.

5. Place one piece of foil, greased side down, on top of each can. Secure foil with rubberbands or cotton string. Place upright in slow cooker.

6. Pour boiling water into slow cooker to come halfway up sides of cans. (Make sure foil tops do not touch boiling water).

7. Cover cooker. Cook on low 4 hours, or until skewer inserted in center of bread comes out clean.

8. To remove bread, lay cans on their sides. Roll and tap gently on all sides until bread releases. Cool completely on wire racks.

9. Serve with butter or cream cheese, and bowls of soup.

* To substitute for buttermilk, pour 1 Tbsp. lemon juice into 1-cup measure. Add enough milk to fill the cup. Let stand 5 minutes before mixing with molasses.

Date and Nut Loaf

Jean Butzer
Batavia, NY

Makes 16 servings

1 1/2 cups boiling water
1 1/2 cups chopped dates
1 1/4 cups sugar
1 egg
2 tsp. baking soda
1/2 tsp. salt
1 tsp. vanilla
1 Tbsp. melted butter
2 1/2 cups flour
1 cup walnuts, chopped
2 cups hot water

1. Pour 1 1/2 cups boiling water over dates. Let stand 5-10 minutes.
2. Stir in sugar, egg, baking soda, salt, vanilla, and butter.
3. In separate bowl, combine flour and nuts. Stir into date mixture.
4. Pour into 2 greased 11.5-oz. coffee cans or one 8-cup baking insert. If using coffee cans, cover with foil and tie. If using baking insert, cover with its lid. Place cans or insert on rack in slow cooker. (If you don't have a rack, use rubber jar rings instead.)
5. Pour hot water around cans, up to half their height.
6. Cover slow cooker tightly. Cook on high 3 1/2-4 hours.
7. Remove cans or insert from cooker. Let bread stand in coffee cans or baking insert 10 minutes. Turn out onto cooling rack. Slice. Spread with butter, cream cheese, or peanut butter.

Banana Loaf

Sue Hamilton
Minooka, IL

Makes 6-8 servings

3 very ripe bananas
1/2 cup margarine, softened
2 eggs
1 tsp. vanilla
1 cup sugar
1 cup flour
1 tsp. baking soda

1. Combine all ingredients in an electric mixing bowl. Beat 2 minutes or until well blended. Pour into well greased 2-lb. coffee can.
2. Place can in slow cooker. Cover can with 6 layers of paper towels between cooker lid and bread.
3. Cover cooker. Bake on high 2-2 1/2 hours, or until toothpick inserted in center comes out clean. Cool 15 minutes before removing from pan.

Cheery Cherry Bread

Shirley Sears
Tiskilwa, IL

Makes 6-8 servings

6-oz. jar maraschino cherries
1 1/2 cups flour
1 1/2 tsp. baking powder
1/4 tsp. salt
2 eggs
3/4 cup sugar
3/4 cup coarsely chopped pecans

1. Drain cherries, reserving ⅓ cup syrup. Cut cherries in pieces. Set aside.

2. Combine flour, baking powder, and salt.

3. Beat eggs and sugar together until thickened.

4. Alternately add flour mixture and cherry syrup to egg mixture, mixing until well blended after each addition.

5. Fold in cherries and pecans. Spread in well greased and floured baking insert or 2-lb. coffee can. If using baking insert, cover with its lid; if using a coffee can, cover with 6 layers of paper towels. Set in slow cooker.

6. Cover cooker. Cook on high 2-3 hours.

7. Remove from slow cooker. Let stand 10 minutes before removing from pan.

8. Cool before slicing.

Gingerbread with Lemon Sauce

Jean Butzer
Batavia, NY
Marie Shank
Harrisonburg, VA

Makes 8 servings

½ cup butter or margarine, softened
½ cup sugar
1 egg, lightly beaten
1 cup sorghum molasses
2½ cups flour
1½ tsp. baking soda
1 tsp. cinnamon
2 tsp. ground ginger
½ tsp. ground cloves
½ tsp. salt
1 cup hot coffee or hot water
½ cup powdered sugar
2 tsp. cornstarch
pinch of salt
juice of 2 lemons
½ cup water

1 Tbsp. butter
powdered sugar for garnish

1. Cream together ½ cup butter and sugar.

2. Add egg. Mix well.

3. Add molasses. Mix well.

4. Sift together flour, baking soda, cinnamon, ginger, cloves, and salt. Stir into creamed mixture.

5. Add coffee or water. Beat well.

6. There are two ways to bake the gingerbread:

a. If you have a baking insert, or a 2-lb. coffee can, grease and flour the inside of it. Pour in batter. Place in slow cooker. Pour water around insert or coffee can. Cover insert with its lid, or cover coffee can with 6-8 paper towels.

b. Cut waxed paper or parchment paper to fit bottom of slow cooker. Place in bottom of cooker. Spray paper and sides of cooker's interior with nonstick cooking spray. Pour batter into preheated slow cooker.

7. Cover cooker with its lid slightly ajar to allow excess moisture to escape. Cook on high 1¾-2 hours, or on low 3-4 hours, or until edges are golden and knife inserted in center comes out clean.

8. If you used a baking insert or coffee can, remove from cooker. Cool on cake rack. Let stand 5 minutes before running knife around outer edge of cake and inverting onto serving plate.

If you baked the gingerbread directly in the cooker, cut the cake into wedges after allowing it to cool for 30 minutes, and carefully lift the wedges out of the cooker onto serving plates.

9. In saucepan, mix together ½ cup powdered sugar, cornstarch, and salt. Add lemon juice and water, stirring with each addition. Cook over medium heat until thick and bubbly, about 1 minute. Remove from heat. Stir in butter.

10. If gingerbread has been cooling on a rack, cut it into wedges. To serve, top with sauce and sprinkle with powdered sugar.

Hot Fruit Salad
Sharon Miller
Holmesville, OH

Makes 16 servings

25-oz. jar chunky applesauce
21-oz. can cherry pie filling
20-oz. can pineapple chunks
15½-oz. can sliced peaches
15½-oz. can apricot halves
11-oz. can mandarin oranges
½ cup packed brown sugar
1 tsp. ground cinnamon

1. Combine fruit in slow cooker, stirring gently.
2. Combine brown sugar and cinnamon. Sprinkle over mixture.
3. Cover. Bake on low 3-4 hours.

Variation: If you prefer a less sweet dish, reduce amount of brown sugar to ¼ cup, or to 2 Tbsp.

Baked Fruit
Paula Showalter
Weyers Cave, VA

Makes 8-10 servings

4 cups sliced peaches, drained
4 cups sliced apples
2 cups crushed pineapple, drained
1½ tsp. ground cinnamon
½ tsp. ground nutmeg
1½ cups sugar
2 Tbsp. cornstarch

1. Combine fruit in slow cooker.
2. Sprinkle with spices.

3. Combine sugar and cornstarch. Add to fruit. Mix well.
4. Cover. Cook on high 2 hours or low 4 hours.
5. Serve as a side dish with the main meal, or as a topping for vanilla ice cream.

Curried Fruit
Jane Meiser
Harrisonburg, VA

Makes 8-10 servings

1 can peaches, undrained
1 can apricots, undrained
1 can pears, undrained
1 large can pineapple chunks, undrained
1 can black cherries, undrained
½ cup brown sugar
1 tsp. curry powder
3-4 Tbsp. quick-cooking tapioca,
    depending upon how thickened you'd
    like the finished dish to be
butter or margarine, optional

1. Combine fruit. Let stand for at least 2 hours, or up to 8, to allow flavors to blend. Drain. Place in slow cooker.
2. Add remaining ingredients. Mix well. Top with butter, if you want.
3. Cover. Cook on low 8-10 hours.
4. Serve warm or at room temperature.

Fruit Dessert Topping

Lavina Hochstedler
Grand Blanc, MI

Makes 6 cups

3 tart apples, peeled and sliced
3 pears, peeled and sliced
1 Tbsp. lemon juice
1/2 cup packed brown sugar
1/2 cup maple syrup
1/4 cup butter or margarine, melted
1/2 cup chopped pecans
1/4 cup raisins
2 cinnamon sticks
1 Tbsp. cornstarch
2 Tbsp. cold water

1. Toss apples and pears in lemon juice in slow cooker.
2. Combine brown sugar, maple syrup, and butter. Pour over fruit.
3. Stir in pecans, raisins, and cinnamon sticks.
4. Cover. Cook on low 3-4 hours.
5. Combine cornstarch and water until smooth. Gradually stir into slow cooker.
6. Cover. Cook on high 30-40 minutes, or until thickened.
7. Discard cinnamon sticks. Serve over pound cake or ice cream.

We also like this served along with pancakes or an egg casserole. We always use Fruit Topping for our breakfasts at church camp.

Dried Fruit

Janet Roggie
Lowville, NY

Makes 3-4 servings

2 cups mixed dried fruit
1/4 cup water

1. Place dried fruit in slow cooker. Add water.
2. Cover. Cook on low 4-8 hours.
3. Serve warm with a spoonful of sour cream on each individual serving and a dash of ground nutmeg.

Variations and Notes:
1. To do more than plump the fruit, and to increase juiciness, increase water to 1/2 cup.

2. This is a good alternative to fresh fruit in the wintertime.

3. Use a single dried fruit, or put together your own choice of mixed fruits.

Zesty Pears

Barbara Walker
Sturgis, SD

Makes 6 servings

6 fresh pears
1/2 cup raisins
1/4 cup brown sugar
1 tsp. grated lemon peel
1/4 cup brandy
1/2 cup sauterne wine
1/2 cup macaroon crumbs

1. Peel and core pears. Cut into thin slices.
2. Combine raisins, sugar, and lemon peel. Layer alternately with pear slices in slow cooker.
3. Pour brandy and wine over top.
4. Cover. Cook on low 4-6 hours.
5. Spoon into serving dishes. Cool. Sprinkle with macaroons. Serve plain or topped with sour cream.

Southwest Cranberries

Bernita Boyts
Shawnee Mission, KS

Makes 8 servings

16-oz. can whole berry cranberry sauce
10 1/2-oz. jar jalapeno jelly
2 Tbsp. chopped fresh cilantro

1. Combine ingredients in slow cooker.
2. Cover. Cook on low 2-3 hours.
3. Cool. Serve at room temperature.
4. Serve these spicy cranberries as a side dish or as a marinade for poultry or pork.

Slow-Cooker Spoon Peaches

Jeanette Oberholtzer
Manheim, PA

Makes 6 servings

1/3 cup sugar
1/2 cup brown sugar
3/4 cup buttermilk baking mix
2 eggs
2 tsp. vanilla
2 tsp. butter or margarine, melted
half a 12-oz. can evaporated milk
2 cups mashed peaches, fresh, frozen,
   or canned (if canned, drain slightly)
3/4 tsp. cinnamon

1. Combine sugar, brown sugar, and baking mix.
2. Add eggs and vanilla. Mix well.
3. Add margarine and milk. Mix well.
4. Add peaches and cinnamon. Mix well. Pour into greased slow cooker.
5. Cover. Cook on low 6-8 hours.
6. Serve warm with whipped cream or vanilla ice cream.

This is a great warm dessert for a cold winter evening.

Cranberry Baked Apples

Judi Manos
West Islip, NY

Makes 4 servings

4 large cooking apples
1/3 cup packed brown sugar
1/4 cup dried cranberries
1/2 cup cran-apple juice cocktail
2 Tbsp. butter, melted
1/2 tsp. ground cinnamon
1/4 tsp. ground nutmeg
chopped nuts, optional

1. Core apples. Fill centers with brown sugar and cranberries. Place in slow cooker.
2. Combine cran-apple juice and butter. Pour over apples.
3. Sprinkle with cinnamon and nutmeg.
4. Cover. Cook on low 4-6 hours.
5. To serve, spoon sauce over apples and sprinkle with nuts.
6. This is a great accompaniment to vanilla ice cream.

This was one of our favorite recipes while growing up. When it's cooking, the house smells delicious. I'm suddenly full of memories of days gone by and a much more relaxing time. My mother passed away in October and I re-found this recipe among her collection of favorites.

Baked Apples

Donna Lantgen
Rapid City, SD

Makes 4 servings

4 baking apples, cored and unpeeled
1 tsp. cinnamon
1/4 cup brown sugar
4 Tbsp. butter

1. Place apples in slow cooker.
2. Combine cinnamon and brown sugar. Stuff into apples.
3. Top each apple with 1 Tbsp. butter.
4. Cover. Cook on low 4-5 hours.
5. Delicious as a side dish served warm, or as a topping for waffles, pancakes, or ice cream.

221

Wagon Master Apple-Cherry Sauce

Sharon Timpe
Mequon, WI

Makes 12-15 servings

2 21-oz. cans apple pie filling
2-3 cups frozen tart red cherries
1 Tbsp. butter or margarine
1/2 tsp. ground cinnamon
1/2 tsp. ground nutmeg
1/8 tsp. ground ginger
1/8 tsp. ground cloves

1. Combine all ingredients in slow cooker.
2. Cover. Heat on low 3-4 hours, until hot and bubbly. Stir occasionally.
3. Serve warm over vanilla ice cream, pudding, pound cake, or shortcake biscuits. Top with whipped cream.

Spiced Apples

Michelle Showalter
Bridgewater, VA

Makes 8-10 servings

2 qts. peeled, sliced apples
2 1/2 cups water
1/4 cup cinnamon candy
1/2-3/4 cup sugar, according to your taste preference
1/3 cup Therm-flo or Clearjell
1/2 tsp. ground cinnamon
1/8 tsp. salt
1/8 tsp ground nutmeg

1. Place apples in slow cooker.
2. Combine remaining ingredients and stir until thickening agent dissolves. Pour over apples.
3. Cover. Cook on high 3 hours.
4. Serve hot with your main meal, or chill and serve with whipped cream and chopped pecans, or as a topping for ice cream, or as a base for apple crisp.

Hosting Idea

"End of the Trail Cook-Out"

To help create a casual setting I use large bandanas as napkins. I also tie bandanas around pots of flowering plants for centerpieces and add small cowboy hats and horse shoes on the table. I use spattered enamel-ware dishes. If it is a large party I switch to aluminum pie plates for dishes.
—Sharon Timpe

Caramel Apples

Becky Harder
Monument, CO
Jeanette Oberholtzer
Manheim, PA

Makes 8-10 servings

2 14-oz. bags of caramels
1/4 cup water
8-10 medium apples
sticks
waxed paper
granulated sugar

1. Combine caramels and water in slow cooker.
2. Cover. Cook on high for 1-1 1/2 hours, stirring every 5 minutes.
3. Wash and dry apples. Insert a stick into stem end of each apple. Turn cooker to low. Dip apple into hot caramel, turning to coat entire surface.
4. Holding apple above cooker, scrape off excess accumulation of caramel from bottom of apple.
5. Dip bottom of caramel-coated apple in granulated sugar to keep it from sticking. Place apple on greased waxed paper to cool.

This is a good recipe for Fall/Harvest/Halloween parties. Children won't forget the hands-on experience of dipping their own apples. Room mothers can make the caramel mix ahead of time and bring into the classroom. This recipe is also a fun intergenerational activity for church groups or family reunions.

In the late 1950s and early 1960s, my sister and I were rewarded with a store-bought caramel apple, only after our Saturday night baths and our Sunday school lessons had been completed. I remember that the waxed paper wrapped around each apple had colorful clowns printed on it, and they sold for less than 50¢ each.
—Becky Harder

Apple Caramel Dessert

Jeanette Oberholtzer
Manheim, PA

Makes 7 servings

2 medium apples, peeled, cored, and cut in wedges
1/2 cup apple juice
7 ozs. caramel candy
1 tsp. vanilla
1/8 tsp. ground cardamom
1/2 tsp. ground cinnamon
1/3 cup creamy peanut butter
7 slices angel food cake
1 qt. vanilla ice cream

1. Combine apple juice, caramel candies, vanilla, and spices. Place in slow cooker.
2. Drop peanut butter, 1 tsp. at a time, into slow cooker. Stir.
3. Add apple wedges.
4. Cover. Cook on low 5 hours.
5. Stir well.
6. Cover. Then cook 1 more hour on low.
7. Serve 1/3 cup warm mixture over each slice of angel food cake and top with ice cream.

Hosting Idea

For those times when you can't have everything done, don't spend a lot of time apologizing. It might actually make your guests feel more comfortable if there are a few toys on the floor.
—Michelle Showalter

Apple Schnitz

Betty Hostetler
Allensville, PA

Makes 6-8 servings

1 qt. dried apples
3 cups water
1 cup sugar
1 tsp. ground cinnamon
1 tsp. salt

1. Combine apples, water, sugar, cinnamon, and salt in slow cooker.
2. Cover. Cook on low 6 hours or on high 2½ hours.
3. Serve warm as a side dish with bean soup, or as filling for Half Moon Pies (see below).
4. For pie filling, remove apples from slow cooker. Mash until smooth with potato masher or put through food mill. Cool.

Pie Crust:
4 cups flour
2 tsp. salt
4 Tbsp. shortening
¼ cold water, or more

1. Combine flour and salt. Cut in shortening until mixture resembles small peas.
2. Add ¼ cup cold water to dough, adding more by tablespoonfuls as needed to make a soft pie dough.
3. Pinch off small pieces of dough, each about the size of a large walnut. Roll into round pieces, each about 8" in diameter.
4. Jag one half of the circle a few times with a sharp fork to create holes for the steam to escape while baking. On the other half place a heaping tablespoon of apple filling. Fold one-half of dough up over the half holding the pie filling, shaping the pie like a half moon. Press edges of dough together. Cut off remaining dough and crimp edges.
5. Bake at 350° for 30 minutes.

On a cold winter day, Mother would prepare dried beans to make soup. After the beans were soft, she added milk to the soup pot. She heated the mixture to the boiling point, then added rivels. While the beans were cooking, she cooked dried apples until they were soft. She served these Half Moon Pies as a side dish/dessert with the soup.

Menu Idea

Bean Soup (pages 149-156)
Cheese Cubes
Sour Pickles
Celery and Carrot Sticks
Half Moon Pies

Apple Crisp

Michelle Strite
Goshen, IN

Makes 6-8 servings

1 qt. canned apple pie filling, or
  ⅔ cup sugar
  1¼ cups water
  3 Tbsp. cornstarch
  4 cups sliced, peeled apples
  ½ tsp. ground cinnamon
  ¼ tsp. ground allspice
¾ cup quick oatmeal
½ cup brown sugar
½ cup flour
¼ cup butter or margarine, at room temperature

1. Place pie filling in slow cooker. If not using prepared filling, combine ⅔ cup sugar, water, cornstarch, apples, cinnamon, and allspice. Place in cooker.
2. Combine remaining ingredients until crumbly. Sprinkle over apple filling.
3. Cover. Cook on low 2-3 hours.

Applescotch Crisp

Mary Jane Musser
Manheim, PA

Makes 6 servings

4 cups cooking apples, peeled and sliced
2/3 cup brown sugar
1/2 cup flour
1/2 cup quick-cooking oats
3 1/2-oz. pkg. cook-n-serve butterscotch
   pudding mix
1 tsp. ground cinnamon
1/2 cup cold butter or margarine

1. Place apples in slow cooker.
2. Combine remaining ingredients. Cut in butter until mixture resembles coarse crumbs. Sprinkle over apples.
3. Cover. Cook on low 5-6 hours.
4. Serve with ice cream.

Variation: For a less-sweet dish, use only 1/4 cup brown sugar.

Steamed Chocolate Pudding

Evelyn L. Ward
Greeley, CO

Makes 8 servings

1/2 cup butter, softened
3/4 cup sugar
3/4 cup flour
3 Tbsp. cocoa powder
1/4 tsp. salt
3 eggs
1/2 tsp. vanilla
1/4 cup half-and-half

1. Cream together butter and sugar in electric mixer.
2. Sift together flour, cocoa powder, and salt. Add alternately with eggs to creamed mixture. Beat well.
3. Add vanilla and half-and-half. Beat well.
4. Spoon into greased and floured slow cooker baking insert*. Cover tightly with lid or double layer of foil. Place insert on a rack in slow cooker. Add boiling water to slow cooker, halfway up sides of insert.
5. Cover slow cooker. Cook on high 2 1/2 hours.
6. Remove insert from cooker. Cool 2 minutes. Unmold.
7. Slice and serve with frozen whipped topping, thawed, or ice cream.

Hint: A coffee can that fits inside your slow cooker serves as a good pudding mold. You can use a jar ring for a rack under the can or baking insert.

Steamed Carrot Pudding

Evelyn L. Ward
Greeley, CO

Makes 12 servings

1/2 cup butter, softened
3/4 cup sugar
1 tsp. ground cinnamon
1 tsp. ground nutmeg
1/2 tsp. ground cloves
1 1/2 cups day-old bread crumbs
1 cup grated carrots
1 cup grated cooked potatoes
1 cup raisins
1/2 cup chopped nuts

Lemon Sauce:
1/2 cup sugar
1 1/2 Tbsp. cornstarch
1/8 tsp. salt
1 cup boiling water
2 Tbsp. butter, at room temperature
3 Tbsp. lemon juice
1 tsp. grated lemon rind

1. Cream together butter and sugar. Stir in spices.
2. Add remaining ingredients, mixing well.
3. Fill a greased baking insert 2/3 full. Cover tightly with lid or double layer of foil. Place on rack or rubber jar rings in slow cooker. Pour boiling water into cooker, so that it comes halfway up sides of baking insert.
4. Cover cooker. Steam 3-4 hours on high.
5. Remove insert and uncover. Let stand 5 minutes, then unmold. Serve warm with Lemon Sauce.
6. To make lemon sauce, mix together dry ingredients in saucepan. Add boiling water. Cook over medium heat until thickened, stirring constantly. Remove from heat.
7. Add butter, lemon juice, and rind. Mix together well. Serve hot over pudding.

Note: A 11.5-oz. coffee can, if it fits into your slow cooker, is a good pudding mold.

Fifty-two years ago I was a guest at a Christmas luncheon, and the hostess served this dessert "flaming." She had soaked sugar cubes in lemon extract, placed one on each serving and lighted it.

Dried Cranberry Pudding

Evelyn L. Ward
Greeley, CO

Makes 8 servings

1/4 cup butter, softened
1/2 cup brown sugar
1/2 cup molasses
1 egg
1/2 tsp. baking soda
1/2 cup hot water
1 1/2 cups flour, divided
1 tsp. baking powder
1/2 cup dried cranberries

Butter Sauce:
1/2 cup sugar
1 Tbsp. flour
1/2 cup water
pinch salt
1 Tbsp. butter
2 tsp. vanilla

1. Cream together butter, sugar, and molasses.
2. Add egg. Beat well.
3. Dissolve baking soda in hot water. Stir into creamed mixture until well mixed.
4. Beat in 1 cup flour and baking powder.
5. Combine cranberries with 1/2 cup flour. Stir into batter.
6. Pour into well-greased baking insert. Cover tightly with lid or double layer of foil. Place on rack in slow cooker.

7. Pour boiling water into cooker, halfway up the sides of the insert.

8. Cover cooker. Steam 3 hours on high.

9. Remove insert from water. Cool 2 minutes. Run knife around edge of insert, turn upside down, and unmold.

10. Serve with hot Butter Sauce.

11. To make butter sauce, combine sugar, flour, water, and salt in saucepan. Cook over medium heat, stirring constantly until thickened. Remove from heat. Stir in butter and vanilla. Serve hot.

Hint: A coffee can that fits your slow cooker works as a good pudding mold. You can use a jar ring as a rack under the mold.

Deluxe Tapioca Pudding

Michelle Showalter
Bridgewater, VA

Makes 16 servings

2 qts. milk
3/4 cup dry small pearl tapioca
1 1/2 cups sugar
4 eggs, beaten
2 tsp. vanilla
3-4 cups whipped cream, or frozen
    whipped topping, thawed
chocolate candy bar

1. Combine milk, tapioca, and sugar in slow cooker.

2. Cook on high 3 hours.

3. Add a little of the hot milk to the eggs. Stir. Whisk eggs into milk mixture. Add vanilla.

4. Cover. Cook on high 20-30 minutes.

5. Cool. Chill in refrigerator. When fully chilled, beat with hand mixer to fluff the pudding.

6. Stir in whipped cream or whipped topping. Garnish with chopped candy bar.

Rice Pudding

Vera Schmucker
Goshen, IN

Makes 4-6 servings

2 1/2 cups cooked rice
1 1/2 cups evaporated milk, or scalded milk
2/3 cup sugar
2 tsp. butter or margarine, melted
1/2-1 tsp. ground nutmeg
whipped cream
maraschino cherries

1. Combine all ingredients. Pour into lightly greased slow cooker.

2. Cover. Cook on high 2 hours or on low 4-6 hours. Stir after first hour.

3. Serve topped with whipped cream and maraschino cherries.

Slow-Cooker Rice Pudding

Dede Peterson
Rapid City, SD

Makes 5 servings

1 pkg. vanilla cook-and-serve pudding mix
1 cup cooked white rice
1 cup raisins
1 tsp. cinnamon
2 tsp. vanilla
3 cups half-and-half or milk

1. Combine ingredients in slow cooker.
2. Cover. Cook on low 3-4 hours.

Chocolate Rice Pudding

Michele Ruvola
Selden, NY

Makes 4 servings

4 cups cooked white rice
¾ cup sugar
¼ cup baking cocoa powder
3 Tbsp. butter, melted
1 tsp. vanilla
2 12-oz. cans evaporated milk
whipped cream
sliced toasted almonds
maraschino cherries

1. Combine first 6 ingredients in greased slow cooker.
2. Cover. Cook on low 2½-3½ hours, or until liquid is absorbed.
3. Serve warm or chilled. Top individual servings with a dollop of whipped cream, sliced toasted almonds, and a maraschino cherry.

Simple Bread Pudding

Melanie L. Thrower
McPherson, KS

Makes 6-8 servings

6-8 slices of bread, cubed
2 cups milk
2 eggs
¼ cup sugar
1 tsp. ground cinnamon
1 tsp. vanilla

Sauce:
6-oz. can concentrated grape juice
1 Tbsp. cornstarch

1. Place bread in slow cooker.
2. Whisk together milk, eggs, sugar, cinnamon, and vanilla. Pour over bread.
3. Cover. Cook on high 2-2½ hours, or until mixture is set.
4. Combine cornstarch and concentrated juice in saucepan. Heat until boiling, stirring constantly, until sauce is thickened. Serve drizzled over bread pudding.
5. This is a fine dessert with a cold salad main dish.

Home-Style Bread Pudding

Lizzie Weaver
Ephrata, PA

Makes 4-6 servings

2 eggs, beaten
2¼ cups milk
½ tsp. cinnamon
¼ tsp. salt
½ cup brown sugar
1 tsp. vanilla
2 cups 1" bread cubes
½ cup raisins or dates

1. Combine all ingredients in bowl. Pour into slow cooker baking insert. Cover baking insert. Place on metal rack (or rubber jar ring) in bottom of slow cooker.
2. Pour ½ cup hot water into cooker.
3. Cover slow cooker. Cook on high 2-3 hours.
4. Serve pudding warm or cold topped with cherry pie filling and whipped topping.

Apple-Nut Bread Pudding

Ruth Ann Hoover
New Holland, PA

Makes 6-8 servings

8 slices raisin bread, cubed
2-3 medium-sized tart apples, peeled and sliced
1 cup chopped pecans, toasted
1 cup sugar
1 tsp. ground cinnamon
½ tsp. ground nutmeg
3 eggs, lightly beaten
2 cups half-and-half
¼ cup apple juice
¼ cup butter or margarine, melted

1. Place bread cubes, apples, and pecans in greased slow cooker and mix together gently.
2. Combine sugar, cinnamon, and nutmeg. Add remaining ingredients. Mix well. Pour over bread mixture.
3. Cover. Cook on low 3-4 hours, or until knife inserted in center comes out clean.
4. Serve with ice cream.

Peach or Pineapple Upside Down Cake

Vera M. Kuhns
Harrisonburg, VA

Makes 10 servings

1/2 cup butter or margarine, melted
1 cup brown sugar
1 medium-sized can pineapple slices,
    drained, reserving juice
6-8 maraschino cherries
1 box yellow cake mix

1. Combine butter and brown sugar. Spread over bottom of well greased cooker.

2. Add pineapple slices and place cherries in the center of each one.

3. Prepare cake according to package directions, using pineapple juice for part of liquid. Spoon cake batter into cooker over top fruit.

4. Cover cooker with 2 tea towels and then with its own lid. Cook on high 1 hour, and then on low 3-4 hours.

5. Allow cake to cool for 10 minutes. Then run knife around edge and invert cake onto large platter.

No Fat Apple Cake

Sue Hamilton
Minooka, IL

Makes 8 servings

1 cup flour
1 cup sugar
2 tsp. baking powder
1 tsp. ground cinnamon
1/4 tsp. salt
4 medium-sized cooking apples, chopped
2 eggs, beaten
2 tsp. vanilla

1. Combine flour, sugar, baking powder, cinnamon, and salt.

2. Add apples, stirring lightly to coat.

3. Combine eggs and vanilla. Add to apple mixture. Stir until just moistened. Spoon into lightly greased slow cooker.

4. Cover. Bake on high 2 1/2-3 hours.

5. Serve warm. Top with frozen whipped topping, thawed, or ice cream and a sprinkle of cinnamon.

Variation: Stir 1/2 cup broken English or black walnuts, or 1/2 cup raisins, into Step 2.

The slow cooker is great for baking desserts. Your guests will be pleasantly surprised to see a cake coming from your slow cooker.

Creamy Orange Cheesecake

Jeanette Oberholtzer
Manheim, PA

Makes 10 servings

Crust:
¾ cup graham cracker crumbs
2 Tbsp. sugar
3 Tbsp. melted butter

Filling:
2 8-oz. pkgs. cream cheese, at room
   temperature
⅔ cup sugar
2 eggs
1 egg yolk
¼ cup frozen orange juice concentrate
1 tsp. orange zest
1 Tbsp. flour
½ tsp. vanilla

1. Combine crust ingredients. Pat into 7" or 9" springform pan, whichever size fits into your slow cooker.
2. Cream together cream cheese and sugar. Add eggs and yolk. Beat for 3 minutes.
3. Beat in juice, zest, flour, and vanilla. Beat 2 minutes.
4. Pour batter into crust. Place on rack in slow cooker.
5. Cover. Cook on high 2½-3 hours. Turn off and leave stand for 1-2 hours, or until cool enough to remove from cooker.
6. Cool completely before removing sides of pan. Chill before serving.
7. Serve with thawed frozen whipped topping and fresh or mandarin orange slices.

Carrot Cake

Colleen Heatwole
Burton, MI

Makes 6-8 servings

½ cup salad oil
2 eggs
1 Tbsp. hot water
½ cup grated raw carrots
¾ cup flour
¾ cup sugar
½ tsp. baking powder
⅛ tsp. salt
¼ tsp. ground allspice
½ tsp. ground cinnamon
⅛ tsp. ground cloves
½ cup chopped nuts
½ cup raisins or chopped dates
2 Tbsp. flour

1. In large bowl, beat oil, eggs, and water for 1 minute.
2. Add carrots. Mix well.
3. Stir together flour, sugar, baking powder, salt, allspice, cinnamon, and cloves. Add to creamed mixture.
4. Toss nuts and raisins in bowl with 2 Tbsp. flour. Add to creamed mixture. Mix well.
5. Pour into greased and floured 3-lb. shortening can or slow cooker baking insert. Place can or baking insert in slow cooker.
6. Cover insert with its lid, or cover can with 8 paper towels, folded down over edge of slow cooker to absorb moisture. Cover paper towels with cooker lid. Cook on high 3-4 hours.
7. Remove can or insert from cooker and allow to cool on rack for 10 minutes. Run knife around edge of cake. Invert onto serving plate.

Dump Cake

Janice Muller
Derwood, MD

Makes 8-10 servings

20-oz. can crushed pineapple
21-oz. can blueberry or cherry pie filling
18½-oz. pkg. yellow cake mix
cinnamon
½ cup butter or margarine
1 cup chopped nuts

1. Grease bottom and sides of slow cooker.
2. Spread layers of pineapple, blueberry pie filling, and dry cake mix. Be careful not to mix the layers.
3. Sprinkle with cinnamon.
4. Top with thin layers of butter chunks and nuts.
5. Cover. Cook on high 2-3 hours.
6. Serve with vanilla ice cream.

Variation: Use a pkg. of spice cake mix and apple pie filling.

Lemon Poppy Seed Upside-Down Cake

Jeanette Oberholtzer
Manheim, PA

Makes 8-10 servings

1 pkg. lemon poppy seed bread mix
1 egg
8 ozs. light sour cream
½ cup water

Sauce:
1 Tbsp. butter
¾ cup water
½ cup sugar
¼ cup lemon juice

1. Combine first four ingredients until well moistened. Spread in lightly greased slow cooker.
2. Combine sauce ingredients in small saucepan. Bring to boil. Pour boiling mixture over batter.
3. Cover. Cook on high 2-2½ hours. Edges will be slightly brown. Turn heat off and leave in cooker for 30 minutes with cover slightly ajar.
4. When cool enough to handle, hold a large plate over top of cooker, then invert.
5. Allow to cool before slicing.

Chocolate Peanut Butter Cake

Ruth Ann Gingerich
New Holland, PA

Makes 6-8 servings

2 cups (half a package) milk chocolate
    cake mix
1/2 cup water
6 Tbsp. peanut butter
2 eggs
1/2 cup chopped nuts

1. Combine all ingredients. Beat 2 minutes
in electric mixer.
2. Pour into greased and floured 3-lb.
shortening can. Place can in slow cooker.
3. Cover top of can with 8 paper towels.
4. Cover cooker. Bake on high 2-3 hours.
5. Allow to cool for 10 minutes. Run knife
around edge and invert cake onto serving
plate. Cool completely before slicing and
serving.

Graham Cracker Cookies

Cassandra Ly
Carlisle, PA

Makes 8 dozen cookies

12-oz. pkg. (2 cups) semi-sweet chocolate
    chips
2 1-oz. squares unsweetened baking
    chocolate, shaved
2 14-oz. cans sweetened condensed milk
3¾ cups crushed graham cracker crumbs,
    divided
1 cup finely chopped walnuts

1. Place chocolate in slow cooker.
2. Cover. Cook on high 1 hour, stirring
every 15 minutes. Continue to cook on low
heat, stirring every 15 minutes, or until
chocolate is melted (about 30 minutes).
3. Stir milk into melted chocolate.
4. Add 3 cups graham cracker crumbs,
1 cup at a time, stirring after each addition.
5. Stir in nuts. Mixture should be thick but
not stiff.
6. Stir in remaining graham cracker crumbs
to reach consistency of cookie dough.
7. Drop by heaping teaspoonfuls onto
lightly greased cookie sheets. Keep remaining
mixture warm by covering and turning the
slow cooker to warm.
8. Bake at 325° for 7-9 minutes, or until
tops of cookies begin to crack. Remove from
oven. Cool 1-2 minutes before transferring to
waxed paper.

Note: These cookies freeze well.

*This delectable fudge-like cookie is a family
favorite. The original recipe (from my maternal
grandmother) was so involved and yielded so few
cookies that my mom and I would get together to
make a couple of batches only at Christmas-time.
Adapting the recipe for using a slow cooker,
rather than a double boiler, allows me to prepare
a double batch without help.*

Chocolate Fondue

Vera Schmucker
Goshen, IN
Vicki Dinkel
Sharon Springs, KS

Makes 8-10 servings

1 Tbsp. butter
16 1-oz. chocolate candy bars with
    almonds, broken
30 large marshmallows
1⅓ cups milk, divided

1. Grease slow cooker with butter. Turn to high for 10 minutes.
2. Add chocolate, marshmallows, and ⅓ cup milk.
3. Cover. Turn to low. Stir after 30 minutes; then continue cooking for another 30 minutes, or until melted and smooth.
4. Gradually add additional milk.
5. Cover. Cook on low 2-6 hours.
6. Bring the cooker to the table, along with cubes of angel food cake, strawberries, chunks of pineapple, bananas, apples, and oranges, and pretzels for dipping.

Chocolate Covered Pretzels

Beth Maurer
Harrisonburg, VA

Makes 10-12 servings

1 lb. white chocolate bark coating
2 blocks chocolate bark coating
1 bag pretzel rods

1. Chop white chocolate into small chunks. Place in slow cooker.
2. Cover. Heat over low setting, stirring occasionally until melted. Turn off cooker.
3. Using a spoon, coat ¾ of each pretzel rod with chocolate. Place on waxed paper to cool.
4. Chop chocolate bark into small chunks. Microwave on high for 1½ minutes. Stir. Microwave on high for 1 minute. Stir. Microwave on high in 30-second intervals until chocolate is smooth when stirred. (Do not allow chocolate to get too hot or it will scorch.)
5. Put melted chocolate in small bag. Snip off corner of bag. Drizzle chocolate over white chocolate-covered pretzels.

These are easy to make; they taste wonderful and are good holiday gifts when placed in small gift bags!

Appetizers, Snacks, and Spreads

Hot Artichoke Dip

Mary E. Wheatley
Mashpee, MA

Makes 7-8 cups dip

2 14³/4 oz. jars marinated artichoke hearts,
  drained
1 cup mayonnaise
1 cup sour cream
1 cup water chestnuts, chopped
2 cups grated Parmesan cheese
1/4 cup finely chopped scallions

   1. Cut artichoke hearts into small pieces.
Add mayonnaise, sour cream, water chestnuts,
cheese, and scallions. Pour into slow cooker.
   2. Cover. Cook on high 1-2 hours or on low
3-4 hours.
   3. Serve with crackers or crusty French
bread.

Red Pepper-Cheese Dip

Ann Bender
Ft. Defiance, VA

Makes 12-15 servings

2 Tbsp. olive oil
4-6 large red peppers, cut into 1″ squares
1/2 lb. feta cheese
crackers or pita bread

   1. Pour oil into slow cooker. Stir in peppers.
   2. Cover. Cook on low 2 hours.
   3. Serve with feta cheese on crackers.

Chili Con Queso

Arlene Leaman Kliewer
Lakewood, CO

Makes 12-16 servings

2 Tbsp. oil
1 medium onion, chopped
2 4-oz. cans chopped green chilies
14½-oz. can Mexican-style stewed
  tomatoes, drained
1 lb. Velveeta cheese, cubed

1. In skillet saute onion in oil until transparent. Add chilies and tomatoes. Bring to boil.
2. Add cheese. Pour into slow cooker on low. Cook for 2 hours.
3. Keep warm in slow cooker, stirring occasionally.
4. Serve with tortilla chips.

Chili Bean Dip

Glenna Fay Bergey
Lebanon, OR

Makes 10 appetizer servings

15-oz. can chili
1 small green or red sweet pepper, diced
8-oz. jar Cheese Whiz
1 lb. cheddar cheese, cubed

1. Combine all ingredients in slow cooker.
2. Cover. Cook on high 45-60 minutes, or until cheese is melted. Turn cooker to low for up to 6 hours.
3. Serve dip warm from the cooker with nacho chips.

Hot Chili Dip

Lavina Hochstedler
Grand Blanc, MI
Anna Stoltzfus
Honey Brook, PA
Kathi Rogge
Alexandria, IN

Makes 2 cups

24-oz. jar hot salsa
15-oz. can chili with beans
2 2¼-oz. cans sliced ripe olives, drained
12 ozs. mild cheese, cubed

1. Combine all ingredients in slow cooker.
2. Cover. Cook on low 1-2 hours, or until cheese is melted, stirring halfway through.
3. Serve with tortilla chips.

Chili Dip

Sue Tjon
Austin, TX

Makes 8 servings

1 large can chili without beans
8-oz. pkg. cream cheese
10-oz. pkg. jalapeno Jack cheese, shredded
tortilla chips

1. Pour chili into slow cooker.
2. Cut cream cheese into chunks and add to chili.
3. Add shredded cheese. Stir well.
4. Cover. Cook on low 4 hours.
5. Serve with tortilla chips.

This is best served warm, so I keep it in the slow cooker to serve. You can refrigerate leftovers and reheat them.

Cheesy Hot Bean Dip

John D. Allen
Rye, CO

Makes 4-5 cups dip

16-oz. can refried beans
1 cup salsa
2 cups (8 ozs.) shredded Jack and cheddar
    cheeses, mixed
1 cup sour cream
3-oz. pkg. cream cheese, cubed
1 Tbsp. chili powder
1/4 tsp. ground cumin
tortilla chips

1. Combine all ingredients except chips in slow cooker.
2. Cover. Cook on high 2 hours. Stir 2-3 times during cooking.
3. Serve warm from the cooker with chips.

This bean dip is a favorite. Once you start on it, it's hard to leave it alone. We have been known to dip into it even when it's cold.

Mexican
Bean and Cheese Dip

Mary Sommerfeld
Lancaster, PA

Makes about 5 cups dip

15-oz. can refried beans
8-oz. jar taco sauce
1 lb. Velveeta cheese, cubed
1 pkg. dry taco seasoning

1. Combine ingredients in slow cooker.
2. Cover. Cook on low 2-3 hours, or until cheese is melted.
3. Serve warm from the cooker with tortilla chips.

Note: If you're cautious about salt, choose minimally salted chips.

Mexican Meat Dip

Deborah Swartz
Grottoes, VA

Makes 20 servings

1 lb. ground beef
3/4-1 cup chopped onions
15-oz. can refried beans
1 pkg. dry taco seasoning mix
1 cup sour cream
1 1/2 cups grated mozzarella cheese

1. Brown ground beef and onions in skillet. Drain. Place meat and onions in slow cooker.
2. Add beans and taco seasoning mix. Mix together well.
3. Spread sour cream over mixture. Sprinkle cheese over top.
4. Cover. Cook on low 1 1/2 hours or on high 3/4 hour.
5. Serve warm from the cooker with tortilla chips.

Hamburger Cheese Dip
Carol Eberly
Harrisonburg, VA

Makes about 6 cups dip

1 2-lb. box Velveeta cheese, cubed
1 lb. ground beef
1 onion, chopped
10³/4-oz. can cream of mushroom soup
14.5-oz. can diced tomatoes with green
  chilies

1. While cutting up cheese, brown beef and onions in skillet. Drain meat mixture and place in slow cooker.
2. Place all remaining ingredients in slow cooker and combine.
3. Cover. Cook on low 2 hours, or until cheese is melted, stirring occasionally.
4. Serve over baked potatoes or with tortilla chips.

Variation: For more snap, add 4.5-oz. can green chilies in Step 2.

Hot Hamburger Dip
Kristi See
Weskan, KS

Makes 10-12 servings

1 lb. ground beef
1 small onion, chopped
1 lb. Velveeta cheese, cubed
8-oz. can green chilies and tomatoes
2 tsp. Worcestershire sauce
1/2 tsp. chili powder
1 tsp. garlic powder
1/2 tsp. pepper

10³/4-oz. can tomato soup
10³/4-oz. can cream of mushroom soup

1. Brown ground beef and onions in skillet. Drain and place in slow cooker.
2. Add remaining ingredients and stir well.
3. Cover. Simmer until cheese is melted.
4. Serve with corn chips and little barbecue smokies.

TNT Dip
Sheila Plock
Boalsburg, PA

Makes 8 cups

1¹/2 lbs. ground beef, browned
10³/4-oz. can cream of mushroom soup
1/4 cup butter, melted
1 lb. Velveeta, cubed
1 cup salsa
2 Tbsp. chili powder

1. Combine all ingredients in slow cooker.
2. Cover. Cook on high 1-1¹/4 hours, or until cheese is melted, stirring occasionally.
3. Serve with tortilla chips, corn chips, or party rye bread.

Variation: To change the balance of flavors, use 1 lb. browned ground beef and 1¹/2 cups salsa.

My son has hosted a Super Bowl party for his college friends at our house the past two years. He served this dip the first year, and the second year it was requested. His friends claim it's the best dip they've ever eaten. With a bunch of college kids it disappears quickly.

Nacho Dip

Beth Maurer
Harrisonburg, VA

Makes 10-12 servings

2 lbs. ground beef, browned
1 lb. sausage, browned
16-oz. jar medium-hot salsa
1 pkg. dry taco seasoning mix
2-lb. box Velveeta cheese, cubed
10¾-oz. can cream of mushroom soup

1. Stir salsa and seasoning mix into meat.
Then spread in bottom of slow cooker.
2. Cover and cook on high one hour.
3. Stir in cheese and soup.
4. Cover. Cook on low 3-4 hours, until
ingredients are hot and cheese and soup are
melted.
5. Serve with unsalted chips, tortilla or
nacho chips, pita wedges, chopped tomatoes,
refried beans, onions, and sour cream.

*This is a delight at any party or get-together.
We serve it at every Christmas party.*

Hot Beef Dip

Paula Showalter
Weyers Cave, VA

Makes about 3 cups dip

2 8-oz. pkgs. cream cheese, softened
8 ozs. mild cheddar cheese, grated
1 green pepper, chopped fine
1 small onion, chopped fine
¼ lb. chipped dried beef, shredded

1. Combine cheeses.
2. Fold in onions, peppers, and beef.
3. Place in slow cooker.
4. Cover. Cook on low 2-3 hours.
5. Serve hot with crackers.

Variation: *For more kick, add a few finely diced
chili peppers to Step 2.*

Hearty Beef Dip Fondue

Ann Bender
Ft. Defiance, VA
Charlotte Shaffer
East Earl, PA

Makes 2 1/2 cups dip

1 3/4 cups milk
2 8-oz. pkgs. cream cheese, cubed
2 tsp. dry mustard
1/4 cup chopped green onions
2 1/2 ozs. sliced dried beef, shredded or
   torn into small pieces
French bread, cut into bite-sized pieces,
   each having a side of crust

1. Heat milk in slow cooker on high.
2. Add cheese. Stir until melted.
3. Add mustard, green onions, and dried beef. Stir well.
4. Cover. Cook on low for up to 6 hours.
5. Serve by dipping bread pieces on long forks into mixture.

Variations: Add 1/2 cup chopped pecans, 2 Tbsp. chopped olives, or 1 tsp. minced onion in Step 3.

I make this on cold winter evenings, and we sit around the table playing games.

Menu Idea

Hearty Beef Dip Fondue
French Bread Cubes
Tossed Salad with a variety of greens,
   slivered almonds, mandarin oranges,
   and purple onion rings, topped with
   a Vidalia Onion Dressing
Strawberry Rhubarb Custard Pie

Cheesy Sausage Dip

Reba Rhodes
Bridgewater, VA

Makes 12-14 servings

1 lb. smoked sausage, chopped
1 lb. Velveeta cheese, cubed
1 1/4 cups salsa

1. Brown sausage in skillet. Drain and place in slow cooker.
2. Add cheese. Pour salsa over top.
3. Cover. Cook on low 1 1/2-2 hours.
4. Serve with tortilla chips or party rye bread.

Sausage Cheese Dip

Fannie Miller
Hutchinson, KS

Makes 20 servings

1 lb. sausage, either sliced thin, or with
   casings removed and crumbled
1 medium onion, chopped
1 green pepper, chopped
2 lbs. Velveeta or American cheese, cubed
16-oz. jar medium salsa

1. Brown sausage and onions in skillet. Drain of drippings and transfer meat and onions to slow cooker.
2. Add remaining ingredients to slow cooker and stir well.
3. Cover. Cook on low 4-5 hours.
4. Serve warm from cooker with tortilla chips.

Barbara Jean's Pizza Dip

Barbara Jean Fabel
Wausau, WI

Makes 8-10 servings

4 ozs. mozzarella cheese, shredded
4 ozs. cheddar cheese, shredded
1 green pepper, minced
5-oz. can sliced black olives
5-oz. jar sliced stuffed green olives
4 ozs. sliced mushrooms
1 cup mayonnaise
pepperoni slices, cut up

1. Combine all ingredients except pepperoni in slow cooker.
2. Top with pepperoni.
3. Cover. Cook on low 2 hours.
4. Stir well before bringing to the buffet or table.
5. Serve with snack crackers, or pour over steamed cauliflower and broccoli.

Slow Cooker Reuben Dip

Allison Ingels
Maynard, IA

Makes 8-12 servings

8-oz. carton sour cream
2 8-oz. pkgs. cream cheese, softened
8-oz. can sauerkraut, drained
3 2½-oz. pkgs. dried corned beef,
    finely chopped
6-oz. pkg. shredded Swiss cheese

1. Combine ingredients in slow cooker.
2. Cover. Heat on low 3-4 hours, or until cheeses are melted.

3. Serve from cooker with rye crackers or rye party bread.

Reuben Appetizer

Joleen Albrecht
Gladstone, MI

Makes 12 servings

½ cup mayonnaise
10 ozs. Swiss cheese, shredded
½ lb. chipped or thinly sliced corned beef
16-oz. can sauerkraut, drained and cut up
sliced party rye bread

1. Combine all ingredients except bread in slow cooker.
2. Heat until cheese is melted.
3. Serve hot on rye bread.

Black-Eyed Pea Dip

Audrey Romonosky
Austin, TX

Makes 12 snack-sized servings

8 ozs. Velveeta cheese, cubed
15.5-oz. can black-eyed peas, drained
4.5-oz. can chopped green chilies
1/2 cup (1 stick) butter, melted
4 chopped green onions
tortilla chips

1. Combine cheese, peas, chilies, butter, and onions in slow cooker.
2. Cover. Cook on low, stirring occasionally, until cheese melts. Cook an additional 1½ hours on low.
3. Serve warm from cooker with tortilla chips.

Cheese and Crab Dip

Donna Lantgen
Rapid City, SD

Makes 10-12 servings

3 8-oz. pkgs. cream cheese, at room
   temperature
2 6-oz. cans crabmeat, drained
1 can broken shrimp, drained
6 Tbsp. finely chopped onions
1 tsp. horseradish
1/2 cup toasted almonds, broken

1. Combine all ingredients in slow cooker.
2. Cover. Cook on low 2 hours.
3. Serve with crackers or bread cubes.

Hot Crab Dip

Cassandra Ly
Carlisle, PA
Miriam Nolt
New Holland, PA

Makes 15-20 servings

1/2 cup milk
1/3 cup salsa
3 8-oz. pkgs. cream cheese, cubed
2 8-oz. pkgs. imitation crabmeat, flaked
1 cup thinly sliced green onions
4-oz. can chopped green chilies
assorted crackers or bread cubes

1. Combine milk and salsa. Transfer to greased slow cooker.
2. Stir in cream cheese, crabmeat, onions, and chilies.
3. Cover. Cook on low 3-4 hours, stirring every 30 minutes.
4. Serve with crackers or bread.

Crab Dip

Rebecca Plank Leichty
Harrisonburg, VA

Makes 8-10 servings

2 eggs, beaten
1 green pepper, diced
2 Tbsp. diced pimento
1/2 tsp. ground mustard
1/8 tsp. pepper
1 tsp. salt
10³/4-oz. can cream of celery soup
1-lb. can white crabmeat, or imitation
    crabmeat
toasted bread crisps

1. Beat eggs with whisk in greased slow cooker.
2. Add green pepper, pimento, seasonings, and soup. Mix well.
3. Fold in crabmeat.
4. Cover. Cook on high 3 hours.
5. Serve with toasted bread crisps for dipping.

Note: To make bread crisps, cut crusts off bread slices. Cut remaining bread into triangles. Toast on baking sheet in 350° oven. Turn once to brown evenly.

This is an easy way to serve an appetizer before a meal.

Liver Paté

Barbara Walker
Sturgis, SD

Makes 1¹/2 cups paté

1 lb. chicken livers
1/2 cup dry wine
1 tsp. instant chicken bouillon
1 tsp. minced parsley
1 Tbsp. instant minced onion
1/4 tsp. ground ginger
1/2 tsp. seasoning salt
1 Tbsp. soy sauce
1/4 tsp. dry mustard
1/4 cup soft butter
1 Tbsp. brandy

1. In slow cooker, combine all ingredients except butter and brandy.
2. Cover. Cook on low 4-5 hours. Let stand in liquid until cool.
3. Drain. Place in blender or food grinder. Add butter and brandy. Process until smooth.
4. Serve with crackers or toast.

Pear Butter

Betty Moore
Plano, IL

Makes 2-3 pints

10 large pears (about 4 lbs.)
1 cup orange juice
2½ cups sugar
1 tsp. ground cinnamon
1 tsp. ground cloves
½ tsp. ground allspice

1. Peel and quarter pears. Place in slow cooker.
2. Cover. Cook on low 10-12 hours. Drain and then discard liquid.
3. Mash or puree pears. Add remaining ingredients. Mix well and return to slow cooker.
4. Cover. Cook on high 1 hour.
5. Place in hot sterile jars and seal. Process in hot water bath for 10 minutes. Allow to cool undisturbed for 24 hours.

Snack Mix

Yvonne Boettger
Harrisonburg, VA

Makes 10-14 servings

8 cups Chex cereal, of any combination
6 cups from the following: pretzels, snack crackers, goldfish, Cheerios, nuts, bagel chips, toasted corn
6 Tbsp. butter or margarine, melted
2 Tbsp. Worcestershire sauce
1 tsp. seasoning salt
½ tsp. garlic powder
½ tsp. onion salt
½ tsp. onion powder

1. Combine first two ingredients in slow cooker.
2. Combine butter and seasonings. Pour over dry mixture. Toss until well mixed.
3. Cover. Cook on low 2 hours, stirring every 30 minutes.

Beverages

Hot Apple Cider

Joan Rosenberger
Stephens City, VA

Makes 21 servings

4 qts. cider
4 sticks cinnamon
2 tsp. whole cloves

1. Combine ingredients in 6-qt. slow cooker.
2. Cover. Cook on high 2 hours. Turn to low and simmer until ready to serve.

Spicy Hot Cider

Marcia S. Myer
Manheim, PA

Makes 16 servings

1 gallon cider
4 cinnamon sticks
2 Tbsp. ground allspice
1/2 cup brown sugar

1. Combine all ingredients in slow cooker.
2. Cover. Cook on low 3 hours.

Red Hot Apple Cider

Allison Ingels
Maynard, IA

Makes 16 servings

1 gallon apple cider or apple juice
1¼ cups cinnamon candy hearts
4-5 cinnamon sticks

   1. Combine ingredients in slow cooker.
   2. Cover. Cook on low 1½-2 hours.
   3. Serve hot with a cinnamon stick in each cup.

Our family enjoys this recipe on cold winter evenings and especially Christmas Eve. The smell creates a very relaxing atmosphere.

Matthew's Hot Mulled Cider

Shirley Unternahrer Hinh
Wayland, IA

Makes 12 servings

2 qts. apple cider
¼-½ cup brown sugar, according to your
   taste preference
½ tsp. vanilla
1 cinnamon stick
4 cloves

   1. Combine ingredients in slow cooker.
   2. Cover. Cook on low 5 hours. Stir.

Our kids just tried hot mulled cider for the first time this past Christmas. They loved it. It's fun to try new old things.

Cider Snap

Cathy Boshart
Lebanon, PA

Makes 12-16 servings

2 qts. apple cider or apple juice
4 Tbsp. red cinnamon candies
at least 16 apple slices
at least 16 cinnamon sticks

   1. Combine cider and cinnamon candies in slow cooker.
   2. Cover. Cook on high for 2 hours until candies dissolve and cider is hot.
   3. Ladle into mugs and serve with apple slice floaters and cinnamon stick stirrers.

This is a cold-winter-night luxury. Make it in the morning and keep it on low throughout the day so its good fragrance can fill the house.

Menu Idea

Cider Snap
Ginger Cookies
Popcorn
Cheeseball and Crackers

Maple Mulled Cider
Leesa Lesenski
Wheately, MA

Makes 8-10 servings

1/2 gallon cider
3-4 cinnamon sticks
2 tsp. whole cloves
2 tsp. whole allspice
1-2 Tbsp. orange juice concentrate,
   optional
1-2 Tbsp. maple syrup, optional

1. Combine ingredients in slow cooker.
2. Cover. Heat on low for 2 hours. Serve warm.

Serve at Halloween, Christmas caroling, or sledding parties.

Hot Spicy Cider for a Crowd
Lydia A. Yoder
London, OH

Makes 32 servings

1 gallon apple cider
1 cup sugar
2 tsp. ground cloves
2 tsp. ground allspice
2 3"-long cinnamon sticks
2 oranges studded with cloves

1. Combine all ingredients in slow cooker.
2. Cover. Cook on low 5-6 hours or on high 2-3 hours.

Variation: You can replace apple cider with apple juice, especially if cider is out of season, and 1/4 cup orange juice for the oranges.

Deep Red Apple Cider
Judi Manos
West Islip, NY

Makes 8-9 servings

5 cups apple cider
3 cups dry red wine
1/4 cup brown sugar
1/2 tsp. whole cloves
1/4 tsp. whole allspice
1 stick cinnamon

1. Combine all ingredients in slow cooker.
2. Cover. Cook on low 3-4 hours.
3. Remove cloves, allspice, and cinnamon before serving.

Variation: You can use 8 cups apple cider and no red wine.

Orange Cider Punch

Naomi Ressler
Harrisonburg, VA

Makes 9-12 6-oz. servings

1 cup sugar
2 cinnamon sticks
1 tsp. whole nutmeg
2 cups apple cider or apple juice
6 cups orange juice
fresh orange

1. Combine ingredients in slow cooker.
2. Cover. Cook on low 4-10 hours or high 2-3 hours.
3. Float thin slices of an orange in cooker before serving.

Wassail

Virginia Bender
Dover, DE

Makes 16-18 servings

1 gallon cider
6-oz. container orange juice concentrate
6-oz. container lemonade concentrate
1/2-1 cup brown sugar
1 tsp. whole nutmeg
1 Tbsp. whole cloves
1 Tbsp. whole allspice
orange slices
cinnamon sticks

1. Combine cider, orange juice and lemonade concentrates, and brown sugar. Mix well.
2. Place nutmeg, cloves, and allspice in cheesecloth bag or spice ball. Add to juices in slow cooker.
3. Cover. Cook on low 2-8 hours.
4. Float orange slices and cinnamon sticks on top. Ladle from slow cooker to serve.

Wassail Hot Cider

Ruth Hershey
Paradise, PA

Makes 18 6-oz. servings

3 tea bags, your choice of flavors
1 qt. boiling water
2 qts. cider
1 qt. cranberry juice
2 cups orange juice
½ cup sugar
3 cinnamon sticks
12 whole cloves
thin orange slices, optional

1. Steep tea in boiling water for 5 minutes. Remove tea bags and pour tea into cooker.
2. Combine all remaining ingredients in slow cooker.
3. Cover. Cook on low 4 hours.
4. Float orange slices in cider when ready to serve. Keep warm in cooker while serving.

Hot Cranberry Cider

Kristi See
Weskan, KS

Makes 10-12 servings

2 qts. apple cider or apple juice
1 pt. cranberry juice
½-¾ cup sugar, according to your taste
 preference
2 cinnamon sticks
1 tsp. whole allspice
1 orange, studded with whole cloves

1. Put all ingredients in slow cooker.
2. Cover. Cook on high 1 hour, then on low 4-8 hours. Serve warm.
3. Serve with finger foods.

Note: To garnish wassail with an orange, insert 10-12 ½"-long whole cloves halfway into orange. Place studded orange in flat baking pan with ¼ cup water. Bake at 325° for 30 minutes. Just before serving, float orange on top of wassail.

I come from a family of eight children, and every Christmas we all get together. We eat dinner, and then set around playing games and drinking Hot Cranberry Cider.

Fruity Wassail

Kelly Evenson
Pittsboro, NC

Makes 20 cups

6 cups apple cider
1 cinnamon stick
¼ tsp. ground nutmeg
¼ cup honey
3 Tbsp. lemon juice
1 tsp. grated lemon rind
46-oz. can pineapple juice

1. Combine ingredients in slow cooker.
2. Cover. Cook on low 1-2 hours.
3. Serve warm from slow cooker.

Variation: Use 3 cups cranberry juice and reduce the amount of pineapple juice by 3 cups, to add more color and to change the flavor of the wassail.

Johnny Appleseed Tea

Sheila Plock
Boalsburg, PA

Makes 8-9 cups

2 qts. water, divided
6 tea bags of your favorite flavor
6 ozs. frozen apple juice, thawed
¼ cup, plus 2 Tbsp., firmly packed
  brown sugar

1. Bring 1 quart water to boil. Add tea bags.
Remove from heat. Cover and let steep
5 minutes. Pour into slow cooker.
2. Add remaining ingredients and mix well.
3. Cover. Heat on low until hot. Continue
on low while serving from slow cooker.

I serve this wonderful hot beverage with
cookies at our Open House Tea and Cookies
afternoon, which I host at Christmas-time for
friends and neighbors.

Hot Fruit Tea

Kelly Evenson
Pittsboro, NC

Makes 20 servings

5-6 tea bags, fruit flavor of your choice
2 cups boiling water
1¾ cups sugar
2 cinnamon sticks
2½ qts. water
1¼ tsp. vanilla
1¼ tsp. almond extract
juice of 3 lemons
juice of 3 oranges

1. Steep tea bags in boiling water for
5 minutes.
2. Bring tea water, sugar, cinnamon sticks,
and 2½ qts. water to boil in saucepan. Remove
from heat and add remaining ingredients.
3. Pour tea into slow cooker and keep warm
there while serving.

Variation: *Float thinly cut fresh lemon and/or*
orange slices in tea.

Spicy Autumn Punch

Marlene Bogard
Newton, KS

Makes 16 servings

2 oranges
8 whole cloves
6 cups apple juice
1 cinnamon stick
1/4 tsp. ground nutmeg
3 Tbsp. lemon juice
1/4 cup honey
2 1/4 cups pineapple juice

1. Press cloves into oranges. Bake at 350° for 30 minutes.
2. Meanwhile, combine apple juice and cinnamon stick in slow cooker.
3. Cover. Cook on high 1 hour.
4. Add remaining ingredients except oranges.
5. Cover. Cook on low 2-3 hours. Add oranges at end, either whole or in quarters.

Hot Buttered Lemonade

Janie Steele
Moore, OK

Makes 5-6 servings

4 1/2 cups water
3/4 cup sugar
1 1/2 tsp. grated lemon peel
3/4 cup lemon juice
2 Tbsp. butter
6 cinnamon sticks

1. Combine water, sugar, lemon peel, lemon juice, and butter in slow cooker.
2. Cover. Cook on high for 2 1/2 hours, or until well heated through.
3. Serve very hot with a cinnamon stick in each mug.

Fruity Hot Punch

Evelyn L. Ward
Greeley, CO

Makes 12 servings

2 16-oz. cans cranberry sauce, mashed
4 cups water
1 qt. pineapple juice
3/4 cup brown sugar
1/4 tsp. salt
1/4 tsp. ground nutmeg
3/4 tsp. ground cloves
1/2 tsp. ground allspice
12 cinnamon sticks
butter, optional

1. Combine all ingredients in slow cooker.
2. Cover. Heat on low 4 hours.
3. Serve in mugs with cinnamon stick stirrers. Dot each serving with butter if you wish.

My daughter is a teacher and has served this at faculty meetings when it's her turn to treat.

Hot Cranberry Punch

Janie Steele
Moore, OK

Makes 15-16 8-oz. servings

1 cup water
1 1/4 cups brown sugar
3/8 tsp. salt
3/8 tsp. nutmeg
3/8 tsp. cinnamon
3/4 tsp. allspice
1 1/8 tsp. cloves
46-oz. can unsweetened pineapple juice
64-oz. bottle cranberry juice
rum flavoring, optional
red food coloring, optional
15-16 cinnamon sticks

1. Combine water and sugar in slow cooker. Bring to boil.
2. Place salt and spices in bag or tea ball. Add spice ball to cooker.
3. Cover. Cook on high 1 hour.
4. Add juices, and rum flavoring and food coloring, if desired.
5. Cover. Cook on high 2-3 hours until hot.
6. Serve in cups, each with a cinnamon-stick stirrer.

Christmas Wassail

Dottie Schmidt
Kansas City, MO

Makes 6-8 servings

2 cups cranberry juice
3¼ cups hot water
⅓ cup sugar
6-oz. can lemonade concentrate
1 stick cinnamon
5 whole cloves
2 oranges, cut in thin slices

1. Combine all ingredients except oranges in slow cooker. Stir until sugar is dissolved.
2. Cover. Cook on high 1 hour. Strain out spices.
3. Serve hot with an orange slice floating in each cup.

Hot Chocolate

Colleen Heatwole
Burton, MI

Makes 10-12 servings

8 cups water
3 cups dried milk
⅓ cup non-dairy coffee creamer
1 cup instant hot chocolate mix (the kind you mix with milk, not water)
marshmallows

1. Pour water into slow cooker.
2. Gradually stir in dried milk until blended.
3. Cover and cook on high 2-3 hours, or until milk is hot.
4. Stir in coffee creamer and hot chocolate mix.
5. Turn on low until serving time, up to 3-4 hours.
6. Serve in mugs topped with marshmallows.

Hot Chocolate with Stir-Ins

Stacy Schmucker Stoltzfus
Enola, PA

Makes 12 6-oz. servings

9½ cups water
1½ cups hot chocolate mix
Stir-ins:
    smooth peanut butter
    chocolate-mint candies, chopped
    candy canes, broken
    assorted flavored syrups: hazelnut,
        almond, raspberry, Irish creme
    instant coffee granules
    cinnamon
    nutmeg
whipped topping
candy sprinkles

1. Pour water into slow cooker. Heat on high 1-2 hours. (Or heat water in tea kettle and pour into slow cooker.) Turn cooker to low to keep hot for hours.
2. Stir in hot chocolate mix until blended.
3. Arrange stir-ins in small bowls.
4. Instruct guests to place approximately 1 Tbsp. of desired stir-in in mug before ladling hot chocolate in. Stir well.
5. Top with whipped topping and candy sprinkles.

Crockery Cocoa

Betty Hostetler
Allensville, PA

Makes 9-12 servings, depending on size of mugs

½ cup sugar
½ cup unsweetened cocoa powder
2 cups boiling water
3½ cups nonfat dry milk powder
6 cups water
1 tsp. vanilla
marshmallows
1 tsp. ground cinnamon

1. Combine sugar and cocoa powder in slow cooker. Add 2 cups boiling water. Stir well to dissolve.
2. Add dry milk powder, 6 cups water, and vanilla. Stir well to dissolve.
3. Cover. Cook on low 4 hours or high 1-1½ hours.
4. Before serving, beat with rotary beater to make frothy. Ladle into mugs. Top with marshmallows and sprinkle with cinnamon.

Variations:

1. Add ⅛ tsp. ground nutmeg, along with ground cinnamon in Step 4.

2. Mocha-style—Stir ¾ tsp. coffee crystals into each serving in Step 4.

3. Coffee-Cocoa—Pour half-cups of freshly brewed, high quality coffee; top with half-cups of Crockery Cocoa.

Breakfast Dishes

Breakfast Skillet

Sue Hamilton
Minooka, IL

Makes 4-5 servings

3 cups milk
5.5 oz. box au gratin potatoes
1 tsp. hot sauce
5 eggs, lightly beaten
1 Tbsp. prepared mustard
4-oz. can sliced mushrooms
8 slices bacon, fried and crumbled
1 cup cheddar cheese, shredded

1. Combine milk, au gratin-sauce packet, hot sauce, eggs, and mustard.
2. Stir in dried potatoes, mushrooms, and bacon.
3. Cover. Cook on high 2½-3 hours or on low 5-6 hours.
4. Sprinkle cheese over top. Cover until melted.

Menu Idea

For Brunch: Breakfast Skillet
Toast or Muffins

Western Omelet Casserole

Mary Louise Martin
Boyd, WI

Makes 10 servings

32-oz. bag frozen hash brown potatoes
1 lb. cooked ham, cubed
1 medium onion, diced
1½ cups shredded cheddar cheese
12 eggs
1 cup milk
1 tsp. salt
1 tsp. pepper

1. Layer one-third each of frozen potatoes, ham, onions, and cheese in bottom of slow cooker. Repeat 2 times.
2. Beat together eggs, milk, salt, and pepper. Pour over mixture in slow cooker.
3. Cover. Cook on low 8-9 hours.
4. Serve with orange juice and fresh fruit.

Mexican-Style Grits
Mary Sommerfeld
Lancaster, PA

Makes 10-12 servings

1½ cups instant grits
1 lb. Velveeta cheese, cubed
½ tsp. garlic powder
2 4-oz. cans diced chilies
½ cup (1 stick) butter or margarine

1. Prepare grits according to package directions.
2. Stir in cheese, garlic powder, and chilies, until cheese is melted.
3. Stir in butter. Pour into greased slow cooker.
4. Cover. Cook on high 2-3 hours or on low 4-6 hours.

Menu Idea

Mexican-Style Grits
Fried or Scrambled Eggs
Bacon or Sausage
Toast

Cornmeal Mush
Betty Hostetler
Allensville, PA

Makes 15-18 servings

2 cups cornmeal
2 tsp. salt
2 cups cold water
6 cups hot water

1. Combine cornmeal, salt, and cold water.
2. Stir in hot water. Pour into greased slow cooker.
3. Cover. Cook on high 1 hour, then stir again and cook on low 3-4 hours. Or cook on low 5-6 hours, stirring once every hour during the first 2 hours.
4. Serve hot with butter as a side dish.

Variations:
1. Pour cooked cornmeal mush into loaf pans. Chill until set. Cut into ½-inch slices. Coat with flour and fry in butter.

2. Serve warm with milk, butter, and syrup or chili.

3. Serve slices for breakfast with maple syrup, bacon, sausage, or ham and eggs.

When we lived on the farm, Mother would prepare boiled mush for the evening meal. The rest she poured into pans and fried for supper the next evening. I adapted this recipe for the slow cooker several years ago when Mother was living with us and I needed to go to work.

4. Allow to cool in cooker, stirring every 30 minutes or so, or spread onto cookie sheet. When thoroughly cooled, break into chunks and store in airtight container.

Slow Cooker Oatmeal

Betty B. Dennison
Grove City, PA

Makes 2 servings

1 cup uncooked rolled oats
2 cups water
salt
1/3-1/2 cup raisins
1/4 tsp. ground nutmeg
1/4 tsp. ground cinnamon

1. Combine ingredients in slow cooker.
2. Cover. Cook on low 6-8 hours.
3. Eat with milk and brown sugar.

Peanut Butter Granola

Dawn Ranck
Harrisonburg, VA

Makes 16-20 servings

6 cups dry oatmeal
1/2 cup wheat germ
1/2 cup toasted coconut
1/2 cup sunflower seeds
1/2 cup raisins
1 cup butter
1 cup peanut butter
1 cup brown sugar

1. Combine oatmeal, wheat germ, coconut, sunflower seeds, and raisins in large slow cooker.
2. Melt together butter, peanut butter, and brown sugar. Pour over oatmeal in cooker. Mix well.
3. Cover. Cook on low 1 1/2 hours, stirring every 15 minutes.

Hot Wheatberry Cereal

Rosemarie Fitzgerald
Gibsonia, PA

Makes 4 servings

1 cup wheatberries
5 cups water
butter
milk
honey

1. Rinse and sort berries. Cover with water and soak all day (or 8 hours) in slow cooker.
2. Cover. Cook on low overnight (or 10 hours).
3. Drain, if needed. Serve hot with honey, milk, and butter.

Variations and Notes:
1. Eat your hot wheatberries with raisins and maple syrup as a variation.

2. Wheatberries can also be used in pilafs or grain salads. Cook as indicated, drain and cool.

Breakfast Apple Cobbler

Anona M. Teel
Banga, PA

Makes 6-8 servings

8 medium apples, cored, peeled, sliced
¼ cup sugar
dash of cinnamon
juice of 1 lemon
¼ cup (½ stick) butter, melted
2 cups granola

1. Combine ingredients in slow cooker.
2. Cover. Cook on low 7-9 hours (while you sleep!), or on high 2-3 hours (after you're up in the morning).

Hot Applesauce Breakfast

Colleen Konetzni
Rio Rancho, NM

Makes 8 servings

10 apples, peeled and sliced
½-1 cup sugar
1 Tbsp. ground cinnamon
¼ tsp. ground nutmeg

1. Combine ingredients in slow cooker.
2. Cover. Cook on low 8-10 hours.

Variations and Notes:
1. Yummy over oatmeal or with vanilla yogurt. Or serve it over pancakes or waffles.

2. Add chopped nuts for an extra treat.

Breakfast Prunes

Jo Haberkamp
Fairbank, IA

Makes 6 servings

2 cups orange juice
¼ cup orange marmalade
1 tsp. ground cinnamon
¼ tsp. ground cloves
¼ tsp. ground nutmeg
1 cup water
12-oz. pkg. pitted dried prunes (1¾ cups)
2 thin lemon slices

1. Combine orange juice, marmalade, cinnamon, cloves, nutmeg, and water in slow cooker.
2. Stir in prunes and lemon slices.
3. Cover. Cook on low 8-10 hours, or overnight.
4. Serve warm as a breakfast food, or warm or chilled as a side dish with a meal later in the day.

Variation: If you prefer more citrus flavor, eliminate the ground cloves and reduce the cinnamon to ½ tsp. and the nutmeg to ⅛ tsp.

Dulce Leche (Sweet Milk)
Dorothy Horst
Tiskilwa, IL

Makes 2¹/2 cups

2 14-oz. cans sweetened condensed milk

1. Place unopened cans of milk in slow cooker. Fill cooker with warm water so that it comes above the cans by 1¹/2-2 inches.
2. Cover cooker. Cook on high 2 hours.
3. Cool unopened cans.
4. When opened, the contents should be thick and spreadable. Use as a filling between 2 cookies or crackers.

When on a tour in Argentina, we were served this at breakfast time as a spread on toast or thick slices of bread. We were also presented with a container of prepared Dulce Leche as a parting gift to take home. This dish also sometimes appears on Mexican menus.

Breakfast Wassail
Lori Berezovsky
Salina, KS

Makes 4 quarts

64-oz. bottle cranberry juice
32-oz. bottle apple juice
12-oz. can frozen pineapple juice concentrate
12-oz. can frozen lemonade concentrate
3-4 cinnamon sticks
1 qt. water, optional

1. Combine all ingredients except water in slow cooker. Add water if mixture is too sweet.
2. Cover. Cook on low 3 hours.

Even though the name of this recipe conjures up thoughts of Christmas, it is the perfect breakfast substitute for juice, especially when entertaining a houseful of overnight guests.

Index

Z

Notes

About the Authors

Phyllis Pellman Good and Dawn J. Ranck collaborated on the highly successful *Fix-it and Forget-It Cookbook* which has been the topselling cookbook throughout the country and has appeared for months on *The New York Times* bestseller list.

Good has been part of many cookbook projects, authoring *The Best of Amish Cooking* and *The Festival Cookbook*, and co-authoring *Recipes from Central Market, Favorite Recipes with Herbs, The Best of Mennonite Fellowship Meals,* and *From Amish and Mennonite Kitchens.*

Good and her husband, Merle, live in Lancaster, Pennsylvania, and are co-directors of The People's Place, a heritage interpretation center in the Lancaster County village of Intercourse, Pennsylvania.

Ranck has been a convinced slow-cooker user for years. She, along with her many friends, have been lining up their various-sized cookers on their kitchen counters before they set off each morning—and coming home to richly flavored full dinners.

Ranck, who lives in Harrisonburg, Virginia, is the co-author of *A Quilter's Christmas Cookbook* and *Favorite Recipes with Herbs.*